MEDICATION

COMPLIANCE

A BEHAVIORAL MANAGEMENT APPROACH

Edited by

IVAN BAROFSKY

Department of Behavioral Sciences
Massachusetts College of Pharmacy
Boston, Massachusetts

Library of Congress catalog card number: 77-771-61

ISBN 0-913590-50-9
Printed in the United States of America by

 Charles B. Slack, Inc.
6900 Grove Road
Thorofare, N.J. 08086

Contributors

I. Barofsky, Ph.D.
Department of Behavioral Sciences
Massachusetts College of Pharmacy
Boston, Massachusetts

B. Blackwell, M.D.
Department of Psychiatry
School of Medicine
Wright State University
Dayton, Ohio

S.W. Budman, Ph.D.
Harvard Community Health
Harvard Medical School
Boston, Massachusetts

P.J. Curry, M.P.H.
School of Medicine
Stanford University
Palo Alto, California

P.G. Ensor, Ph.D.
Department of Health Science
Towson State College
Towson, Maryland

F.S. Finnerty, M.D.
Department of Medicine
School of Medicine
Georgetown University
Washington, D.C.

V.J. Gagliardi, M.D.
Bureau of Drugs
Food and Drug Administration
Washington, DC

R.L. Grissom, M.D.
Division of Cardiovascular Medicine
The University of Nebraska Medical
  Center
Omaha, Nebraska

R.W. Hingson, Ph.D.
Department of Socio-medical Sci-
  ences
Boston University School of Medi-
  cine
Boston, Massachusetts

C.D. Jenkins, Ph.D.
Department of Behavioral Epidem-
  iology
Division of Psychiatry
Boston University School of Medi-
  cine
Boston, Massachusetts

A.R. Kasachkoff, Ph.D., S.M. in
  Hyg.
American Health Foundation
New York, New York

C.E. Lewis, M.D.
Department of Medicine
School of Medicine
University of California
Los Angeles, California

A. Mahoney, R.N.
Department of Nursing
Massachusetts General Hospital
Boston, Massachusetts

M.-'V. Marston, Ph.D.
Graduate Community Health Nursing Program
School of Nursing
Boston University
Boston, Massachusetts

M. Michnich, M.D.
Department of Medicine
School of Medicine
University of California
Los Angeles, California

L.A. Morris, Ph.D.
Bureau of Drugs
Food and Drug Administration
Washington, DC

S.G. Rosenberg, M.A., M.P.H.
Division of Long Term Care
National Center for Health Services Research
Rockville, Maryland

T.R. Sharpe, Ph.D.
Department of Health Care Administration
University of Mississippi
University, Mississippi

K.F. Tempero, M.D., Ph.D.
Director, Clinical Pharmacology
Merck, Sharpe and Dohme Research Laboratories
Rahway, New Jersey

W.B. Whiston, Ph.D.
Center for Business Administration
University of Massachusetts
Amherst, Massachusetts

P. Yurchak, M.D.
Department of Medicine
Harvard Medical School
Massachusetts General Hospital
Boston, Massachusetts

S. Zifferblatt, Ph.D.
National Heart and Lung Institute
National Institutes for Health
Bethesda, Maryland

I.K. Zola, Ph.D.
Department of Sociology
Brandeis University
Waltham, Massachusetts

Preface

This book is one in what we hope will be a continuing effort, by ourselves and others, to focus attention on various aspects of the problem of compliance with medication regimens. It is a book of ideas, proposals, research accomplished, research in progress, and the experiences of various health practitioners. It reflects the state of the art in a field that is bound to grow and become increasingly important as the problems of health care delivery shift from acute to chronic illnesses, and the demands for improved health care quality shift to include the patient and his contribution to his own health care.

The book is meant to be a manual: a summary statement of the behavioral management procedures available at this time that can be used to help patients and various practitioners help patients with their medication regimen. The content of this book comes from several sources. Ten of the nineteen papers represent revisions of papers originally presented at a Workshop held February 23, 1974, at the Countway Library of the Harvard Medical School. Additional papers were invited, some of which were sponsored by the National High Blood Pressure Education Program, to insure complete coverage of topics.

We acknowledge with thanks, but cannot list by name, the many colleagues who contributed either as speakers or moderators at the Workshop, or reviewed portions of the text.

The financial support of the following institutions and pharmaceutical firms is gratefully acknowledged:

Massachusetts College of Pharmacy
Merck, Sharpe and Dohme, Inc.
Smith, Kline and French, Inc.
CIBA Pharmaceutical
National High Blood Pressure Education Program

In addition, I would like to acknowledge that permission has been given by Heldref Publications to reproduce Figure 1 and by J.B. Lippincott Co. to reproduce Figures 2 and 3 in the article by Barofsky. The American Psychological Association has permitted Budman to quote from a paper of his own in *Professional Psychology* and Lewis and Michnich from a paper by Sulzer in the *Journal of Counseling Psychology*. Ensor and Rosenberg quote from a book by Roark and Stanford published by Allyn and Bacon and their permission to quote is acknowledged. Finally, Hingson quotes from a paper by Pratt *et al* published in the *American Journal of Public Health;* the American Public Health Association has granted permission to quote from this article.

If an editor is permitted to dedicate the work of others, as well as his own, then I would like to dedicate this volume to my parents and my wife, who taught me that competency is more than the sum of individual capabilities or skills, but rather the integration of such factors. The encouragement and active support of my colleagues at the College, in particular R.A. Gosselin, President of the College, and Albert I. Edlin, Associate Professor of Pharmacology, are also gratefully acknowledged.

I. BAROFSKY
Boston, Massachusetts
June, 1976

Table of Contents

vii **Preface**

xv **Introduction**

Ivan Barofsky
Department of Behavioral Science, Massachusetts College of Pharmacy,
Boston, Massachusetts

1 **PART ONE** **Specification Of The Problem**

3 **Taking Your Medication — Problem for Doctor or Patient**

Irving Kenneth Zola
Department of Sociology, Brandeis University, Waltham, Massachusetts

9 **Cultural Differences in Concepts of Disease and How These Affect Health Behavior**

C. David Jenkins
Department of Behavioral Epidemiology, Division of Psychiatry, School
of Medicine, Boston University, Boston, Massachusetts

19 **PART TWO** **Factors Determining Compliance**

21 **Some Economic Issues in Medication Compliance**

William B. Whiston
Center for Business and Economic Research, School of Business
Administration, University of Massachusetts, Amherst, Massachusetts

29 Sociological and Psychological Aspects of Medication Compliance

I. Barofsky
Department of Behavioral Science, Massachusetts College of Pharmacy, Boston, Massachusetts

45 Biological Variability and Drug Response Variability as Factors Influencing Patient Compliance: Implications for Drug Testing and Evaluation

K.F. Tempero
Merck, Sharp & Dohme Research Laboratories, Rahway, New Jersey

53 PART THREE Intervention Techniques Available To Increase Compliance

55 A. Focus on the Patient

57 Chemical Coping, Self-Control and Compliance in Hypertension

B. Blackwell
Department of Psychiatry, School of Medicine, Wright State University, Dayton, Ohio

69 Contracts as a Means of Improving Patient Compliance

Charles E. Lewis
Marie Minich
Department of Medicine, University of California, Los Angeles, California

77   **Patient Self-Management of Hypertension Medication**

Steven M. Zifferblatt
National Heart and Lung Institute, National Institutes of Health,
Bethesda, Maryland

Pamela J. Curry
Stanford University, School of Medicine, Stanford, California

95   **The Patient Package Insert as Drug Education**

Louis A. Morris
Vincent J. Gagliardi
Bureau of Drugs, Food and Drug Administration, Washington, D.C.

105   **Patient Self-care in Hypertension: A Physician's Perspective**

R.L. Grissom
Division of Cardiovascular Medicine, The University of Nebraska
Medical Center, Omaha, Nebraska

115   **B. Focus on the Practitioner**

117   **The Physician's Problems in Identifying Potentially Non-compliant Patients**

R.W. Hingson
Department of Socio-Medical Sciences, Boston University
School of Medicine, Boston, Massachusetts

133   **The Pharmacist's Potential Role as a Factor in Increasing Compliance**

Thomas R. Sharpe
Research Institutes of Pharmaceutical Sciences, School of
Pharmacy, University of Mississippi, University, Mississippi

139   **Nursing Management of Compliance with Medication Regimens**

Mary-'Vesta Marston
School of Nursing, Boston University, Boston, Massachusetts

165 **C. Focus on Educational Interventions**

167 **Principles of Learning, Patient Education and Hypertension**
P.G. Ensor
Department of Health Sciences, Towson State College,
Towson, Maryland

S.G. Rosenberg
Division of Long Term Care, National Center for Health Services
Research, Rockville, Maryland

181 **Group Treatment and Management of the Hypertensive Patient**
Alisa Rosa Kasachkoff
American Health Foundation, New York, New York

189 **Psychoeducational Groups with Medical Patients**
Simon H. Budman
Harvard Community Health Plan, Harvard Medical School,
Boston, Massachusetts

195 **Patient Education: A Nurse's Perspective**
A. Mahoney
Massachusetts General Hospital, Boston, Massachusetts

203 **One Physician's Approach to the Teaching of Patients**
P. Yurchak
Massachusetts General Hospital, Harvard Medical School,
Boston, Massachusetts

209 ## D. Focus on the Health Delivery Systems:

211 ### The D.C. General Hospital Experience

Frank A. Finnerty, Jr.
Georgetown University School of Medicine and the Georgetown
University Medical Division, Washington, D.C.

215 # Summary

I. Barofsky
Department of Behavioral Sciences, Massachusetts College of
Pharmacy, Boston, Massachusetts

Introduction

I. BAROFSKY

Department of Behavioral Sciences
Massachusetts College of Pharmacy
Boston, Massachusetts

We are all aware of the data that demonstrate that the incidence of mortality and morbidity in the patient with high blood pressure (HBP) can be significantly reduced by antihypertensive drugs.[1,2] The application of these observations to the treatment of the hypertensive patient, however, has only been partially successful,[3-5] primarily because of:

1. Incomplete screening and detection of patients with HBP,
2. The dropping-out of patients following initiation of treatment, and
3. The noncompliance of patients with their established medication regimens.

As a result, a situation exists in which the successful treatment of a disease is dependent not on the availability of appropriate prophylactic agents, but rather on the techniques available to implement and maintain the therapy. Thus, progress in the treatment of the hypertensive patient requires the development and identification of techniques which will reduce patient drop-out and noncompliance. The purpose of this book is to provide help to any practitioner interested in starting on this task.

However, the problem of medication noncompliance is not limited to hypertensive patients. A large literature exists [6,7] demonstrating that noncompliance occurs in both chronic and acute illnesses, with or without symptoms. We have focused our attention on noncompliance in the hypertensive patient because uncontrolled HBP, being asymptomatic and chronic, approaches being a major public health problem afflicting approximately 10 percent of the population, and noncompliance greatly complicates the successful management of the disease. In addition, most currently available methods of managing noncompliance in hypertensive patients have been palliative (*e.g.,* fear motivation), if that, and thus need exists for a thorough investigation of alternative approaches.

We can predict that, on the one hand, the public will accept methods for improving their self-care which will be minimally disruptive of their current life-styles, and, on the other, that changes in life-styles will be required for proper control of potential and real health problems. We, in this book, do not solve the profound ethical and social problems of how you encourage patients to increase their self-care without appearing manipulative or directed. Medicine, and the behavioral sciences as well, assume that the directed activities of the practitioner is in the interest of patients, thus justifying whatever violence may occur to a person's "freedom" to act. I hope, however, that all the contributors to this book, no matter how much they view behavior as determined, would agree that attempts in changing patient behavior can only occur *after* the patient has indicated an interest in change.

The book consists of three major sections. The first section defines the context within which the problem of medication noncompliance occurs. The papers presented are meant to tell us that compliance is basically a behavioral problem that is affected by the social and cultural context within which it occurs. The second section is designed to review a number, but not all, of the factors that may contribute to the problem of noncompliance. Do people not comply with their physician-initiated medication regimen because it costs too much to comply, because of patient variability in drug response, because of variability in drug potency, or to the psychological consequences of taking drugs? What do we know about how these factors contribute to noncompliance? Can we estimate the magnitude that each of these factors attains in determining noncompliance? Are there interesting research questions that remain to be answered? The purpose of the third section is to consider approaches that could be taken in managing the noncompliant hypertensive patient, irrespective of what we know about what determines noncompliance. The techniques considered vary over a wide range. Their inclusion reflects both their potential applicability in managing medication noncompliance and their past success in dealing with related problems.

As this book will demonstrate, medication compliance is a unique health care problem that requires the integrated efforts of several sciences, as well as practitioners at several levels of the health care process. The opportunity to integrate these various efforts around a common health care problem is sufficient justification for the book, but the possibility of making progress in this area makes such efforts almost an imperative. The book itself can be looked upon as identifying the elements and techniques of what may become an integrated, team approach to primary care, although how this is to occur remains to be determined.

REFERENCES

1. VA Cooperative Study, Effects of treatment on morbidity in hypertension: I. Results in patients with diastolic blood pressures averaging 115 through 129 mm Hg. JAMA 202:1028-1034, 1967.
2. VA Cooperative Study, Effects of treatment on morbidity in hypertension: II. Results in patients with diastolic blood pressure averaging 90 through 114 mm Hg. JAMA 213:1143-1152, 1970.
3. Finnerty FA, Mattie EC, Finnerty FA III: Hypertension in the inner city. Circulation 47:73-75, 1973.
4. Schoenberger JA, Shekelle RB, Shekelle S, Stamler J: Current status of hypertension control in an industrial population. JAMA 222:559-562, 1972.
5. Wilber JA: Detection and control of hypertensive diseases in Georgia, USA. *In* Stamler JR,

Pullman TH (eds): The Epidemiology of Hypertension. New York, Grune and Stratten, 1967, pp 439-448.
6. Haynes RB, Sackett DL: An Annotated Bibliography. *In* Sackett DL, Haynes RB (eds): Compliance with Therapeutic Regimens. Baltimore, Johns Hopkins Press, 1976.
7. Marston M: Compliance with medical regimens: a review of the literature. Nurs Res 19:312-323, 1970.

PART ONE

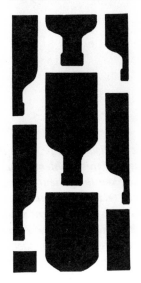

Specification
Of The Problem

Medication noncompliance is a problem that people have, but what is the source of this problem? Does it come from the patient himself; is the key the patient's physician, the patient's regimen, the patient's relationship with the physician or other health professionals, or is it the patient's cultural background, beliefs concerning his illness, etc? Drs. Zola and Jenkins help us narrow and focus our attention to the fact that medication noncompliance refers, first and foremost, to the behavior of patients and that social and cultural factors are important contributors that determine this behavior.

Taking Your Medication — Problem for Doctor or Patient

1

IRVING KENNETH ZOLA

Department of Sociology
Brandeis University
Waltham, Massachusetts

From a medical perspective, compliance involves getting patients to follow a regimen which is in their best interests. Despite, however, the most intense efforts, large numbers of patients fail to take medical advice. Perhaps then, it is time to re-examine some traditional ways that we have responded to this problem.

The first reworking is in where we have sought an answer — namely, in studying the who's, the why's, and the wherefore's of noncompliers and how to alter their "inappropriate" behavior. The logic is sound but the efforts to change patterns of smoking, eating, working, or playing have been largely unsuccessful. Taking a page from anthropological studies of public health programs,[1] I note that most programs were rejected when they tried to impose a set of beliefs and actions unfamiliar, unintegrated, if not antithetical, to a group's way of life. On the other hand, projects were accepted to the degree they were compatible, or were made compatible, with existing traditions. So too with medical compliance. Surely it has been reported often enough that much of what is required is perceived to be too disruptive of current life styles. Thus we need analogs in people's lives compatible with medical compliance. At least one such realm of behavior — self-medication — seems to satisfy this requirement.

Since most medical compliance takes place outside the hospital and doctor's office, it might fruitfully be regarded as self-medication. That we know so little about the extent, let alone the dynamics, of this behavior is amazing. While there has been a continuing tradition of research into the patient's keeping to a prescribed regimen [2-4] and many reports of physicians' prescribing patterns,[5-8] there have been few systematic studies and even fewer publications of what the lay individual does to, and for, himself. An example of this is seen in the monograph, *Home Medication and the Public Welfare,* published as the 1969 Annals of the New York Academy of Sciences.[9] In this document, despite the over 30 articles and panel discussions and a welter of references, not a single published study of self-medication is cited. Virtually all the data on which the conclusions are based are inferred from general statistics on drug sales and purchases. It is only within recent years that *Index Medicus* has even begun to note studies having data on self-medication. Thus to most investigators (as judged by the references in their publications and research proposals) the literature has been functionally nonexistent. Moreover, the word "published" needs emphasis for, according to the 1968 pamphlet *Without Prescription,*[10] such data do exist. They are, however, reposing in the files of the marketing divisions of the pharmaceutical industry or in the files of their allied market research firms. The study by Jefferys et al,[11] undertaken in 1953 but published in 1960, is the sole exception. Yet it took over a decade for similar research to be done in the United Kingdom [12] and even longer in the United States.[13]

The reason for such a vacuum is not hard to understand. As with several other areas of sociomedical investigation [14,15] it relates to several hidden and unarticulated assumptions about the prevalence (how much of it exists) and the process (why it takes place). Each tends to play down the existence of any "real" issues to study. But the lack of self-medication research has an additional overlay. As seen in the aphorism, *He who has himself for a physician is being treated by a fool,* self-medication was regarded "bad" in and of itself. It was, therefore, not worth investigating except to "expose" it. As in the investigation of certain psychoactive substances [16] there was the fear that to *even* study it systematically would give the phenomenon some air of legitimacy or, at very least, publicity and therefore unintentionally encourage the "evil" practice.

But let us look at the available data. The earliest investigators were perhaps unwittingly influenced by either the alleged frequency or importance of certain medications. Thus the time period asked of respondents to report self-medication was within the last year and the recall was confined to prescriptions. What gradually emerged was that the deeper our probing, the greater the extent of self-medication. Thus from international surveys asking but a few questions, it was estimated that upwards of one third of the respondents took some medication within the last 48 hours. In the most detailed published study, Dunnel and Cartwright [12] reported that 80 percent of a sample of British adults had taken at least one kind of medicine in a two-week span. When the time was narrowed to 24 hours, nearly half of the adults had self-medicated. Moreover, while a quarter of the adults had taken only one kind of medicine fully a fifth had taken four or more.

Lest one think such high use is peculiarly English let me cite some U.S. data. Over the past few years I have collected health diaries of college students — a group generally regarded by vital statistics, utilization rates, and self-ratings as perhaps the 'healthiest' population. Yet my findings closely resemble those of Dunnell and Cartwright. Thus within the past 36 hours, from 67 to 80 percent of my subjects reported ingesting or applying some medicament to their bodies. This figure included what one would ordinarily call medical substances but omitted marihuana or other psychoactive, but supposedly nontherapeutic, drugs. Although some of this self-medication is done with prescription drugs, this should not be interpreted as medical compliance. Much consisted of using a previously prescribed drug (theirs or someone else's) for a current ill and still more was used essentially when the individual deemed it necessary and not according to any fixed schedule.

The relevance of these data to the study of compliance should be obvious. Such a high prevalence indicates that the U.S. population as a whole is not averse to using drugs on a regular basis. What it must be averse to is the circumstances and purposes under which *some* drugs *must* be taken. The question now becomes why and under what circumstances people self-medicate and then how to build upon this use.

This focusing on self-treatment and its prevalence leads to an additional way of studying compliance. Rather than dividing populations into groups of compliers and noncompliers, we should focus more intensively on the individual as the unit of study. Thus within each individual we could, for example, research the specific contingencies under which he does or does not take drugs, uses over-the-counter remedies, resorts to a previous prescription or seeks outside help, continues a treatment or ends it, follows instructions exactly, modifies them or tapers off. As with studies of medical decision-making [15,17] the decision to self-medicate is probably also a social one influenced by friends, family and social circumstance. The more continuous the required action — such as in a long treatment regimen — the more important the social context and the more necessary social support.

As stated in my title, the issue of compliance or taking one's medicine is the responsibility of the physician as well as the patient. Yet all the papers in this conference — inferred from the titles — and frankly all conferences on medical compliance which I have recently attended focus on the issue as a *patient problem*. As such our research inevitably emphasizes seeking out characteristics of the patient (usually negative ones) or factors in relation to his physician. One study [18] noted that 67 percent of physicians attributed noncompliance to the patient's uncooperative personality and a further 40 percent specifically blamed the patient's inability to understand their recommendations. In fact the individual physician seems extraordinarily well-defended against closely examining the problem of noncompliance. Not only do doctors generally underestimate the rates of noncompliance in their practices but they are also inaccurate in identifying noncompliant individuals.[19] Davis [18] further found that of a group of senior-board physicians, 42 percent claimed that almost all *their* patients adhered to medical advice. An additional 47 percent claimed that at least three fourths of their patients were compliant. Thus while almost all clinicians believe there *is* a problem, it seems to be someone else's.

The truth is, of course, closer to home. General studies of learning indicate the important role played by the transmitter of information. This role may not even be a conscious one. Thus several reports have noted that experimenter attitudes have even influenced the results of animal research.[20] Surely the behavior and beliefs of prescribing physicians about their patients, their problems, and their treatment must similarly influence the actions of those very patients.

As, however, suggested in the study of self-medication we should focus on the dynamics of compliance, the actual situation in which advice and instructions are given. For heuristic purposes, based on my own observations of the doctor-patient interaction, I am amazed that the patient follows *any* of the doctor's advice! Over the past several years I have conducted several informal studies of this interface. They were not done in a situation in which there was a marked discrepancy in the doctor-patient status. In several instances the social status of the patient was indeed higher. They were not scenes of rushed consultations but of relaxed ones. They were not with patients who were dissatisfied with their care but on the contrary with patients who were quite satisfied and felt they had every opportunity to discuss and ask questions. Yet, in anywhere from six hours to one week, a sense of disquiet had set in. These patients began to realize that they did not fully understand all they were told. Sadder still, they felt too embarrassed or guilty to recheck with the doctor. They did not want to bother him. It did not seem worth the trouble. So, gradually they altered their treatment. In the frame of reference of this conference, they began to noncomply.

What happened in these atypical situations where seemingly the conditions were best suited for understanding? I would speculate that there are certain structural barriers in the treatment situation which specifically impede good communication. In short, the traditional doctor-patient consult is ill suited for learning to take place. I mention but three contributing elements.

The doctor-patient encounter is perhaps the most anxiety-laden of all lay-expert consultations. Rarely does one go for a reaffirmation of a good state. At best one is told that he is indeed in good health and thus a previous worry should be dismissed.[17] More likely one learns that a particular problem is not as serious as he fears. Given all the medical complaints uncovered by epidemiological surveys, a doctor's help is not the most frequent response to symptoms.[14, 17, 21] The visit to a doctor is likely approached with considerable caution. Delay is the statistical norm. Thus few are cool and calm when seeing a doctor. While some anxiety has been found conducive to learning, the amount in the traditional doctor-patient encounter is surely excessive! It is also not without significance that recall of the timing if not frequency of doctor visitation is found to be notoriously unreliable. In the large majority of instances this may well have been an experience to be finished as quickly as possible; and the best way to deal with unpleasant events is to suppress them. In such a situation is it any surprise that a patient is likely to forget much that happened, including his physician's orders?

A second impediment to communication is the amount of information transmitted. Regardless of the potentially upsetting advice, there is quite simply the problem of *data-overload.* The patient is asked to remember too much with too few tools in too short a time. In most other teaching situations, the learner is encouraged to find such ways of remembering as taking notes. But the traditional position of the patient — without the 'set' or the implements — negate this possibility. Giving patients a printed sheet of instructions, as done occasionally in pediatric practice, is not the answer, but it is at least a start.

Finally there is the manner of communication. This is a situation in which the physician attempts to distill in several minutes the knowledge and experience accumulated in decades. I have spent much of my professional life at medical schools and teaching hospitals but have yet to see this problem explicitly discussed. As in college teaching, we often assume that the degree guarantees or is at least positively correlated with the ability to communicate what was learned. But the task is not so simple. There is, for example, not merely the confusion of a technical jargon but a different or more specific (and I would argue, thus unshared) meaning to the same common terms. This is a rather insidious process. When heard by the patient, the dictionary meaning is absolutely clear. The confusion sets in only after the consultation when he is at home and must operationalize the instructions. Let me illustrate with several routine incidents.

> *Take this drug four times a day.* Does this mean I must wake up in the middle of the night? What if I forget? Should I take two when I remember?

> *Keep your leg elevated most of the day.* How high is elevated? Is it important that it be above my waist or below? How long is "most"? What about when I sleep?

> *Take frequent baths.* Are they supposed to be hot or cold? Should I soak for a while? Is four times a day frequent? Does it matter when?

> *Come back if there are any complications.* What is a complication? Must it be unbearable? What if my fingers feel a little numb? Which feelings are related to my problem and which to my treatment?

I am sure there are other elements of the doctor-patient encounter detrimental to a good learning situation. My purpose is simply to offer an alternative perspective from which to understand medical compliance.

So ends my plea for new directions. They were, however, recommendations born not merely out of social observation but social necessity. There is at long last in this country a consumer movement. In its wake is the demand to share power in decisions affecting one's life. Problems like taking one's medicine will not disappear but the context of discussion will change. At some future conference, the panel and the audience will consist of lay as well as professional experts. There will be less talk of persuasion and more of negotiation. Moreover, the title of the meeting will not be *Medication Compliance* but *Therapeutic Alliance.*

REFERENCES

1. Paul B (ed): Health, Culture and Community. New York, Russell Sage, 1955.
2. Barofsky I: A reasonably complete bibliography on aspects of medication compliance. Presented at the Boston Area Workshop on Medication Compliance, February 1974.
3. Rabin DL: Use of medicines: a review of prescribed and non-prescribed medicine use. Med Care Rev 6:668-699, 1972.
4. Sacket DL, Haynes RB (eds): Newsletter on Compliance with Therapeutic Regimens, Number 1, Dept. of Clinical Epidemiology and Biostatistics, Faculty of Medicine, McMaster University, Hamilton, Ontario, Canada, June 1973.
5. Coleman J, Katz E, Menzel H: Medical Innovation. Indianapolis, Indiana, Bobbs-Merrill, 1966.
6. Lee JAH, Draper PA, Weatherall M: Primary medical care: prescribing in three English towns. Milbank Mem Fund Q 43:285-290, 1965.
7. Martin JP: Social Aspects of Prescribing. London, England, Heineman, 1957.
8. Parrish P: The prescribing of psychotropic drugs in general practice. Roy Coll Gen Pract 21:(Suppl 4), 1971.
9. Parrish P: Home medication and the public welfare. Ann New York Acad Sci 120:807-1024, 1969.
10. Office of Health Economics: Without Prescription — A Study of the Role Of Self-Medication. London, England, 1968.
11. Jefferys M, Brotherstan JHF, Cartwright A: Consumption of medicines on a working class housing estate. Br J Prev Soc Med 14:64-76, 1960.
12. Dunnell K, Cartwright A: Medicine Takers, Prescribers, and Hoarders. London, England, Routledge and Kegan Paul, 1972.
13. Knapp DA, Knapp DE, Engel JR: The public, the pharmacist and self-medication. J Amer Ph A NS6:460-462, 1966.
14. Zola IK: Culture and symptoms — an analysis of patients presenting complaints. Amer Soc Rev 31:615-630, 1966.
15. Zola IK: Pathways to the doctor — from person to patient. Soc Sci Med 7:677-684, 1973.
16. Efron D (ed): Ethnopharmacologic Search for Psychoactive Drugs. Washington, D.C.: U.S. Government Printing Office, PHS Publ. No. 1645, 1967.
17. Zola IK: Studying the decision to see a doctor: Review, critique, corrective. Adv Psychosom Med 8:216-236, 1972.
18. Davis MS: Variations in patients' compliance with doctors' orders. J Med Educ 41:1037-1048, 1966.
19. Barsky A, Gillum R: The diagnosis and management of patient non-compliance. JAMA 228:1563-1567, 1974.
20. Freeman N: The Social Nature of Psychological Research. New York, Basic Books, 1967.
21. Zola IK: The Medicalizing of Society. Leiden, Netherlands Institute of Preventive Medicine, 1972.

Cultural Differences in Concepts of Disease and How These Affect Health Behavior

2

C. DAVID JENKINS

Department of Behavioral Epidemiology
Division of Psychiatry
School of Medicine
Boston University
Boston, Massachusetts

Why do so many people fail to take the necessary steps to maintain their health? This question is particularly awesome when applied to the epidemic of hypertension in the United States. It is commonly estimated that 22 million Americans have high blood pressure.[1,2] Only half of these are aware of their problem. Of those who know they have hypertension only half are receiving treatment for it, and an additional half of these are receiving treatment which for one reason or another is not adequately lowering their blood pressures. Thus, despite pharmacological breakthroughs in discovering effective drugs for lowering blood pressure, 7/8 of all hypertensives are not being successfully treated according to HEW estimates.[3,4] This is not a doctor-patient problem; it is a public health problem. The behavioral sciences can offer approaches to its solution.

Studies of preventive health behavior have been conducted in scattered locations for nearly 20 years, but no adequately financed, continuing large-scale program has ever been undertaken. Most of these studies have dealt with public response to short-term campaigns for prevention or screening such as the polio vaccine or chest X-ray programs. Relatively few studies have been done of continued compliance with health regimens. Continuing compliance becomes a matter of concern only after the health problem is discovered and treatment is prescribed. If the federal figures for hypertension are correct, there are two undiscovered hypertensives for every known patient not currently under treatment. This is but one reason for broadening the scope of concerns to include all three stages of medical care: namely, the initial response to a health screening appeal, the decision of those persons screened positive as to whether or not they will accept referral for treatment, and finally the issues of embarking upon and continuing with a lengthy treatment program. This is a sequence of health-related acts which has common social and cultural antecedents and common psychological determinants.

In order to organize effectively either research or intervention programs dealing with failure to take health maintenance measures, one needs a theory about what is causing noncompliance. The alternative to a hypothesis-testing approach is the aimless and often noncumulative making of surveys, assembling of "expert committees," and the mounting of "hit or miss" action programs. Let me briefly outline a sequence of theories or explanations which have been offered in past years to explain noncompliance.

The first commonly invoked explanation for failure to take a health measure is its cost in money. It is certainly true that persons with very little money need to spend it on food, housing, or emergency medical care rather than on preventive medical care, particularly if the latter seems less than essential.* Middle-class people may not rank their priorities much differently but rather have enough funds to purchase even low priority items.

A more telling argument against the "financial cost" explanation of failure to participate in health programs is the fact that even those programs which give their services free of charge fail to reach a large fraction of the susceptible population. These failure rates are associated with education and social class levels just like the compliance rates for those programs which charge for their medical care. Inevitably, free health service reaches more people than one that has a cost in money, but removing monetary costs removes only one of many barriers to health compliance.

A second often-cited explanation for failure to take health maintenance actions is that people are uninformed. The remedy prescribed is health education. In studies of public response to a free oral polio vaccine program in Florida some years ago, it was learned that many persons who obtained the oral polio vaccine had little knowledge about the disease or about why the vaccine worked.[5] This particular program had so broad-gauged an outreach that it became easier to accept the vaccine than to avoid it, and so many people with relatively little knowledge and relatively little motivation participated in the program. Thus health knowledge in the usual sense was neither necessary nor sufficient for participation in this program. Another example of the inadequacy of health

---

*See Whiston's paper in this book for an expanded discussion of this issue.

information alone is the failure of most antismoking campaigns in the United States to achieve lasting results in stopping the habit of cigarette smoking. Most cigarette smokers can tell you the facts relating their habit to risks of cancer and heart disease — and they take another cigarette to calm their fears.[6]

A more sophisticated explanatory model of health behavior is the "health belief" model offered by Rosenstock, Hochbaum and their associates.[7,8] This model holds that what people do in response to preventive or casefinding programs aimed at a specific disease is largely influenced by the way they perceive that disease. Specifically, people are more likely to seek to prevent a disease if they perceive it as being severe and see themselves as being susceptible to it. Similarly response is influenced by how effective the preventive measure is believed to be. This particular model makes room for social, cultural, and convenience factors but places clearly the greatest emphasis on changing people's perceptions of diseases and perceptions of health measures, both in terms of research and program intervention measures.

Once we accept that beliefs and feelings about a disease are important in planning public health programs, it becomes necessary to devise means for measuring these beliefs and feelings. Standard questionnaire items have many limitations: they are usually unable to detect slight differences in intensity of feeling, the substantial wording involved may tend to bias responses, and they may not communicate equally to persons of widely different educational backgrounds. Open-ended or projective questioning techniques are difficult to score and often elicit only fragmentary responses from people who are not particularly interested or talkative. To overcome these problems about a decade age we constructed a substantially revised form of the semantic differential for use in health studies.[9] Respondents were presented a series of lines each five inches long containing "hash marks" each quarter inch and labeled with verbal anchors at several locations along their length. Respondents were asked to check the strength of their belief or feeling by marking that spot anywhere along the line which best represented the position they held. Sixteen such scales were presented for each disease. In the initial research a probability sample of the population of one county in Florida was studied for its perceptions of four diseases: tuberculosis, poliomyelitis, cancer, and mental illness.

The sample differed substantially in its perception of the four diseases, and in ways that were predictable. The three ethnic groups in the county were blacks, Spanish-speaking whites, and "Anglos" (including all persons neither black nor Spanish-speaking). They differed substantially in certain perceptions of each of the four diseases, but the number and extent of differences were particularly marked for tuberculosis, a disease which had vastly different morbidity and mortality rates in the three ethnic categories.[10]

The figures illustrate selected scales of the Semantic Differential for Health and show the frequency distribution of responses for each of the three ethnic groups. Figure 1 is intended to elicit perceptions of the prevalence of a disease and, by implication, susceptibility to it. It will be noted, that 55 percent of the black respondents answered in the "many people get it" category. They perceived a much greater frequency of tuberculosis than did their Latin and Anglo counterparts.

Responses to another scale are shown in Figure 2. This scale is labeled: *Clean, Sort of Clean, Sort of Dirty, Dirty.* The respondent is asked: "Where would you put tuberculosis?" We find the black population listing tuberculosis as a relatively unclean disease, and the Spanish-speaking population more commonly believing it to be clean. Again, the ethnic groups differed sharply at the $p <$ 0.001 level in their distribution of these responses, which are part of a broader social acceptability dimension. For these two ethnic minority groups tuberculosis was considered much more common, and still a much more socially undesirable experience.

One scale was designed to determine whether people felt there was some moral quality to the diseases under study, whether these diseases were perhaps punishment for sin, or a special tragedy that happens particularly to good people. By and large, most respondents of all three groups took a moralistically neutral position, feeling that disease struck irrespective of whether a person was good or bad, but Figure 3 indicates that both the black and the Spanish-speaking groups had a larger minority that took extreme positions than did the Anglo group, clustered in the middle. This suggests that certain groups have substantial minorities that may consider disease related to the moral qualities of the patient.

The scale in Figure 4 pertains to the salience of the disease, or how much it is discussed and thought about in the community. Here it was found that the black subpopulation did a lot of talking about the disease; the Spanish and Anglos did very little talking about it.

If one combines the implications of these scales together with some of the others not displayed, one could infer that in the black community tuberculosis was considered to be very common, it was talked about a lot, it occurs particularly to bad people, and it is sort-of a dirty disease, one that is socially undesirable, one to be ashamed about. Quite converse perceptions were held by the Anglo community. It follows that one would be wise to approach these two subcommunities in sharply different ways in a health promotion, a health screening, or a medication compliance program.

We are illustrating first that ethnic groups or social cultural groups see diseases differently and that therefore, they need to be approached differently with regard to compliance; and second, that the Semantic Differential for Health (SDH) is a technique that can tap perceptions and feelings about the disease, even those perceptions which do not seem immediately pertinent to the medication compliance issue. The value of this, of course, is in gaining better insight into the social and cultural determinants of medication compliance.

The three ethnic groups were combined into the total sample; this was successively divided first by social class levels and second by an educational index, number of years of school attended. The differences between socioeconomic and educational levels in response to the SDH were considerably smaller than when the population was divided along ethnic lines. This suggests that for many features of belief and feeling about certain diseases, ethnic

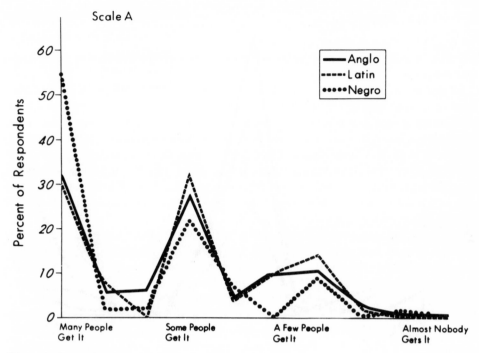

Figure 1: Perceptions of tuberculosis by three ethnic groups. Scale A: A perception of community prevalence of the disease.

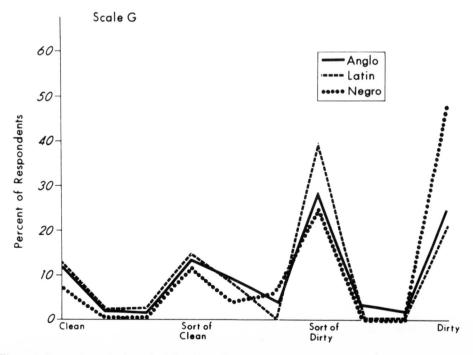

Figure 2: Perceptions of tuberculosis by three ethnic groups. Scale G: Perceptions of "uncleanness" of the disease.

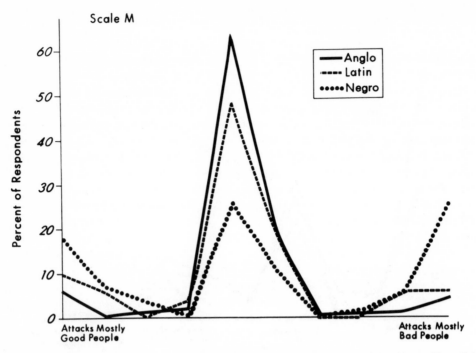

Figure 3: Perceptions of tuberculosis by three ethnic groups. Scale M: Perceptions of "moral" qualities of victims of the disease.

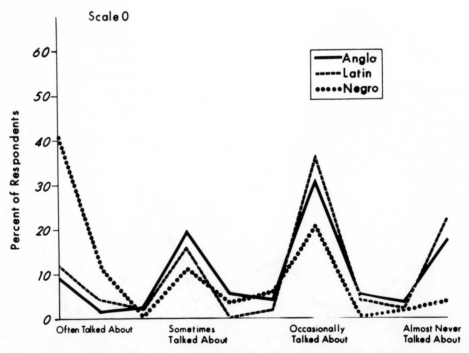

Figure 4: Perceptions of tuberculosis by three ethnic groups. Scale O: Perceptions of community salience of the disease.

subcultural influences are more important than economic and educational differences.

The differences in perceptions of disease elicited by this new measuring technique were not strongly predictive of whether individuals would take preventive health actions for polio or tuberculosis, although some associations between perceptions and health behaviors could be discerned.[11] Thus, although the health belief model is attractive because it seems to fall in line with common sense, it has not proved to be an adequately effective predictor of health-related behavior, whether measured by this technique or simple questions. It is only a partial answer because the model assumes that human behavior is largely determined by reason and the cognitive weighing of alternatives. Both depth psychology and behavioristic research over the past fifty years have substantially eroded this 19th century belief. Unconscious feelings and fears, unexpressed desires, and impulsive behavior triggered by social and environmental circumstances override goal-directed, reasonable behavior in all of us more often than we care to admit. Health programs need to take this into account, even as mass media, advertising, and marketing have done.

A sociological approach to the prediction of health behavior starts from the position that group values, pressures for conformity, normative behavior, and situational factors of convenience in the delivery of a health procedure are the primary determinants of its public acceptance. The processes involved are indexed by such social structural variables as socioeconomic status, social participation, exposure to information media, family living arrangements, and primary group cohesiveness. Other papers in this book will expand these points. Even as the health belief model is incomplete without consideration of social influences, so also this latter theory needs to be complemented by those psychological considerations which contribute to the determination of health behavior.

A still more advanced formulation of the theory of health behavior uses an epidemiologic framework of host, agent, and environment.[12] It lists a series of personal readiness factors: psychological tendencies of the host; the circumstances and nature of the health-related action itself, including convenience, effectiveness and attractiveness; and finally, influences from the social and physical environment which facilitate or hinder a health response. This formulation leaves us with a wide array of variables but no yardstick for evaluating their relative strengths or organizing them into a linked system for prediction of behavior.

A "reward-cost" theory provides these advances. Such a theory holds that each of the above categories of variables is important but that their impact on sustaining appropriate health behavior is determined primarily by the balance between the total array of rewards associated with the health measure, as contrasted with the total array of costs, efforts, and negative side effects. In this theory rewards are defined broadly as including not only the effectiveness of the action, its pleasure, and the social approval associated with it, but also personal feelings of reduced tension, enhanced self-esteem, and the recognitions that come from friends, community leaders, health professionals, and others. "Costs" are broadly defined to include the efforts needed to obtain the health measure, the alternative ways of spending the time and resources which must be given up, inconveniences associated with the act, negative side effects (including feelings of sluggishness, depression, stuffy nose, dizziness and the like), the change in self-image which comes with acknowledging that something might be wrong with one's health, and the feeling of being "put down" associated with having to "come for help."

Perhaps not all of these variables are really important in predicting compliance to a specific health regimen such as that for reducing high blood pressure. In any event, all the kinds of beliefs and feelings and fears just mentioned have the potential for being measured by means of interviews, questionnaires, symptom checklists, and modified semantic differential approaches. These then could be related empirically to direct measures of compliance and the genuinely important issues can thus be identified.

Different subcultures, occupations, and other reference groups attach widely differing valences to various costs and inconveniences associated with a medication program. Transient dizziness may be quite acceptable to a housewife but be grounds for loss of one's career for an airline stewardess. Similarly, occasional impotence may be a far greater blow to a younger bachelor than to an older widower. There are many other important kinds of differences both in costs and rewards which are group-mediated but which are far less obvious than these two examples. Hence, cultural and group differences strongly affect the reward-cost equation in ways that health professionals may not recognize unless their frame of reference is closely attuned to that of the subgroup for whom they are providing health services.

The form in which a pharmacologic agent is provided may also influence the popular view of its efficacy. In fieldwork on the Upper Surinam River we learned that any injection, no matter what its content, was thought to be far more powerful medication than any drug taken by mouth.

What does one do when the pertinent rewards and costs associated both with the disease and its treatment have been measured and compared? That is the time for a program of action. Intervention may take one of two major directions. First, one may decide to use health education or other promotional techniques to modify the beliefs, feelings, and action tendencies of the target population. Second, one could design or reformulate the health care delivery program to better reach the target population in their current state of beliefs and feelings. It is generally much easier to modify a health program to fit a subpopulation than to modify the culture and values of a subpopulation to fit a health program. Sometimes both efforts need to be undertaken simultaneously. Comprehensive studies of health delivery programs often reveal that the barriers interfering with adequate response of the target population have been created by health professionals themselves. This can be most clearly seen in examples of international programs in which Western medicine has attempted to provide health services to populations of vastly different cultures. The same principle holds in considering the ways that upper- and middle-class health professionals have failed to be aware of the cultural variety within the American population.

Behavioral science studies can guide us in appropriate modification of our health education and health administration systems using the "reward-cost" model as a guide. Health professionals planning preventive screening and mass treatment programs can develop their health promotion and care delivery systems so as to maximize "rewards" for the recipient population and minimize the "costs" of their participation and continued compliance. It must also be remembered that individuals and groups may take health-related actions largely due to motives quite unrelated to health. More toothpaste is sold to promote sex appeal and reduce socially disapproved odors than to reduce dental caries or periodontitis.

Both positive and negative values are learned by individuals in an interpersonal setting. These learnings differ markedly in different social environments. In order to maximize compliance with health regimens, health professionals must get into the frame of reference of their patient groups. They must learn what turns them on and what turns them off and govern plans for medical treatment accordingly.

Pharmacists have an important role to play in health service delivery because of their unique position as intermediaries between medical administrators and prescribing physicians on the one hand, and the lay recipients of medical care on the other. Many persons go to pharmacists for first-line health information. The information that is given, and also the way in which it is given, can have great impact on beliefs and feelings about diseases, medications, and personal health care habits, as well as attitudes toward the professionals who provide the health services. Many patients also bring the pharmacist complaints about their medical regimens which they hesitate to take to physicians. In response to this pharmacists can help prescribing physicians to make their orders more convenient and easy to follow. Similarly, they can help patients find handy systems to take the right medications at the right times and perhaps even help them to avoid or minimize some of the side effects. Pharmacists should seek out the opportunity to participate in the planning of large-scale screening and intervention programs because they are in a position to harmonize the pharmacologic prerequisites of effective treatment with the treatment-relevant personal and social characteristics of community groups. The behavioral sciences can assist the profession of pharmacy in conceptualizing and measuring those perceptions, values, behaviors, rewards, and costs which go into the complex equation determining health behavior.

REFERENCES

1. Gordon T, Devine B: Hypertension and hypertensive heart disease in adults 1960-1962 — data from National Health Survey. Vital Health Statistics Series No. 11, 1966.
2. National Heart, Blood Vessel, Lung and Blood Program. Vol IV, Part 1. Report of the Heart and Blood Vessel Diseases Panel pp 2-25. DHEW Publication (NIH)73-518, April 6, 1973.

 3. Lille RD, Gould J, Viera M et al: The management of hypertension in an inner city area. Clin Res
    21:538, 1973.
 4. Wilber JA, Millward D, Baldwin A, Capion B, Silverman D, Levy JM, Wolbert T, McCombs NJ:
    Atlanta community high blood pressure program: methods concerning hypertension screening. Cir
    Res 31(Supp 2):1-102, 1972.
 5. Johnson AL, Jenkins CD, Patrick RC et al: Epidemiology of Polio Vaccine Acceptance: A Social
    and Psychological Analysis. Florida State Board of Health. Monograph No. 3, February 1972.
 6. Macoby N, Farquhar JW: Communication for health: unselling heart disease. J Commun 25:114-
    126, 1975.
 7. Hochbaum G: Health Behavior. Belmont, California, Wadsworth Publ, 1970.
 8. Rosenstock IM: Why people use health services. Milbank Mem Fund Q 64:94-127, 1966.
 9. Jenkins CD: The semantic differential for health: a technique for measuring beliefs about
    diseases. Pub Health Rep 81:549-558, 1966.
10. Jenkins CD: Group differences in perception: a study of community beliefs and feelings about
    tuberculosis. Am J Sociol 71:417-429, 1966.
11. Jenkins CD: Views of disease: actions toward health, identification of public beliefs about health
    problems as a basis for predicting use of health services. Final Project Report to DHEW, USPHS,
    Division of Community Health Services. Chapel Hill, N.C., University of North Carolina,
    Department of Epidemiology, pp x-187, 1964.
12. Suchman EA: Preventive health behavior: a model for research on community health campaigns.
    J Health and Soc Behav 8:197-209, 1967.

PART TWO

Factors Determining Compliance

In assessing factors that determine compliance, some fairly obvious questions can be asked. Do people not comply because of the cost of the medications? Do people not comply because of some unique sociological or psychological problems underlying compliance? Finally, do people not comply because biological differences lead to variability in drug responses?

We will learn that the cost of medication is rarely a reason for noncompliance, that there are almost too many sociological and psychological "explanations" of medication noncompliance, and that individual differences in biological processes may yet account for some of the reasons why patients do not comply.

Some Economic Issues in Medication Compliance

1

WILLIAM B. WHISTON

Center for Business and Economic Research
School of Business Administration
University of Massachusetts
Amherst, Massachusetts

THE RELATIVE COST OF PRESCRIPTIONS AND HEALTH CARE

Prescription drug prices are a lively issue and the subject of much debate. Health care costs have climbed more rapidly than most other components of the cost of living index. Presently nearly ten cents of every dollar of national income is spent on health care.[1] While only about one tenth of this is for prescription drugs, this one tenth has high visibility to the public for several reasons.

Most members of the health care delivery system escape identification as profit centers. Hospitals are perceived as nonprofit or even charitable institutions. The medical profession, partly because of the spectacular skills of some of its members, has preserved an image of high professionalism. Only the pharmacist is perceived to be a merchant by most consumers of health care services.

THE MERCHANT OF THE HEALTH CARE SYSTEM

It is very possible that the pharmacist himself is largely responsible for this mercantile image. The typical pharmacy is a retail establishment with the majority of sales outside the dispensary or pharmacy department. Pricing, costing, and budgeting procedures developed for the "front store" are very often applied to the dispensary. The front store prices are often set by percentage markup. This percentage is determined by the distribution of store overhead and target return on investment according to dollar volume. This method is widely used in retailing and it is inevitable that the markup pricing method is extended to cover prescription drugs in most pharmacies. As a result, the pharmacist is seen by himself and his customers as primarily a merchant when pricing is discussed.

The rapid rise in prices of medical care in the past fifteen years is a source of serious concern to all. For the United States during the five-year period ending in June 1971, medical care rose 46.2 percent and hospital daily service charges rose 95 percent. The consumer price index for this period rose but 25.1 percent. But prescription drug prices actually declined 0.5 percent during this same five-year period.[2] This price stability was attained although new and sophisticated products were introduced and all other costs of doing business in the pharmacy were rising.

This record of cost control in the retail pharmacies was not easily accomplished. Many neighborhood pharmacies have been forced to close. Much of the prescription drug business has moved to high-volume self-service outlets in strategic high traffic locations such as shopping centers. Although the pharmacist has controlled costs and prices better than any other element of the health care delivery system he still receives open condemnation for his pricing practices.

Since the pharmacist is perceived by most to be the only private profit center in the health care delivery chain, much of the wrath over rising medical expense is visited upon him, even though he has held costs in line. The purchase of the prescription is a highly visible cash transaction less often covered by insurance or other third-party payment plans than the physician or hospital expense, and one of the few aspects of the health care process that the patient can exert some control over. Not too surprisingly, therefore, the purchasing of medications and the person involved in distributing the medications (i.e., the pharmacist) become involved in the process of patient self-care. The linking of economic issues with the process of patient self-care occurs readily, but whether this linkage is incidental or determined remains a question for debate. However, there is little doubt that patient consciousness over prescription drug prices can become an obstacle to compliance with a medication regimen.

DISPARITIES IN INCOME AND
THIRD-PARTY PAYMENT COVERAGE

A very important source of economic pressure working against "purchase compliance" is the poor insurance and third-party payment coverage for prescription drugs. In spite of the many comprehensive health insurance plans and the introduction in the U.S. of Medicare and Medicaid, very little progress has been made in third-party payment of prescription drugs among the poor and aged. Much of what progress there has been is due to various welfare programs in several states. In the U.S. during calendar 1970, 87 per cent of hospitalization and 61 per cent of physician services were paid by private insurance or by government programs; but only 11 per cent of drugs and sundries were so financed.

Among the elderly and the very poor this problem of payment coverage is even more serious. Many health insurance plans are available only for those employed (or retired from employment) in an establishment with a group plan. To the unemployed or the marginally employed such sources may be unavailable. The full benefits of Social Security are unavailable to those elderly who did not fulfill certain employment requirements during their working years. Recent medical assistance plans of the Federal government have attempted to fill this gap. But the paperwork and "knowhow" to qualify for new health programs is more than many educated, healthy, middle-class citizens can fathom! As a result, those who most need third-party coverage for payment of prescription drugs are without such provision except through welfare. All too often the administration of welfare is too degrading for those who may be sick but still carry themselves with pride.

As noted earlier, the average third-party coverage for prescription payments of 11 per cent is about one eighth that for hospital payments which are 87 per cent. As the level of third-party payment for hospital insurance changes with age, sex, income, and minority status, some similar change would be expected for coverage for prescription expense. The figures for hospital insurance coverage of all types in the U.S. in 1970 are given in Table I. As this table shows, the poor are largely without hospital insurance. If this is the case they surely have virtually no prescription drug coverage since it has already been shown that drug coverage is only one eighth as prevalent as hospital coverage for the U.S. population as a whole.

Many of the poor in the U.S. are aged. In 1970, the median income of the aged in the U.S.A. was $2,044. In that year the "poverty level" was set at $1,855 income per year; 38.4 per cent of all males and 60.9 per cent of all females aged 65 years or older fell below this poverty level. Median income for aged single females was only $1,522. It is not only the aged that are heavily concentrated below the poverty line; 51.6 per cent of all blacks and 62.7 per cent of all blacks aged 65 and over had incomes below the poverty level.[3]

TABLE I

HOSPITAL INSURANCE COVERAGE[6]

Family's Income	Those With No Hospitalization Coverage (%)
< $3000	64
$3000-5000	43
$5000-7000	22
$7000-10,000	11
> $10,000	8

It is among these — the poor, the aged and the minority citizens of the U.S. — where an economic basis for medication noncompliance is apparent. Not only are these groups without adequate income or coverage, as shown above, but the medical needs of these groups are usually greater than for the general population. Much of the medical and prescription requirements for these groups goes unmeasured because they lack the economic means to register their needs in the health care system.

THE DISTRIBUTION OF PRESCRIPTION COSTS

In 1971 the per capita expenditure for drugs and drug sundries was $30.02 for those under 65 years of age. For those 65 years and older the average per capita expenditure for these same items was $86.98.[4] The expense for prescription drugs and sundries is nearly three times as large for the aged as for the general population. Since these data represent drugs actually purchased, allowance for economic hardship among the aged leads to the conclusion that their drug needs may be more than three times that of the general population.

Among the very poor health needs are found to be greater than for the general population. The report of the National Health Survey shows a higher incidence of bed-disability days of persons with chronic disorders in families of $5000 annual income or less.[2]

Averages such as these often conceal the personal hardships and tragedies of individuals. The health-care requirements of these aged, poor and minority citizens are distributed very unevenly. A study in Lawrence County, Pennsylvania,[5] revealed that 2 per cent of the aged account for 20 per cent of all prescriptions and that 40 per cent of the aged have virtually no prescription drug expense! If 21 per cent of the prescriptions go to persons whose drug requirements are ten times that of their age group, the $86.98 U.S. annual average requirement indicates a very burdensome level of prescription drug requirement for such individuals. It is, of course, improper to compound percentages and averages in this way since these measures of age, income and registered drug usage are not independent. But as the Lawrence County study shows, a substantial percentage of medication prescription goes to individuals for whom it is a heavy burden.

A very much earlier report (1962) by the National Center for Health Statistics indicated that 18 per cent of the aged had prescription drug expenses of $100 or more. If we allow for the increased frequency of prescriptions and the somewhat higher prescription prices, this figure might approach $200 today. This amounts to 10 per cent of the median income for all aged and 13 per cent of the median income for the aged female. Similar burdens exist for other poverty groups.

Averages are very misleading measures if individual medication compliance and individual financial hardship are at issue. While an average burden may be tolerable even for some members of these low income groups, the average burden is experienced by few. Great hardship is experienced among a minority of individuals but these few individuals represent a substantial percentage of all prescribed medication in their group. Substantial medication noncompliance inevitably results.

POSSIBLE REDUCTION IN
ECONOMIC NONCOMPLIANCE

It may be appropriate to discuss possible allocation of the economic problems discussed previously. Three come to mind:
1. Improvement in the pharmacist role,
2. Assistance in extension of third party payment coverage,
3. Product selection.

The Role of the Pharmacist

It was observed earlier in this paper that the pharmacist may have been unfairly selected as a target for those attacking the increase in health care costs. Careful cost analysis in pharmacy dispensaries indicates that the typical pharmacist fills drug prescriptions at a lower overall cost than a public dispensary. Most pharmacists are unconscious of the degree of their underpricing even though each knows that without the "front store" he could not survive.

But to raise prescription prices is to increase any economic basis for medication noncompliance and will further alienate the consumer. The only viable alternative is to lower costs. This will not be done easily or without dislocation of present personnel, practices, and facilities. High volume outlets should probably continue to replace smaller neighborhood pharmacies. Allocation of peripheral duties in the dispensary to semiskilled support personnel may increase. Restrictions and regulations that unnecessarily increase the expenses of the pharmacy department should be amended.

Pharmacist members of regulatory boards should abstain from voting on regulations where conflict of financial interest is possible. Other health-care professionals on the board should be trusted to vote for the good of the public and of the pharmacies, which should be inseparable. There are many alternatives to high pharmacy costs that become available once job preservation for the pharmacist is not the subject of regulation. "Lock and leave" for the pharmacy and "on call" pharmacist availability are two of many alternatives that might be examined for the reduction of dispensary overhead.

Extension of Third-Party Drug Programs

Third-party payment paperwork is a burden to those professionals who work every day within the system. Just consider how difficult it must be for the uninitiated, the poor, the aged and those from different cultures to obtain the financial aid that is properly theirs to claim. Professional health care advice requires more than a page torn from a prescription pad. Why not accompany prescription slips with instruction sheets showing a check mark to indicate the appropriate program(s) and methods by which that individual patient could receive reimbursement or payment for the expense of that prescription?

Personnel in doctor's offices, in clinics, and in pharmacies must assume responsibility for the training and counsel of patients in the appropriate third-party payment system for which the patient may be eligible. This responsibility may not seem to be a medical responsibility, but if noncompliance is a medical problem, who else should be more interested in the solution?

Drug Product Selection and Substitution

The opportunity for cost reduction in the dispensary has been shown to be limited. But the acquisition cost of the drug itself is about 60 per cent of the retail price. There are opportunities for reduction of this portion of the prescription price also. At present about 90 per cent of all prescriptions are written for a branded product. In many cases a generic equivalent for the drug is available at a fraction of the cost. There has been much discussion of required generic prescriptions and some welfare programs have initiated such requirements. But the institution of generic substitution requires careful study and administration if it is to be equal to brand product prescription.

The American Pharmaceutical Association issued a white paper in March 1971 entitled "The Pharmacist's Role in Product Selection." The pharmacy profession has taken a timely and intelligent position on this issue. Any delays in the implementation of product substitution are not due to the pharmacy profession. Barriers are not to be found in government. The drug manufacturers are decreasingly vocal on the issue as they become increasingly conscious of public relations.

If institutional and political barriers are not the real reasons, are there any remaining issues unsolved? If the barriers are pharmacological and therapeutic, then this work should proceed. Our leading drug manufacturers may be quite right when they say that a generic equivalent is not necessarily a dependable therapeutic equivalent. There may be wide differences in form, grain size, rate of solution, etc, but such differences are easily resolved by scientists, physicians and engineers.

The rewards to the poor and aged for a vigorous product selection program are readily calculable. A one third reduction in material cost or 75 cents a prescription is readily available. The present pricing practice of the retail pharmacist would add to this saving. A saving of 85 cents per prescription is one and one half billion dollars a year in the U.S. alone. Let me describe the PARCOST system, now operating in the province of Ontario, Canada, as a possible basis for a U.S. program.

The Ontario PARCOST Program

The PARCOST program in the province of Ontario, Canada, has offered an interesting experiment in product selection. The Ontario Pharmacists' Association has cooperated with the provincial health ministry in promotion of the program. As many as 70 per cent of the pharmacists joined the program. Each volunteer pharmacy agrees to a maximum professional fee, currently $2.20, and to "product select." These pharmacies are permitted to display a seal designating their shop as a PARCOST member.

Product selection under the PARCOST agreement means that the pharmacist fills every prescription with the lowest cost-equivalent product in his dispensary, unless specifically instructed otherwise. The medical advisors to the health ministry specify exactly which products are complete therapeutic equivalents and list them in order of decreasing cost in a manual available to both the pharmacist and his customer.

The resultant savings through product selection were unofficially estimated by the Health Ministry of Ontario to be in the millions of dollars annually for a single product in the province of Ontario alone.

CONCLUDING COMMENTS

The prescription drug sector of the health care industry of the U.S. can take pride in what it has done. The cost of a prescription has risen less than any of the major indices and far less than hospital and doctor fees. The quality and complexity of the product dispensed has risen. Everyone from manufacturer to retail pharmacist can share in the credit for what has been accomplished to date. But more needs to be done if we are to adequately meet the needs of the financially underprivileged.

REFERENCES

1. U.S. Department of Health, Education and Welfare, Social Security Administration, Office of Research and Statistics, Prescription Drug Data Summary, 1972, DHEW Publication No. (SSA) 73-11900, p 7.
2. U.S. Department of Health, Education and Welfare, Public Health Service, Health Characteristics of Low-Income Persons, DHEW Publication No. (HSM) 73-1500, Rockville, Md., July 1972, pp 12, 17 and 19.
3. U.S. Department of Commerce, Social and Economic Statistics Section, Bureau of the Census, Statistical Abstract of the United States, 1972, p 332.
4. U.S. Department of Health, Education and Welfare, Social Security Administration, Office of Research and Statistics, Prescription Drug Data Summary, 1972, DHEW Publication No. (SSA) 73-11900, p 7.
5. U.S. Department of Health, Education and Welfare, Task Force on Prescription Drugs, Background Papers, The Drug Users, Washington, D.C., December, 1968, p 25.
6. U.S. Congress, National Health Insurance Proposals, Hearings before the Committee on Ways and Means, House of Representatives, 92nd Congress, Part 13, November 19, 1971, Washington, D.C.: U.S. Government Printing Office, 1972, p 3210.

Sociological and Psychological Aspects of Medication Compliance*

2

I. BAROFSKY

Department of Behavioral Sciences
Massachusetts College of Pharmacy
Boston, Massachusetts

The purpose of this paper is to apply selected sociological and psychological principles to the problem of social compliance. In so doing I hope to provide a perspective on how various aspects of the problem of compliance can be approached and studied, and provide some information on the role social and psychological processes play in the more specialized phenomena of compliance with therapeutic regimens. We will start by classifying the behavior patterns that reflect a person's state of health, proceed to discuss several principles of social interaction, and then discuss several mechanisms that appear to control behavior (*e.g.*, cognitive dissonance, attribution, interoceptive conditioning). In each case, we will discuss how compliance with a medication regimen may be viewed and defined.

*Drs. R. Hingson and D. Rowden were kind enough to read the text of this paper and to make some conceptual and literary suggestions. Their efforts are acknowledged, although the consequences remain the author's.

THE SOCIOLOGY OF COMPLIANCE

The social processes and behaviors characteristic of the health care process have been divided by Kasl and Cobb [1] into three reasonably distinct classes (Figure 1). Each class differs in terms of health status of the person and the degree and nature of the intervention by various health professionals. *Health behavior,* for example, was defined by Kasl and Cobb [1] as "any activity undertaken by a person who believes himself to be healthy, for the purpose of preventing disease or detecting disease in an asymptomatic stage," and involves minimal intervention by a health professional. *Illness behavior* was defined as "any activity undertaken by a person who feels ill, for the purpose of defining the state of his health and of discovering a suitable remedy," and usually involves a health professional. *Sick-role behavior* was defined as "the activity undertaken by those who consider themselves ill for the purpose of getting well," and clearly involves health professionals. We will discuss examples of each of these behaviors, and will start by describing a social role approach to compliance.

Social Role Models

The behavior that is expected of an individual by others, as defined by the person's status and culture, has been referred to as the person's *social role.* Ordinarily, we engage in a variety of roles, one of which occurs when we are ill, the so-called *sick role.* The sick role has been described by Parsons,[2-5] as a form of "deviant" behavior in which the person was expected to seek expert (usually medical) advice, could be expected to be exempt from his normal work requirements, could be expected not to be blamed for being ill, and could be blamed if he did not get well. A critical element of Parson's concept of the sick role [5] is that the patient is in continued interaction with some therapeutic agent (*e.g.,* a physician). When the person engages in activities considered socially deviant the *therapeutic agent* uses social control methods to insure that the patient is reintegrated into the social system. Illness, which results in an impairment of a sick person's integration in his relationship with others, is counteracted by therapy which is designed to reintegrate the person into his

Behavior	Health	Illness	Sick Role		
Identity	Healthy	Feel Sick	Am Sick		
Role Performance	Usual Social Roles	Diminished Function	Preparing to Enter Sick Role	Being in Sick Role	Leaving Sick Role
Health	Health	Asymptomatic Disease	Symptoms	Dx	Treatment	Outcome

Figure 1: Kasl and Cobb's [21] continuum relating health to disease at various levels of analysis.

various social roles. Thus, the sick role and the role of therapeutic agent interact to comprise a social system that we recognize as the health care process.

By viewing the sick role as a form of social deviance, Parsons was attempting to place a patient's "motivedness" to recover or not recover in a social context.[5] The function of the therapeutic agent was to restore the social functions of the patient by whatever mechanisms of social control were available. A patient's compliance with a therapeutic regimen may be viewed as a measure of the success of the social system to deal with the patient's "motivedness." This definition of compliance reflects or measures the efficiency of the health care process. It measures the ability of the system to deal with individuals and the disease, socioeconomic and personal characteristics that distinguish individuals. For example, the black hypertensive patient who adheres to some folk medicine practices or the white middle-class patient who knows that some medications are "artificial" means of achieving health both may be noncompliant. On the other hand, if the therapeutic agent is aware of these patient characteristics and adjusts the therapeutic regimen accordingly then noncompliance may not occur and the patient may achieve some therapeutic goal. Thus, compliance with therapeutic regimens, as defined here, is a measure of how well individuals are integrated into the social system we call the *health care process.*

Another perspective to a sick role definition of compliance is not to ask how well the system integrates individuals but how well individuals adapt to the system. We have stated that the sick role can be characterized in terms of a normative set of expectations (*i.e.,* the exemptions and obligations of the sick role) that others have for the patient. Failure of a patient achieving these expectations can occur for a variety of reasons including:

a. a patient failing to assume the sick role,
b. a patient failing to successfully bargain to reduce role strain,[6]
c. a patient not resolving conflict between the sick role and other social roles,
d. a patient adopting a role that is incompatible with the sick role.

Each of the above situations will affect how well the patient adapts to the health care process, and to the extent that the individual fails to adapt to the health care system then noncompliance to the therapeutic regimen may result. For example, evidence supporting the notion that compliance is related to the degree a patient adopts the sick role comes from a recent study by Grey [7] who showed that the extent to which a group of rheumatoid arthritic patients complied with a therapeutic regimen (as measured by physician ratings of the patients) varied inversely with the patient's willingness to adopt a sick role (measured by questionnaire).

The process of taking on the sick role illustrates how a theory of role strain [6] can determine compliance. The steps involved in adopting the sick role starts with the patient assessing the extent and nature of his symptoms, includes the seeking of medical advice for expert diagnosis, and continues with the patient initiating the therapy. One may ask if noncompliance occurs at a particular stage in this process. Does it occur when a patient properly assesses his own symptoms as requiring medical treatment but fails to seek such treatment? Does it occur if the patient avoids visiting a physician because of some distasteful past experience? Does it occur when the patient fails to try to lose weight, or stop smoking or even try the prescribed medication? Each of these examples reflects a stage in a continuous process of adapting one's behavior to what is expected, and to the extent that this does not occur then the patient does not adopt the sick role. Role strain, or the difficulty in meeting role demands, occurs when the individual's total role obligations are overdemanding.[6] Thus the concept of role strain may be applicable at each of the stages in the process of the patient adopting the sick role. For example, a patient may refuse to seek treatment because the conflict between roles exceeds the benefit from relief of symptoms. Hypertension is an example of a disease which is asymptomatic and where the "felt difficulty in fulfilling role obligations"[6] may be such that the patient cannot bargain himself into a sick role.

Conflict between the sick role and other social roles can occur when individuals who possess legitimate authority (e.g., employer, physician, nurse, spouse, etc.) expect particular types of behavior that are incompatible with sick role behavior. Consider the mother who has received a prescription for an antibiotic for the normal ten-day period but who stops taking the drug after five to six days and returns to active management of her family. The patient by returning to work may be fulfilling the expectations that the family has for her, but if the infection returns then clearly the patient has failed to properly execute the sick role. Thus the noncomplementariness of expectations between social roles is a sufficient condition to produce noncompliance to a medicinal or therapeutic regimen.

The role conflict model of noncompliance runs into difficulty when it is applied to such chronic illnesses as hypertension. The problem is that the sick role model assumes that illness, and a patient's experience with it, will be limited in duration. In fact, the model assumes at first glance not only that the disease is limited in duration, but that a cure exists and that the patient knows he has to perform a discrete number of tasks to be cured. However, the hypertensive patient, like many others suffering from chronic illnesses, is told that his disease is life-long, that no cure exists, and that he has to be actively involved in caring for himself the rest of his life. All he can hope for by complying is to reduce the probability of getting sick (e.g., a stroke). The applicability of the sick role model in accounting for noncompliance in the chronically ill apparently limits its usefulness.

Noncompliance itself may constitute a social role. The noncompliant role, like the sick role, is a form of deviant behavior which consists of a limited set of privileges and obligations. The noncompliant role can have a broad social reference but in chronic illness has specific characteristics reflecting the state of being ill. For example, the sick person taking chronic medication is expected to be self-reliant and healthy, and to control his physical ailments. He is not expected to seek medical advice, he remains independent of reliance on medications, he in general avoids physical or psychological treatments, and he does not permit his ailments to limit his activity. Indeed, it is the presence of noncompliance as a clear set of expectations that others have for the ill person (a set of expectations that differ from those that constitute the sick role) that may make noncompliance such a difficult public health problem.

Parsons,[2] in his original formulation, was interested in using the concepts of social deviance and its counterbalancing force, social control, as the principal components of social organization. The sick role and the role of therapeutic agent illustrated this phenomenon. Parsons' interest in it grew out of the observation [8] during the 1930s that "psychic" factors can affect the occurrence, duration, and outcome of (somatic) disease. By conceptualizing illness as a process that was a deviance that elicited control, Parsons was able to account for such social organizations as the hospital, the clinic, etc. Clearly, the model was not formulated to account for individual behavior. Yet inspection of individual cases has convinced some [9,10] that the sick role model has limited utility. Siegler and Osmond,[11] in an attempt to resolve this controversy, suggest that expectations concerning illness can be constituted in a limited number of ways and that these models of illness, eight in all, yield a limited number of sick role models. Such a typological approach to the sick role implies that different patterns of noncompliance also exist.

In summary, we have reviewed Parsons' concept of the sick role to determine where and how it may provide a basis for defining compliance with a therapeutic regimen. Basically, we have defined compliance as a measure of the success whereby a patient is integrated into the health care process, or whereby the patient has successfully adapted to the health care process. Thus, compliance is defined relative to some perspective or within some context, implying that no one definition of compliance exists.

One of the advantages of defining compliance in the context of a discussion of the sick role is that one can pretty much assume that one is dealing with compliance in patients labeled as ill. One of the next questions, however, is whether or not one can discuss compliance in patients who think they are ill but may not be, or in patients who feel healthy and are willing to do something to stay that way.

Illness Behavior, Health Behavior, and the Health Belief Model

The concept of illness behavior was originally proposed by Mechanic [12] and "refers to the ways in which given symptoms may be differentially perceived, evaluated and acted (or not acted) upon by different kinds of persons." Mechanic was, in fact, shifting emphasis from group to individual experiences with illness, permitting a clearer delination of factors that could affect individual illness behavior and a clear exposition of the situational constraints on behavior. In his own research, Mechanic,[12-14] as well as others, has investigated the conditions under which a person becomes defined as ill and seeks medical care.

A patient presenting bodily complaints [8] provides an example of this approach to health-related behaviors. The perception of symptoms appears to be dependent on the degree and nature of personal vulnerability elicited by the symptoms and the ability of the patient to account or attribute the symptoms to some cause. Thus, hypochondriasis may be due to errors in attribution as influenced by social, cultural and experiential factors. Zborowski,[15] in his study of how various groups respond to pain, provided an example of how sociocultural factors can lead to difference in attributional responses. He found that Italian and Jewish patients tended to respond emotionally to pain, "Old Americans" tended to respond stoically, while the Irish patient frequently denied pain. Most interestingly, he found differences between Italian and Jewish patients in their attitudes underlying these responses. Italian patients sought relief from pain and were satisfied when such relief was obtained, but Jewish patients were concerned with the meaning of their pain and tended to be reluctant to accept medication. To the extent that sociocultural factors condition attributional errors, they provide a basis for noncompliance and differences in compliance between groups.

Health behavior and the health belief model grew out of the effort of public health educators to conceptualize the process whereby some people engage in preventative health care.[1,16] The essential element in the health belief model (Figure 2) is the assumption that perceived threat of disease determines health behavior. The threat of disease is dependent on what the patient perceives as his own susceptibility to disease, and the perceived seriousness of the disease (Figure 2). These perceptions are modified by a variety of demographic, sociopsychological and structural variables. However, health behavior requires a cue or a stimulus for initiating action, and these cues may range from a commercial on television advertising the risks of high blood pressure to something someone once said to the patient. With the perceived threat of disease so modified the likelihood of an individual taking action depends on what the patient considers to be the benefit relative to the cost of acting. Thus, the model is an attempt to account for personal health decisions in the absence of clear-cut symptoms.

Since both illness behavior and health behavior do not require the presence of physical symptoms, the question arises whether it is appropriate to discuss compliance with a therapeutic regimen relative to such behaviors. Becker, Drachman and Kirshct[17] provide a partial answer to this question when they suggest that it is possible to use the health belief model as a predictor of compliance, and that it is possible to fit elements of the sick-role model into this "compliance" version of the health belief model. What makes this possible is the fact that in both models patients make subjective probability estimates about some aspect of an illness, and that these estimates determine their behavior. Becker et al[17] state: "There would seem to be no inherent reason why the same type of formulation [referring to the health belief model] should not apply to actions taken by individuals who know that they are ill in order to become well, especially if the concept of susceptibility is extended to mean the probability of progressive effects or of recurrence." Thus, estimating the chances of getting a disease in the absence of any signs of it, or estimating the chances of a recurrence of disease in the presence of symptoms identifies a social

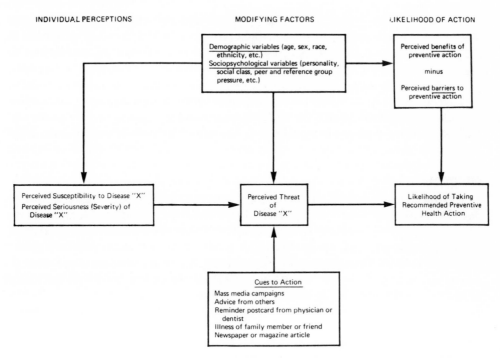

Figure 2: Becker's [17] *summary of the health belief model.*

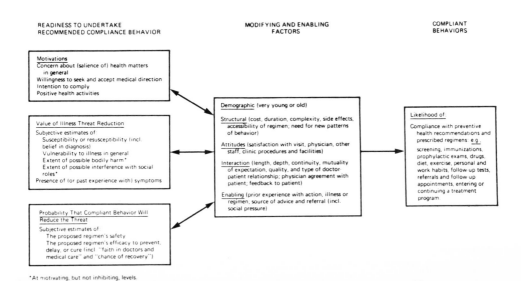

Figure 3: Extension of the health belief model to the problem of compliance to therapeutic regimens.

psychological mechanism which permits a common approach to all three descriptive classes of health-related behaviors.

The model that Becker [18] has proposed to account for patient compliance is illustrated in Figure 3. Note that he lists factors that determine a patient's readiness to undertake recommended compliance behavior, factors that modify or enable compliance behavior, and finally different measures of compliant behavior. Compliance behavior itself is conceived as having a probability of occurring and presumably can be measured quantitatively; other aspects of the model are self-explanatory.

Summary

Sick-role behavior, illness behavior, and health behavior refer to three descriptive categories of health-related behaviors. In discussing how compliance with a therapeutic regimen may be conceptualized we discussed a number of ways that the sick-role model may be formulated to account for compliant behaviors, how analysis of illness behavior can identify mechanisms that produce noncompliance, and how the health belief model provided a model predictive of compliance behavior.

THE PSYCHOLOGY OF COMPLIANCE

We will limit our discussion in this rather vast area of research and study to just five topics: (1) cognitive dissonance theory, (2) attribution theory, (3) coping and adaptation, (4) social reinforcement (or exchange) theory, and (5) interoceptive conditioning (cf, Marston's chapter pp 139-164). Although we are limiting our discussion to these areas, it should be clear that the true breadth of the topic of compliance overlaps with such related psychological issues as conformity, social influence, social control, attitude change, internalization, etc.

Cognitive Theories of Compliance

We shall discuss two such theories: cognitive dissonance theory and attribution theory. *Cognitive dissonance* theory states:

> If a person knows various things that are not psychologically consistent with one another he will, in a variety of ways, try to make them more consistent. Two items of information that psychologically do not fit together are said to be in a dissonant relation to each other. The items of information may be about behavior, feelings, opinions, things in the environment, etc. The word *cognitive* simply emphasizes that the theory deals with relations about items of information.[19]

Cognitive dissonance is assumed to motivate people to resolve dissonance and this in its simplest form may consist of fulfilling unfulfilled expectations. An example may help to illustrate the theory and its applicability to the problem of compliance.

Consider the patient who feels well but has been advised by his physician that he has renovascular hypertension and has to decide between two relatively attractive alternatives designed to manage his ailment. His alternatives are to take antihypertensive medications the rest of his life and reduce the risk of a stroke, or to have a relatively complicated operation and avoid extended self-care. In either case, independent of which decision the patient makes, cognitive dissonance theory predicts that the patient will initially experience dissonance between how he feels and what he has been told by his physician about himself. The resolution of the dissonance will occur by an enhancement of the attractive features of the selected opinion (to be treated), a deemphasis on the attractive features of the selected optionThus, it is not uncommon for a patient who is to be treated to be not quite sure *before* a decision to become an advocate *after* the decision.

What is of interest to us, of course, is that cognitive dissonance may provide a means of predicting compliance with a therapeutic regimen. Unfortunately, the simplicity of the formulation is also its primary defect which, combined with some marginal experimental evidence, has subjected the theory to a range of criticism [20-22] that has essentially shown the theory to be unproved. Still, the logic of using cognitive mechanisms in accounting for compliance remains valid.

An alternative cognitive model that may be applicable to the issue of compliance is ***attribution theory***.[23-25] Attribution is the process of inferring or perceiving properties inherent to entities in the environment. It is the means whereby a person finds constancy in a changing environment. It permits a person to determine the cause of events. The process of attribution involves the use of simple, logical devices by the person "in a way analogous to the experimental method."[23]

The attribution process can, in fact, help account for instances of noncompliance to a therapeutic regimen, since it provides a conceptual model that describes how a person may account for the cause of health-related events. An example of the attribution process is when a drug produces a side effect and the ingested pill is identified by the patient as the cause of the effect. The placebo effect is a corollary to this process: attributing a desirable effect to an extrinsic object.[26] The terminal cancer patient attributing the failure of a therapy to the physician is another example of the attribution process. Thus the attribution process describes a psychological mechanism that could predict a patient's health-related decisions. Unfortunately, there do not appear to be any published experiments that use attribution theory in this particular way.

Coping and Adaptation

One of the most visible aspects of the problem of noncompliance is the fact that subjects differ in how they psychologically adjust the demands of their illness and therapeutic regimens to their life-styles, emotional states, interpersonal relationships, etc. Adapting to (*i.e.,* coping with) the stress of an illness or management of a therapeutic regimen occurs in all patients with varying degrees of success, and may involve a simple solution of some mechanical problem (*e.g.,* how to open up a child-proof container) or may involve use of less rational efforts at mastery, as when various defense mechanisms are elicited.[25,27] The resultant coping, irrespective of illness, helps maximize a patient's sense of personal worth, maintains relationships with other persons of significance to the patient, enhances recovery of bodily functions, and increases likelihood of a patient's returning to or continuing optimal social functions. These goals, which represent the psychological tasks required for the adaptation to an illness, have been observed to occur as a patient recovers from or learns to manage an illness.[28-30]

Lazarus [21] specifically defines coping as one element in a self-regulatory process that characterizes a person's transaction with his stressful environment. Coping permits the person to "alter or master the troubled commerce with the environment, as, for example, when he attempts to demolish, avoid or flee the harmful agent or to prepare somehow to meet the danger."[21] Another kind of self-regulatory process is meant to directly control emotions and includes such diverse modes of control as tranquilizers, alcohol, sleeping pills, ego-defenses, and various types of muscle relaxation or meditation. Such efforts at direct control are designed to reduce the affective, visceral, or motor disturbances that result from emotions and do not focus on the transaction between the person and his environment. Only when the person has sufficient control over his emotions does coping become possible.

The process whereby a patient responds to a life-threatening illness often starts by his *denying* the seriousness of the illness. This is followed by the patient engaging in various *protective strategies* (*e.g.,* my leukemia is nothing more than the flu) and finally progresses to *acceptance.* Coping strategies are used to facilitate this process. Some of the tasks required of the ill or injured individual include accommodating his sense of responsibility for the illness or damage, resolving any separation from family and friends, reconstituting his future plans, overcoming his sexual problems, and managing feelings of personal rejection and hostility.[28] Coping may be facilitated by interaction with other patients, visible support or encouragement from "significant others," and rapid physical recovery. The strategy adopted by the burned patient to cope with the changes in his body appearance and capacity includes a progressive desensitization toward his own appearance, a nonphysical conceptualization of himself, and a blurring of his own image of his physical appearance.[28,31,32] The coping strategy adopted by the parents of a leukemic child has been compared to anticipatory grief.[29] As the disease progresses in its characteristic manner, the parents experience a "narrowing" of hope, and the development of feelings of emotional detachment from the child.[28] Patients become increasingly vigilant or avoidant as they attempt to cope with the stress of surgery.[33] In fact, recovery in the vigilant patient may be impaired if the knowledge of the threatening aspect of surgery is left untempered by denial, while avoidance, if effective, is only so in minor surgery.[33]

The hypertensive patient, who must also cope with a life-threatening illness, does not have the advantage of assuming that a permanent resolution of the stresses created by the illness is possible. Whereas the burned patient will physically recover, the leukemic patient will die, and the surgical patient will have had his operation, whatever the hypertensive patient does in response to his illness he must persist at, usually in the absence of feedback of the consequences of his behavior on his physical condition. Not too surprisingly, therefore, hypertensive patients respond in a variety of ways to the stresses created by their illness. In a preliminary study,[34] we have noticed that the coping strategy used by a patient depends on some combination of the amount of specific knowledge the patient has, some estimate of the risk-to-life from the illness, some notion of the cause of the illness and what, if anything, can be done about the illness. Some patients will view an elevated blood pressure as having an organic base, requiring pharmacological management, and adherence to a therapeutic regimen. Some patients will view hypertension as being due to the quality of their interpersonal relationships and management involves social manipulations (i.e., "it's the aggravation that gives me high blood pressure and, if I could only control it, I would be O.K."). Some will consider themselves impaired by having high blood pressure and make adaptation to a disability the cornerstone of their efforts at coping. Some, out of fear of the consequence of high blood pressure or because they believe they have morally transgressed, will adjust their behavior accordingly. All in all, it is the indeterminancy of the presence of dysfunction and the marginal visibility of the consequence of treatment (except in the presence of adverse effects) that generate the variety of coping styles in the hypertensive. Any individual patient may reflect elements of several of these approaches, and compliance will reflect the adaptive success of the coping strategy.

Viewed from this perspective, compliance with a therapeutic regimen reflects the efficiency and success — the adaptive value — of a person's coping with the psychological consequences of illness and therapy. Although compliance may be measured in terms of specific outcomes (e.g., pill counts, blood pressure control) the nature of a person's psychological response to a therapeutic regimen can be seen as a coping process.

Social Reinforcement Theory

Behavioristic principles have found many application sites and should provide us with a number of approaches to the problem of compliance. A key principle in social reinforcement theory is that behavior is modified by its consequences. This occurs because reinforcement either increases or decreases the probability that a particular behavior will occur again.[35] This principle holds whether the reinforcement is mechanically dispensed or dispensed by another organism, as occurs in social situations.

We will discuss three mechanisms, **reciprocity** (or exchange theory), **coercion** and **modeling,** that have been suggested to be operative in social situations.[36-38] *Reciprocity* occurs when two people positively reinforce each other at approximately equal rates. *Coercion* occurs because one person receives a positive reinforcement, while another is under aversive stimulus control (e.g., avoiding something unpleasant). *Modeling* occurs when a person replicates a behavior engaged in by another person, and when reinforcement is self-initiated.

The notion that social relationships are governed by some reciprocal exchange of goods (which may vary from social approval to money to favors) is not new,[39,40] although it has only of late been formally incorporated into sociological and psychological theory.[38,41] The reciprocity hypothesis [41] assumes that the participants in a social exchange have overlapping repertoires of social behavior that will result in some minimal level of interaction (people, even those from the most diverse backgrounds, have something in common), but the duration and frequency of such interactions depend on the occurrence of reinforcement. Social interaction ceases because of the development of satiation and habituation to the reinforcement, while changes in the form and content of the social interaction occur as a result of differential reinforcement of the behavior of the individuals involved. Evidence supporting the exchange theory includes studies that show that subjects increase their frequency of verbal and nonverbal responses depending on what the experimenter does.[42,43] It has been shown that subjects spend about the same amount of time looking at the experimenter, as the experimenter does looking at them,[44] and vary their behavior according to that of the experimenter.[42]

The coercion hypothesis can be illustrated by the child who makes a demand on his mother in a public place. The mother, who responds to avoid embarrassment, then finds herself faced with another demand from the child sometime later. The mother, by complying with the child's demand, is, of course, encouraging the child to demand again (reinforcing the behavior). To not comply, however, results in a predicted increase in the number of demanding behaviors by the child (as predicted by the process of extinction) and it is the avoidance of this behavior that controls the mother's behavior. Thus, the child is positively reinforced and the mother responds to avoid the aversive stimuli leading to coercion.

The physician-patient relationship has elements of both exchange and coercion. To the extent that the physician is paid for services, one element of an exchange is present, but to the extent that the patient does not receive rewards for like service, reciprocity does not exist. To the extent that the patient may demand and the physician prescribe, coercion may be present. Alternatively, to the extent that the physician may establish a therapeutic regimen and the patient comply, coercion may also be present. Neither hypothesis alone is sufficient to characterize the physician-patient relationship.

If we confine ourselves, however, to one aspect of this relationship — i.e., the physician as the originator of a medication regimen — we are dealing with a situation in which one person is making a demand on another person who is also the beneficiary of the demand. Thus, the physician does not receive direct positive reinforcement if a patient complies; presumably the patient does. This is different from the child making a demand on the mother, since the beneficiary of the demand, if the demand is complied with, is the demander (the child) himself. Rather, it appears that the physician's task is to instruct a patient to engage in some behavior that is primarily reinforcing to the patient. The situation is therefore a form of observational learning, or modeling.[36] Noncompliance in this context is simply defined as incomplete observational learning due to poor stimulus control. Managing this problem becomes the rather technical one of improving the teaching technique of physicians.

Social learning theory permits us to view noncompliance as an operant subject to the same laws that govern any other type of operant behavior (*i.e.,* noncompliant behavior is learned, can be extinguished, can come under stimulus control, etc.). We have investigated briefly three ways of characterizing the social relationship between physician and patient — exchange, coercion and modeling — and have implied that elements of each are present.

Interoceptive Conditioning: It appears obvious, but probably worth stating directly, that behaviors we consider compliant or noncompliant are learned. Not totally obvious, however, is how such behavior is learned and whether knowing that noncompliant behavior is learned provides us with some advantage in its management. If we assume that noncompliant behavior is an operant response, then to determine how we learn to be noncompliant we must investigate (hopefully, experimentally) what specific events reinforce the behavior, and what subjects use as stimuli to elicit noncompliant responses. Just a superficial inspection quickly reveals that a wide variety of individual and social stimuli can elicit noncompliant behaviors, including stimuli associated with the illness of the patient (*e.g.,* the pain of surgery, the headache from high blood pressure), and stimuli dependent on the therapy (*e.g.,* the pain resulting from exercise required for rehabilitation, the drowsiness produced by the drug, etc.). These stimuli with their clear location within the organism, their clear involvement of the internal milieu, suggest that a principal component of the learning underlying noncompliance involves *interoceptive conditioning.*

Interoceptive conditioning is not to be confused with the type of learning that occurs when one learns to recite a poem or learns to find one's way to a place. In those types of learning, stimuli originating outside of the body (including lights, sounds, smells, etc.) become associated with responses and we can refer to this process as *exteroceptive conditioning.* When stimuli originating from within the body is associated with behavior, then we are discussing *interoceptive conditioning.* Behaviors acquired by interoceptive or exteroceptive conditioning procedures differ in several important ways: first, it takes very few trials for interoceptive, as compared to exteroceptive, conditioning to occur; second, the time between associated events must be quite small (measured in seconds) during exteroceptive conditioning as compared to interoceptive conditioning (measured in hours), and third, extinction of the associations occurs quite rapidly for exteroceptively conditioned response. Thus it is harder for us to learn but easier to "forget" exteroceptively as compared to interoceptively conditioned responses.

Of particular interest is the fact that some drugs elicit interoceptive stimuli (*e.g.,* nausea, tachycardia, etc.) that also can be conditioned. This conditioning can occur with or without our awareness of the stimuli being associated. What this implies is that throughout our lives, as we have taken drugs, we have learned good and bad things about them and it does not appear too much of an extension to state that what we have learned about drugs controls our drug-taking or compliance behavior. How this occurs can be illustrated in a standard type of experiment with rats.[45] In this type of experiment rats are first exposed to a novel stimulus — *e.g.,* saccharin solution — and then given a drug. After several pairings when the saccharin is presented prior to the drug, the rats usually avoid drinking the saccharin solution. The aversion seems to occur in the absence of drug or drug effect (*i.e.,* as much as seven days may separate the presentation of the test stimulus following the original pairing [46]). The implication of this work is, therefore, that stimuli that were previously natural and unrelated to any drug effect can acquire properties originally associated with a drug effect, and can control behavior. A popular example of this is the consequence of having a pizza and then a stomach upset; the resultant pairing of the sights and smells of pizza with vomiting will, on the next occasion for having pizza, more than likely seriously curtail the pizza-eating behavior of the subject. From all of the individual's experiences, associating pizza with vomiting does not make sense; yet if one assumes that interoceptive conditioning can occur, it does. Thus the kind of learning that forms the basis for noncompliance is not predictable from a common-sense notion of learning.

Summary

We have learned that noncompliance with a medication regimen may be accounted for in a number of ways. If you will permit some very broad statements, then we have learned (or will learn) from the sociologists what people do when they do not comply, and we have learned from the psychologists the supposed mechanisms that lead to noncompliance. The problem with the sociological approaches to noncompliance is that they too often leave unstated the psychological model that they are using, although it is quite clear that such a model or mechanism forms an important element of how they "explain" the behavior. On the other hand, the psychological approaches to noncompliance often appear irrelevant since they are seldom stated in a form that takes into account the structural limitations that social and cultural factors place on the supposed mechanisms mediating behavior. By bringing some, but probably not all, of the possible sociological and psychological approaches to compliance together, some perspective on the conceptual options available in studying compliance should have been made clear.

REFERENCES

1. Kasl SV, Cobb: Health behavior, illness behavior and sick-role behavior. Arch Environ Health 12:246-266, 1966.
2. Parsons T: The Social System. Glencoe, Free Press, 1951.
3. Parsons T: Patients, Physicians and Illness. New York, Free Press, 1958, p 165-187.
4. Parsons T: Social Structure and Personality. New York, Free Press, 1965.
5. Parsons T: The sick role and the role of the physician reconsidered. Milbank Mem Fund Q 53:257-278, 1975.
6. Goode WJ: A theory of role strain. Am Sociol Rev 25:483-496, 1960.
7. Gray R: Getting sick. Behav Today 5:236, 1974.
8. Mechanic D: Social psychological factors affecting the presentation of bodily complaints. N Engl J Med 286:1132-1139, 1972.

9. Friedson E: Patient's View of Medical Practice. New York: Russell Sage Foundation, 1961.
10. McKinlay J: Problems of Medical Care. London, Tavistoch, 1971.
11. Siegler M, Osmond H: The "sick role" revisited. Hastings Cent Stud 1:41-58, 1973.
12. Mechanic D: The concept of illness behavior. J Chronic Dis 15:189-194, 1962.
13. Mechanic D: Illness and social disabilities some problems in analysis. Pacific Sociol Rev 2:37-41, 1959.
14. Mechanic D: Medical Sociology, A Selective View. New York, Free Press, 1968.
15. Zborowski M: Cultural components in response to pain. J Soc Issues 8:16-30, 1952.
16. Rosenstock IM: Why people use health services. Milbank Mem Fun Q 44:94-124, 1966.
17. Becker MH, Drachman RH, Kirscht JP: A new approach to explaining sick-role behavior in low-income populations. Am J Public Health 64:205-216, 1974.
18. Becker M: Sociobehavioral determinants of compliance. Proceedings of a Workshop/Symposium: Compliance with Therapeutic Regimens (in press).
19. Festinger L: Cognitive dissonance. Sci Am 207:93-102, 1962.
20. Asch SE: A theory of cognitive dissonance. Contemp Psychol 3:194-195, 1958.
21. Chapanis NP, Chapanis A: Cognitive dissonance: five years later. Psychol Bull 61:1-22, 1964.
22. Rhine RJ: Some problems in dissonance theory research on information selectivity. Psychol Bull 68:21-28, 1967.
23. Heider F: The Psychology of Interpersonal Relations. New York: Wiley, 1958.
24. Kelley HH: Attribution theory in social psychology. In D Levine (ed): Nebraska Symposium on Motivation. Lincoln, Nebraska, 1964, pp 192-240.
25. Lazarus RS: A cognitively oriented psychologist looks at biofeedback. Am Psychol 30:553-561, 1975.
26. Valins S, Nisbett RE: Attribution processes in the development and treatment of emotional disorders. In EE Jones, DE Kanouse, HH Kelley, RE Nisbett, S Valins, B Weiner (eds): Attribution: Perceiving the Causes of Behavior. Morristown, NJ, General Learning Press, 1971, 137-150.
27. Lazarus RS, Averill JR, Opton EM: Coping and Adaptation. New York: Basic Books, 1974, pp 249-315.
28. Hamburg DA: Coping behavior in life-threatening circumstances. Psychother Psychosomat 23:13-25, 1974.
29. Lindemann E: Symptomatology and management of acute grief. Psychiatry 101:141, 1944.
30. Visotsky HM, Hamburg DA, Goss ME, Labovits BZ: Coping behavior under extreme stress. Arch Gen Psychiatry 5:423-448, 1961.
31. Andreason NJC, Norris AS: Long-term adjustment and adjustment mechanisms in severely burned adults. J Ner Ment Dis 154:352-362, 1972.
32. Hamburg D, Artz G, Reiss E, Anspacher W, Chambers R: Clinical importance of emotional problems in the care of patients with burns. N Engl J Med 248:355-359, 1953.
33. Cohen F, Lazarus RS: Active coping processes, coping dispositions and recovery from surgery. Psychosomatic Med 35:375-389, 1973.
34. Barofsky I, Sullivan JM: Summary of the Medication Counseling Project (unpublished manuscript), 1973.
35. Skinner BF: Science and Human Behavior. New York, Macmillan, 1953.
36. Bandura A: Principles of Behavior Modification. New York, Holt, Rinehart and Winston, 1969.
37. Homans GC: The sociological relevance of behaviorism. In RL Burgess, D Bushell Jr (eds): Behavioral Sociology: The Experimental Analysis of Social Process. New York, Columbia, 1969, pp 1-24.
38. Patterson GR, Reid JB: Reciprocity and coercion: Two facts of social systems. In C Neuringer, JL Michael (eds): Behavior Modification in Clinical Psychology. New York: Appleton-Century-Crofts, 1970, pp 133-177.
39. Homans GC: Social Behavior: Its Elementary Forms. New York, Harcourt, Brace and World, 1961.
40. Thibout JW, Kelley HH: The Social Psychology of Groups. New York, Wiley, 1959.

41. Emerson RM: Operant psychology and exchange theory. *In* RL Burgess, D Bushell Jr (eds):
42. Rosenfeld HM: Approval-seeking and approval-inducing functions of verbal and nonverbal responses in the aged. J Per Soc Psychol 7:597-605, 1966.
43. Rosenfeld HM: Nonverbal reciprocation of approval: an experimental analysis. J Exp Soc Psychol 3:102-111, 1967.
44. Kendon A: Some functions of gaze direction in social interaction. Unpublished paper, Institute of Experimental Psychology, Oxford University, England, 1965.
45. Garcia J, Hanhins WG, Rusiniah KW: Behavioral regulation of the milieu-interne in man and rat. Science 185:824-831, 1974.
46. Berger BD: Conditioning of food aversions by injections of psychoactive drugs. J Comp Physiol Psychol 81:21-26, 1972.

Biological Variability and Drug Response Variability as Factors Influencing Patient Compliance: Implications for Drug Testing and Evaluation

3

K.F. TEMPERO

Merck, Sharp & Dohme Research Laboratories
Rahway, New Jersey

Recent studies have firmly established that many medical prescriptions are not filled or utilized by the patient in dosage, time sequence, or duration desired by the prescribing physician.[1,2] The influence of various demosociographic factors upon this phenomenon has been studied. Age, sex, religion, income, social class, geographical location, family unit, education, conception of disease, etc., have all been examined and methods of manipulating and influencing several of these factors have been postulated and attempted.[3-5] Less attention has been given to more pharmacologically oriented factors such as dosage form, concurrent therapy, and side effects, but some evaluation of their influence and suggestions on how to change these parameters has been published (as mentioned further in this paper). Even less attention has been paid to variability in pharmacologic response as a factor which may potentially influence compliance. This paper will attempt to point out some of the established conditions in which individuals and/or population groups demonstrate unique reactions to pharmacologic agents.

The implications of this for the practicing physician are multiple. As additional information is generated and codified into usable form, the clinical history will come to contain information which allows the clinician to practice an increasingly important form of preventive medicine as he "tailors" his choice of drugs and dosage to each individual patient. The implications for industrial, academic and governmental research are also manifold and will be developed later in this essay.

FACTORS AFFECTING DRUG ACTION

Multiple factors influence a patient's response to a drug. These factors range from genetic variations (pharmacogenetics), through age (developmental pharmacology), environmental factors influencing intermediary metabolism, and the disease state itself, all of which can potentially affect the realization of any therapeutic goal. When the variance of some of these factors has been studied and established, specific examples will be given.

Pharmacogenetics

This broad term encompasses the entire spectrum of genetically determined (and by conventional usage unique as opposed to common) responses to drugs. While the variability in response may well directly affect the therapeutic efficacy of the drug, it may also exert an indirect influence if a patient experiences a unique side effect which subsequently influences her or his compliance to the therapeutic regimen.[6,7]

The presence or absence of receptors for a given drug may directly influence a patient's response. The fact that some people find phenylthiocarbamide or phenylthiourea tasteless whereas others find these compounds extremely bitter illustrates the potential genetically determined variability in the existence of drug receptor sites. As pointed out by Goldman,[8] this type of effect has not been extensively researched.

Variability in pharmacokinetics (absorption, distribution, metabolism, and excretion) may well be affected by genetics. Even if one assumes a uniform "effective level" in the plasma or tissue, a two- to threefold genetically determined variance in absorption could potentially cause an "average" dose of a drug with a narrow therapeutic range (low therapeutic ratio) to be toxic in some patients. Some of the occasional patients who experience digitalis toxicity on minimal doses of cardiac glycoside may be extremely efficient absorbers. A parallel phenomenon may exist in drug excretion. Two and one-half per cent of the patient population excrete drugs one-third slower than the so-called "average" patient, and fourfold variance in plasma half-lives have been documented.[9,10] The fact that patients may exhibit faster or unusual metabolic drug disposition as well as slower than average distribution and metabolism was documented by Luchi & Gruber [11] and may be expected to affect drug response.

Just as the absorption of nutrition from milk may be influenced by the presence or absence of lactase in the gastrointestinal tract, the characteristics of the patient's intermediary metabolic machinery can influence not only drug metabolism (slow versus rapid acetylators of isoniazid or the prolonged paralysis after succinylcholine administration to a patient lacking pseudocholinesterase) but drug interactions (isoniazid and diphenylhydantoin interaction in slow acetylators) and gross response to a drug, e.g., the intermittent porphyric's response to barbiturates; the response of a patient with a glucose-6-dehydrogenase deficiency to antimalarials or sulfa drugs; the patient who responds to an inhaled anesthetic agent with malignant hyperthermia; or the patient who is extremely resistant to coumarin anticoagulants.[7] Some of these mechanisms are well understood; others such as porphyria and malignant hyperthermia are currently the subjects of active research. Table I delineates some common drugs to which patients may respond differently because of pharmacogenetic factors.

TABLE I

DRUGS UNDERGOING ACETYLATION

Dapsone
Hydralazine
Isoniazid
Phenelzine
Salicylazosulfapyridine
Sulfapyridine
Sulfamethazine

DRUGS AND CHEMICALS WHICH CAN CAUSE
HEMOLYSIS IN PATIENTS WITH A DEFICIENCY
OF GLUCOSE-6-DEHYDROGENASE IN THEIR ERYTHROCYTES

ANALGESICS	ANTIBACTERIAL AGENTS
Acetanilid	Chloramphenicol
Acetophenetidin	Furazolidone
Aminopyrine	Nitrofurantoin
Antipyrine	Para-aminosalicylate
Acetylsalicyclic acid	Sulfa drugs
	Sulfones (including dapsone)

ANTIMALARIALS	OTHER
Pamaquine	British Anti-Lewisite agent
Pentaquine	Mestranol
Primaquine	Napthalene
Quinacrine	Probenecid
	Quinidine
	Quinine

Sex and age can also influence a patient's response to drugs. Females under the age of 60 and all males seem to tolerate heparin therapy with less spontaneous hemorrhage than do females over the age of 60. The cause of this difference has not been determined.

Developmental Pharmacology

Physicians have long been aware that children, metabolically and therapeutically, are not merely "little adults," as is demonstrated by the widespread alertness to the use of opiates, cardiac glycosides, sulfa drugs, and chloramphenicol during the neonatal period. Guides such as Young's and Clark's *Rules* for estimating pediatric doses have attempted to simplify and formalize these differences.

The half-life ($T_{1/2}$) of digoxin varies with age, probably depending on the development of, and during later life loss of, the ability to clear digoxin.[12] Ander's [13] studies have revealed that while the $T_{1/2}$ for cephalothin is similar in the infant and adult, children do not demonstrate a peak of deacetylated metabolite whereas adults always do, and Kaplan et al [14] demonstrated that the plasma $T_{1/2}$ of ampicillin is inversely related to postnatal age. In contrast with many animal species which do not develop cytochrome P-450 and other hepatic drug-metabolizing systems until after birth, man has an appreciable ability to metabolize drugs *in utero* [15] as well as immediately following birth.

The development of drug-metabolizing enzymes shows marked species variation. For instance, guinea pigs develop mixed oxidase systems within two to four days after birth, whereas the rat and rabbit require a period of weeks to develop the same metabolic ability.

Similar to the "greater than adult" capability to metabolize drugs that Alvares et al [16] have reported for certain age groups of human children, young guinea pigs can metabolize some drugs more rapidly than the adult guinea pig despite the fact that the absolute concentrations of cytochrome P-450 in the youthful liver tissue never exceeds that found in adult livers.

Physicians have become aware that geriatric patients often need less medication than younger patients. This has frequently been explained as a decrement in hepatic or renal function with aging, and attempts have been made to correlate renal drug clearance with blood urea nitrogen and/or serum creatinine levels. Much work remains to be done, however, in defining the changes in drug metabolism during aging.

Environmental Factors

Drug interaction phenomena have received widespread attention and, in selected cases, therapeutic regimens are ideally altered or dosages changed in order that the interaction may be avoided or minimized. However, even if the physician and/or the pharmacist carefully monitors the prescription drugs used by a patient in order to control drug interactions, multiple other factors such as over-the-counter medications as well as various social habits and other environmental factors can influence the effects of a drug in any given patient.

Not only can the intake of various drugs which induce hepatic enzymes, such as barbiturates or anticonvulsants, influence a patient's reaction to other drugs, but so can the use of ethanol, tobacco, and the nutritional status of the patient. The "on-off" effect of L-dopa in some Parkinsonian patients [17-19] may be related to the amino acid content of the diet; the benzpyrenes in tobacco smoke can affect liver enzymes sufficiently to alter a patient's clinical response to chlordiazepoxide and diazepam.[8]

We need not knowingly ingest a chemical for it to influence the body's handling of drugs; the use of DDT and other insecticides has been shown to influence drug metabolism in humans as well as animals. Thus, the therapeutic efficacy as well as incidence of side effects may be grossly altered by social habits, concurrent medication, occupation, geography, climate, and urban or rural surroundings.

The Disease State

The particular disease state(s) from which the patient is suffering may influence drug response in several ways. Inflammation in a given tissue — e.g., gut or meninges — can alter membrane permeability and thus influence rates of absorption and other pharmacokinetic parameters as well as the drug distribution space. If, due to inflammation of the meninges, a drug customarily excluded from the central nervous system (CNS) gains entrance to the CNS, a patient may exhibit unusual drug effects.

More mundanely the presence of hepatic and/or renal disease may influence the route and rate of drug elimination and thus the blood and tissue levels of not only the parent drug but also of potentially active metabolites. In the case of salicylazosulfapyridine, the retention of a metabolite, sulfapyridine, is associated with abdominal discomfort, headache, nausea, and, in patients with glucose-6-dehydrogenase deficiency, hemolytic anemia. The implications for patient compliance are as obvious in these cases as they are for the hypertensive patient who associates his impotence with his antihypertensive medication.

PHARMACOLOGIC "TAILORING": THE TASKS AHEAD

Since all drugs must be present in a certain minimum concentration to exert either beneficial therapeutic or undesired side effects, it can be seen that any factor tending to increase drug concentrations above desired concentrations may well lead to increased side effects and thus decreased patient compliance.

While this can become a circle in which one is hard pressed to differentiate "the chicken from the egg," it is clear that increased knowledge will enable the physician to be increasingly cognizant of potential problems and to adjust dosage and/or choice of drugs accordingly.[20] An additional mechanism may be available through the developing science of chronopharmacology in which advantage can be taken of the fact that the body, depending on its rhythmicity, responds differently to some drugs depending on the time of administration. The administration of steroids customarily takes this into account. Professor A. Reinberg [21,22] has published data indicating that some of the pharmacokinetic parameters of aspirin and ethanol are also dependent upon the time of drug administration. Investigation of this phenomenon is needed with regard to other drugs.

Another method of pharmacologic "tailoring" of a drug or drug regimen in order to reduce side effects (and thus, hopefully, increase compliance) is the development of a selective drug delivery system. This has been explored in terms of drug impregnated intrauterine devices, ocular inserts, and automated insulin-dispensing systems. Ghose et al [23,24] have expanded the concept even further into the utilization of tumor immunology to deliver anti-tumor drug to the tumor cell in higher concentrations.

Thus, while many isolated discrete facts are known, currently available information merely begins to demonstrate the importance of the unknown. The implications raised by questions about patient compliance are manifold and important, and involve agencies at all levels (*e.g.,* industrial, academic, and governmental agencies) concerned with drug testing and evaluation of drug safety and efficacy.

IMPLICATIONS FOR DRUG TESTING

Clinical practitioners, industry, academic medical communities, and governmental regulatory agencies are all concerned with the safety and efficacy of drug therapy. Figure 1 is a schematic diagram of the interrelationships and differences in the emphasis of interests of all these members of the medical

Inter-relationships of Clinical Practice, Governmental, Academic and Industrial Groups' Interest in Drug Response Evaluation.

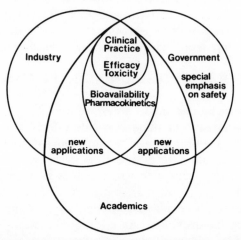

Figure 1: While the direct concerns of the clinical practice community may primarily involve drug efficacy and toxicity as pertaining to the therapeutic aspect of patient care, the governmental, academic and industrial communities will, in addition, concern themselves with additional research and fundamental scientific considerations. Each community will, quite properly, utilize its unique position of interest.

community. Although the emphasis of interest quite properly shifts depending on ultimate goals, the latter three groups especially concern themselves with evaluating and interpreting data to determine the absolute and relative efficacy, toxicity, and side effects of the drug therapy. Overenthusiastic utilization can lead to errors in the assessment of side effects and toxicity and non- or undercompliance can, if unrecognized, lead to errors in evaluation of absolute or relative efficacy. This is especially critical during phase I and IIa studies in which small sample sizes are utilized.[25]

Obviously, no group can accomplish its goals efficiently without excellent subject and patient compliance during the studies from which data are generated. Alternatively, knowledge of the extent of compliance or noncompliance, especially if it is an all-or-none phenomenon, may in the study situation suffice for the evaluation of research data.[26] This latter approach, however, as Blackwell [27] has pointed out is not satisfactory in a clinical situation. Thus, it must be recognized that although the various medical groups may be interested in compliance from varying viewpoints, the problems of documentation, evaluation, and possibly alteration of compliance phenomena are of universal interest and importance.[28,29]

Whether variance in biological response is a major determinant in compliance remains to be determined. Its role may well be overshadowed by socially and culturally determined factors in most instances.

The assessment, utilization, and potential manipulation of motivation may well play an increasingly important role in medical practice as well as in the evaluation of clinical research data. This, in the foreseeable future, will be slowed by our current lack of adequate, nonobtrusive direct methodology by which compliance may be evaluated.[30-35]

Acknowledgment: The author wishes to thank Drs. Bessealaar and Dziewanowska for their assistance in this manuscript.

REFERENCES

1. Ayd FJ: Rational Pharmacotherapy: Once a day drug dosage. Dis Nervous System 34:371-378, 1973.
2. Boyd JR, Covington JR, Stanazek WF et al: Drug defaulting. Part 1: Determinants of compliance. Am J Hosp Pharmacy 31:362-367, 1974.
3. Berry D, Ross A, Huempfner H et al: Self-medication behavior as measured by urine chemical tests in domicilary tuberculosis patients. Am Rev Resp Dis 86:1-7, 1962.
4. Geertsen HR, Gray RM, Ward JR: Patient noncompliance within the context of seeking medical care for arthritis. J Chronic Dis 26:;.26:689-698, 1973.
5. Mikeal RL, Sharpe T: Patient compliance. In Wetheimer AI, Smith MC, (eds): Pharmacy Practice: Social and Behavioral Aspects. Baltimore, University Park Press, 1974, 179-194.
6. Vessel ES: Pharmacogenetics — Introduction: genetic and environmental factors affecting drug response in man. Fed Proc 31:1253-69, 1973.
7. Vessel ES: Medical intelligence: Drug therapy: pharmacogenetics. N Engl J Med 287:904-9, 1972.
8. Goldman P: Patient factors governing response to drugs. Drug Ther 4:50-58, 1974.
9. Waldenstrom JG: Pharmacogenetics (editorial). Acta Med Scand 194:241-3, 1973.
10. WHO Scientific Group on Pharmacogenetics: Pharmacogenetics — the influence of heredity on the response to drugs. WHO Chronicle 28:25-31, 1974.

11. Luchi RJ, Gruber JW: Unusually large digitalis requirements. Am J Med 45:332-338, 1968.
12. Doherty JE: Digitalis glycosides, pharmacokinetics and their clinical implications. Ann Intern Med 79:229-238, 1973.
13. Anders NW, Cooper MJ, Mirkin BL: Application of High Pressure Liquid Chromatography in Pediatric Pharmacology. International Symposium on Perinatal Pharmacology. Milano, Italy, 1974 (in press).
14. Kaplan JM, McCracken H, Horton LF, et al: Pharmacological studies in neonates given large doses of ampicillin. J Pediatrics 84:571-577, 1974.
15. Pelknonen O, Kaltiala EH, Larmi TKT, et al: Comparison of activities of drug metabolizing enzymes in human fetal and adult livers. Clin Pharmacol Ther 14:840-846, 1973.
16. Alvares AP, Kapelner S, Sussa S, et al: Drug metabolism in normal children, lead-poisoned children, and normal adults. Clin Pharmacol Ther 17:179-183, 1975.
17. Cotzias BF, Mena I, Papvasilion PS: Overview of present treatment of parkinsonism with L-DOPA. Adv Neurology 2:265-277, 1973.
18. Mearrick PT, Wase DN: Variability of L-DOPA absorption in man. Aus N Zealand J Med 3:337-338, 1973.
19. Sandler M, Goodwin BL, Ruthven CRJ, et al: Variation of Levodopa metabolism with gastrointestinal absorption site. Lancet II;238-239, 1974.
20. Liblow LS, Mehl B: Self-administration of medications by patients in hospitals or extended care facilities. J Am Geriatrics Soc 18:81-85, 1970.
21. Reinberg A, Zagula Mally A, Ghata J et al: Circadian rhythm in duration of salicylate excretion referred to phase excretory rhythm and routine. Proc Soc Exp Biol Med 124:826-832, 1967.
22. Reinberg A, Clench J, Aymard N et al: Rhythmes circardiens des parametres de l'ethanolemi provoquie chez six hommes adultes, Jaunes et Sains, CR Acad Sci (Paris) 278:1503-1505, 1974.
23. Ghose T, Norvell ST, Gulcu A et al: Immunochemotherapy of cancer with chlorabucil-carrying antibody. Br Med J 3:459-499, 1972.
24. Ghose T, Path MRC, Nigam SP: Antibody as carrier of chlorambucil. Cancer 29:1398-1400, 1972.
25. Rickels D, Briscoe E: Assessment of dosage deviation in outpatient drug research. J Clin Pharmacol 10:153-160, 1970.
26. Joyce CRM: Patient cooperation and the sensitivity of clinical trials. J Chronic Dis 15:1025-1036, 1962.
27. Blackwell B: The drug defaulter. Clin Pharmacol Ther 13:841-848, 1972.
28. Sheiner LB, Rosenberg B, Marathe VV et al: Clin Pharmacol 15:239-246, 1974.
29. Wilson JT: Compliance with instructions in the evaluation of therapeutic efficacy. Clin Pediat 12:333-4, 1973.
30. Gordis L, Markowicz M, Lilienfeld AM: The inaccuracy in using interviews to estimate patient reliability in taking medications at home. Med Care 7:49-54, 1969.
31. Jenkins BW: Are patients true to T.I.D. and Q.I.D. doses? Gen Pract 9:66-69, 1954.
32. Moulding R: The medication monitor for studying the self-administration of oral contraceptives. Am J Ob Gyn 10:1143-1144, 1971.
33. Moulding T, Knight SJ Jr, Colson JB: Vertical pill-calendar dispenser and medication monitor for improving the self-administration of drugs. Tubercle (London) 48:32-37, 1967.
34. Moulding T, Onstad GD, Sbarbaro JA: Supervision of outpatient drug therapy with the medication monitor. Ann Intern Med 73:559-564, 1970.
35. Roth HP, Caron H, Hsi BP: Measuring intake of a prescribed medication. Clin Pharmacol Ther 11:228-237, 1970.

PART THREE

Intervention Techniques Available To Increase Compliance

This section can correctly be considered the core of this book. We have tried to accomplish several things in this section:

(a) To identify the different strategies available to affect change in compliance behavior depending on the various "actors" in the health care process.

(b) To make as explicit as can be done in this type of format how to implement some of these change procedures.

(c) To describe what representative practitioners have accomplished in their own practices.

Reading this material one is naturally impressed by the difference between what can be done and what is being done. But this too is one of the functions of this book, since the discrepancy between the ideal and the reality is the essence of the process of application; only by seeing them contrasted is any individual practitioner able to identify what he can do to improve the management of compliance behavior.

A. Focus on the Patient

The next five papers emphasize patient-related variables as a means of increasing blood pressure control or adherence to the therapeutic regimen. Blackwell compares medication taking with meditation and illustrates how each may succeed for different patients. Lewis and Michnich review what we know about formalizing the patient-physician relationship on a contractual basis, the assumption being that a contract spells out the obligation of each participant to each other and thereby increases the chances that the goals of therapeutic regimen will be achieved. Zifferblatt and Curry spell out in detail how a practitioner can help a patient take his medication. They describe self-control procedures. Morris and Gagliardi review the history of patient package inserts and current experimental applications of the insert to the hypertensive patient. Finally, Grissom describes how he encourages self-care by patients and thus illustrates what one practitioner considers acceptable in his own practice.

Chemical Coping, Self-Control and Compliance in Hypertension

B. BLACKWELL

Department of Psychiatry
School of Medicine
Wright State University
Dayton, Ohio

Once the sphygmomanometer was invented and hypertension was recognized as the most common chronic disease, blood pressure became an obvious and observable end-point for physiologists and psychologists interested in the mind-body interaction and modes to examine it. For almost a century there has been constant speculation on the relationship between life stress, the individual's response, and blood pressure changes.

More recently hypertension has also become a model for studying the complex problems of adherence because it is a life-long, life-threatening disease in which the discomforts of the treatment regimen often exceed the symptoms of disease. These include the side effects of medication as well as the sacrifices involved in reducing risk factors associated with weight, diet, and smoking.

Because hypertension has served as a model for both psychosomatic disorders and adherence problems, it lends itself to an examination of the extent to which chemical coping or self-control procedures, such as meditation, are preferred or effective treatments for individual patients with hypertension who also experience stress.

Drugs and meditational techniques have both been shown to affect blood pressure and anxiety. To understand the place of either in treatment regimens, it is necessary to make an examination first of the interaction between stress, blood pressure and individual coping; second, of the range of individual responses to stress; and finally, the evidence for efficacy of both medication and meditation in the treatment of individuals with hypertension.

STRESS, PERSONALITY AND BLOOD PRESSURE

Popular acceptance that stress plays a possible role in the etiology or aggravation of hypertension followed in the wake of Cannon's "flight or fight" hypothesis [1] and Selye's enunciation of a "General Adaptation Syndrome."[2]

The fact that short-term psychologic stress can provoke physiologic change is well proven, including the observation that individuals differ in which physiologic variable is most altered (pulse rate, skin resistance, respiration, or blood pressure). Betweeen one third and two thirds of the population show a reproducible "response stereotype" to stress.[3] It has also been shown that identified hypertensives exposed to stress display the predictable response stereotype of increased blood pressure.[4] The still incompletely answered question is the extent to which changes that take place under acute experimental conditions also occur following prolonged environmental stress.[5] Resolution of this issue has awaited the development of valid epidemiologic techniques and reliable instruments to measure environmental stress. These strategies are rapidly advancing[6] and appear to confirm the relationship between stressful life events and cardiovascular disease.[7-10] As with the physiologic response to acute experimental stress, the occurrence of disease in response to environmental stress is neither specific or inevitable. Almost any disease may be associated with an increase in recent life events, including psychiatric, medical, and surgical diseases.[11] Epidemiologic evidence has shown an increased incidence of hypertension in airtraffic controllers,[12] but this study also demonstrated that many individuals did not succumb and that others developed ulcers or diabetes rather than hypertension.

This individual variability in response to environmental stress may be accounted for by genetic variables, the presence of contributory risk factors (such as smoking, diet, or obesity), or by personality differences in how people respond psychologically to stress. However, when genetic factors are held constant in studies on monozygotic twins, stress factors remain important in the etiology of cardiovascular conditions.[13]

PSYCHOLOGICAL RESPONSES TO STRESS

Individuals exposed to identical stress respond psychologically in widely differing ways. This variability is based on characteristics that are described in a number of ways as "coping devices," "personality traits," "psychological defenses," or "resistance resources." These different terminologies have been used in attempts to couple specific personal characteristics to particular disease states. In hypertension Franz Alexander maintained that high blood pressure was contributed to by suppressed emotional conflict, particularly aggressive or hostile impulses.[14] A more recent attempt at stereotopy has been the "Type A personality described as impatient, fast-moving, and also aggressive.[15] Such stereotypes are not observed in every individual with hypertension and are not identifiable in all cultures, including some in which cardiovascular disease is rampant, (such as Holland). All the terms that attempt to describe predictable behavior responses to stress can be summarized as an inability to adapt to change. As Theorell [16] has pointed out: "Whether this defective ability should be called 'Type A behavior,' 'Sisyphus syndrome,' 'work addiction,' or 'neuroticism' and whether we are dealing with genetic traits or behavior patterns formed by early childhood circumstances is not known."

The safest conclusion is that stress and change can provoke disease in some genetically predisposed individuals who have defects in psychological adaptation to change. Paradoxically, it may be this defect in psychological adaption that actually results in the detection of the disease, to an overrepresentation of the association between physical and psychological factors, and to the assumption of a causal relationship. This is particularly so in hypertension because it is a "silent" disease. Cases are discovered very often in patients who make somatic complaints in response to psychosocial stress including such symptoms as headaches, lassitude, or tension. In such individuals, high blood pressure is often discovered accidentally on routine physical examination. This response of some individuals to stress has been called "illness behavior."[17] It is more common in people with poor emotional vocabularies who enlist psychological aid from the physician through the medium of physical complaints. Such individuals may also highly value receiving care.[18]

In clinical practice, populations of patients with hypertension are therefore likely to contain an overrepresentation of individuals poor at coping with stress, in some of whom this factor may indeed have a part to play in causation or aggravation of the disease (along with other genetic and risk factors). In contrast, hypertensives discovered through routine screening programs will include fewer individuals in whom psychological factors are an important component, but in whom other risk factors may predominate. This is supported by epidemiologic surveys using measures on "anxiety" or "hostility" which have shown no difference between individuals with previously undetected blood pressure and normal controls.[19]

MEDICATION

Neither patients nor physicians are entirely satisfied with existing drug treatments in hypertension. The efficacy of hypotensive drugs is still equivocal in patients (particularly women) whose diastolic blood pressure is below 115 mm Hg and whose condition is early or uncomplicated.[20] It is this same segment of the hypertensive population that is often termed "labile" and in whom anxiety is assumed to play a causal role. Such individuals with concurrent anxiety and hypertension sometimes self-medicate with alcohol and are often prescribed minor tranquilizers. Sixteen per cent of the fifty million annual prescriptions for diazepam are prescribed to patients with cardiovascular disease.[21] A recent survey in our own hypertension clinic [22] found that 40 per cent of patients were taking a minor tranquilizer. This is over twice the national average for age and sex-comparable groups.

Dissatisfaction with existing hypotensive drugs and their side effects is manifested by a nonadherence rate in several studies of up to fifty per cent.[23,24] Moreover a majority of patients treated with minor tranquilizers are dissatisfied with this means of chemical coping, and feel it is not the best way of dealing with stress.[25]

There are several reasons why dissatisfaction with chemical coping may exist. Individuals with hypertension are mainly discovered by physicians as a consequence of illness behavior (rather than through routine screening). Such people are likely to value caretaking highly. Paradoxically attention from a physician may become contingent on not taking medication since this results in poor control of blood pressure and solicitous manifestations of concern by the physician. There is evidence to show that those who lean most on physicians learn least about medication.[26]

Another component leading to the failure to follow instructions is the reliance that physicians place on fear as a motivating factor: "You will die of a stroke unless you take medication, lose weight, and stop smoking." Disease prevention programs in such conditions as obesity, smoking, and cancer indicate that fear is an inconsistent motivating force.[27] To the extent that an individual views himself as vulnerable, fear may even increase nonadherence. This is because taking medication becomes an intimation of mortality so that forgetting to take it is anxiety-avoiding and reinforcing as a behavior. This may account for a recent finding that half the patients with end-stage hypertension and on renal dialysis were not taking their major medication.[28]

Considered together, these findings indicate that identified hypertensives are a group of individuals in whom problems in coping with stress are frequent but these are often poorly treated by medication, as is the disease itself.

MEDITATION

The probability that inadequate response to stress is one risk factor in hypertension that is overrepresented in the clinical population and is inadequately treated suggests a place for other methods of psychological intervention. As has been pointed out,[29] "to the extent that people have modest aspirations and less intense commitments, they more easily insulate themselves from stress." Most physicians are aware of this when they advise cardiovascular patients to "take it easy." Unfortunately, individual motivations and social pressures make such advice easier to give than to take. What most people seek is some technique by which they can enhance their adaptation to existing life conditions without reducing their commitments. That transcendental meditation (TM) offers precisely this is reflected in the title of its latest book, *Discovering Inner Energy and Overcoming Stress*.[30] In a foreword to this book, Hans Selye himself writes that TM "can help humanity face the crises of modern life." This book was twenty-five weeks on the best-seller list; and many health professionals now are called on to deal with patients who are seeking advice or referral concerning meditation.

Meditational techniques can be traced through the ages in most religions and many have marked similarities to TM. Common components of most meditational techniques are a quiet environment, relaxed posture, passive attitude, and use of a repetitive phrase or word (called the *mantra* in TM), the purpose of which is to shift thought inward, away from logical, externally oriented concerns. In more modern times, such techniques have included progressive muscle relaxation, autogenic training, hypnosis, Zen, and Yoga. TM is a derivative of Yoga, taught and proselytized by Maharishi Maresh Yogi, who introduced it from India to the United States in 1959. Since then, the movement has grown to over an estimated 6,000 teachers and close to half a million meditators as well as a university dedicated to "The Science of Creative Intelligence." Individuals who undertake TM are instructed by qualified teachers at a cost of $125, given a personal mantra, and, after learning to meditate, practice the technique for twenty minutes twice a day.

Evidence for physiologic change associated with meditation was first reported from studies on yogis in India, followed by research in Europe [31] and America.[32] There have now been six well-designed laboratory studies on TM showing consistent physiologic changes including slowing of the electroencephalogram, increased skin resistance, and decreased oxygen consumption. These changes are quite different from those observed in either sleep or hypnosis. A recent review of this research [33] drew attention to design flaws that made it difficult to identify "the specific and dependent variables in causal relationships that account for meditative phenomena." Woolford stated that this was due in part to "a complex framework of expectation, philosophical belief and social influence."

Particular effects on blood pressure have been reported with several types of meditational techniques including Yoga,[3,4] relaxation therapy,[35] and TM.[36-38] These studies all report significant and clinically meaningful reductions in blood pressure. Degree of control and research design have varied, but most have been within-subject designs using extended base lines to limit the effects attributable to focused attention. One study [34] showed significant results compared to a control group of matched hypertensives told to rest on a couch.

In our own study,[38] seven selected hypertensives were stabilized on drugs at a research clinic. After they had learned TM they were seen weekly and also took their own blood pressures several times daily. After twelve weeks of TM, six subjects showed psychologic changes and reduced anxiety scores. Six subjects also showed significant reductions in home and four in clinic blood pressures. Six months later most subjects continued to derive psychologic benefits, and two showed significant blood pressure reductions attributable to TM both at home and in the clinic. It is also important to note that the subjects who failed to benefit from TM subsequently obtained relief for both psychologic complaints and high blood pressure after reverting to more conventional methods of treatment.

An appreciation of the range of effects observed with meditation can be obtained from considering some of the responses of individual subjects who participated in this study. (Original case numbers are retained for cross reference with the earlier communication.[38])

Case 4: This subject was the individual who derived the most benefit from meditation and in whom sustained physiologic and psychologic changes were apparent. He valued self control highly and was able to reduce his dependence on medication and physicians.

He was a 50-year-old accountant who had been a known hypertensive for 20 years treated with diuretics and hypotensive medications. He also took minor tranquilizers regularly but had never seen a psychiatrist. The subject volunteered for the study because his daughter had benefited from meditation and he predicted complete benefit for himself as result of this study. He was enthusiastic about meditation from the start. His instructor noted that he enrolled his wife and son in TM as well. This patient not only kept meticulous blood pressure recordings but graphed them continuously. He reported great benefit from meditation which he felt made him more calm and capable of handling frustrations at work. These changes were accompanied by a reduction in anxiety score and by significant falls in all blood pressure measures. At the end of the study he requested that he be allowed to stop medication as he was convinced he no longer needed it. Following this there was a small increase in blood pressure.

At six months' follow-up the patient was still meditating regularly and monitoring blood pressure. He only took medication rarely if his diastolic blood pressure exceeded 100 mm Hg on three consecutive readings. The clinic systolic and diastolic blood pressures both remained significantly below baseline as did the home diastolic readings. He continued to derive marked psychological benefit.

Case 6: This subject came to the clinic seeking a psychological cure for an allegedly drug-induced side effect. Both his impotence and blood pressures failed to benefit. Following the end of the study his impotence responded to another more specific form of psychological treatment and he was able to resume drugs with benefit to his blood pressure and without the recurrence of side effects.

He is a 43-year-old accountant with a 15-year history of hypertension. He had been treated with diuretics and hypertensive medications and had become impotent during the treatment which discontinued two weeks before the study. This was a major reason for his seeking treatment with meditation and he predicted marked benefit. There was no history of emotional difficulty or psychiatric treatment.

The initial response to meditation was hopeful but it did not improve his impotence and he became increasingly skeptical. His TM instructor noted that he missed only one meeting but his attitude was one of "benign neutrality" in which he seemed neither antagonistic nor enthusiastic. He did not seem to practice TM regularly. These observations were confirmed in the clinic where he stated that he found TM a chore to do and that getting up in the mornings early to meditate made him irritable. He noted his blood pressure had gone down but did not think meditation was responsible. His anxiety scores were also reduced.

At six months' follow-up he had done no meditation and had started back on the same hypotensive drug. He had treated his own impotency by reading

Masters and Johnson's text and had regained full potency while continuing to take medication. Probably as a result of reinstituting medication his home and clinic blood pressures were significantly reduced.

Case 3: This subject responded eagerly to meditation with both psychologic and physiologic benefit. Despite this he failed to persist with meditation once continuous supervision was withdrawn. He eventually rejected self control procedures after a frightening experience and returned to the care of a physician.

He was a 43-year-old director of a purchasing department who had been treated with a diuretic alone for hypertension for seven years' duration. He gave no history of emotional problems or psychiatric treatment. He predicted complete relief of his hypertension as a result of meditation. The patient was also found to have elevated triglycerides during his attendance at the clinic and was placed on a diet as a result of which he lost 12 pounds during the period he was also receiving TM. His meditation instructor reported that he missed only one attendance and maintained a positive attitude throughout.

At the end of the study he reported that he experienced a marked sense of relaxation for brief periods after meditating and also stated that he felt he could read more rapidly (he attributed this to TM and stated he knew of one other person who benefited the same way.) He had stopped biting his fingernails for the first time in seven years. These changes were accompanied by a fall in anxiety score. With regard to his blood pressure, he was skeptical of any benefit and stopped taking his own blood pressure because he felt the results unreliable. He did note some reduction in blood pressure but attributed this to weight loss and considered the cause of his hypertension to be biological. Despite this skepticism, the home systolic and clinic blood pressure showed significant reductions.

At six months' follow-up he had stopped meditation due to "laziness" even though both he and his wife felt he had benefited from it. He had gained back the 12 pounds in weight loss during the study. The patient was asked to begin taking his own blood pressure again during the follow-up period. The next week he telephoned the clinic to state that he would not return. While taking his own blood pressure, he noted that it was elevated with a systolic over 180 mm Hg. He became agitated and developed numbness in the face. Both he and his wife felt concerned that he might be about to have a stroke. He went to an emergency room where his blood pressure was 160/110 and he was sedated with barbiturates. These events were confirmed by the patient's internist. Following this the patient resolved never to take his own blood pressure again and did not return to the clinic.

Case 2: This subject derived marked psychological benefit from meditation but his disease was strongly organically determined. As a result his blood pressure was affected only by medical manipulations and by a subsequent heart attack. However, he continued to meditate and derived considerable psychological benefit.

He was a 42-year-old buyer who was mildly obese and had been treated with diuretics and hypertensive drugs for 10 years. He had heard that TM helped people emotionally and recognized that at times he was tense, for which he had occasionally taken tranquilizers in the past but had never sought psychiatric help. He predicted marked benefit from participation in the study.

After beginning TM himself he enrolled both daughters in the treatment because of the benefit he derived. In his own life he considered that TM helped him become less readily upset at work and that he coped better with family stresses mainly related to one teenage daughter in adolescent turmoil. At the conclusion of the training he still felt that TM had made it much easier for him to cope with pressure and to remain calm in situations where before he would have "blown his stack." His TM instructor confirmed that he attended all meetings and found meditation beneficial. There was no change in blood pressure but he was not concerned about this since he felt benefit might be slow and cumulative. The psychological benefit was reflected in a reduction in anxiety scores.

At six months' follow-up he was still meditating on about half the occasions and the trouble with his daughter had been resolved. He had stopped taking his own blood pressure because "it was always the same." Because he no longer felt that TM benefited his blood pressure, he made an appointment to see a new internist and discovered that his serum triglyceride levels were elevated. Following this he was placed on hypotensive medication and a diet. This probably accounted for the significant reductions in both home and clinic systolic blood pressure follow-up.

A further nine months later this subject experienced a heart attack, lost a great deal of weight, and his blood pressure reverted to normal. He was no longer taking medication but continued to meditate and found it beneficial psychologically.

Case 7: This subject reported marked early benefit physiologically with reduced blood pressure. Later on as a result of careful self-monitoring he concluded that meditation did not persistently reduce his blood pressure. Finally (a year after the end of the study) he ceased meditation completely because, although he felt its benefits emotionally, it was "not worth 20 minutes twice a day.

He was a 59-year-old university professor with a ten-year history of hypertension treated with diuretics and hypotensive medication. He had no history of emotional problems or psychiatric help. His prediction of benefit from meditation was only moderate. Because the initial blood pressure recordings were below the study criteria, all medication was discontinued until he obtained a stable baseline with diastolic pressures above 95 mm Hg.

His meditation instructor reported that he attended all meetings and showed a very positive attitude. At the end of the study he felt that meditation had improved his ability to concentrate and he had less need to sleep during the day. His anxiety score increased slightly but remained within the normal range. He felt his blood pressure had benefited considerably and this was due to changes induced by meditation. This was accompanied by significant reductions in home but not in clinic blood pressures.

At six months' follow-up he was still meditating and recording his own blood pressure regularly. He now appeared more skeptical and said he was "not a deep convert." In keeping with this, his home blood pressure was almost back to baseline and his clinic pressures were slightly elevated.

Considered together, the results of the whole study indicated that most intelligent, motivated subjects derive some psychological benefits from TM; a minority show sustained benefit in blood pressure; some have transitory benefit; and others have none. The presence of psychological benefit, the absence of drug side effects, and the experience of self control may make TM an appealing therapeutic adjunct for some hypertensive individuals, particularly those who have problems adhering with medication regimens. This may be especially true in those for whom a coping device decreases the concept of self-vulnerability so often enhanced by fear. Other may find the time commitment, mystical aspects, payment of a fee, and assumption of personal responsibility less appealing than conventional drug therapy. Some derive benefit from both drugs and TM.

The question of the specificity of the effects attributable to TM remains doubtful in both the clinical and laboratory experiments. This is a subject of controversy among teachers of meditation themselves; strict advocates of TM aver that only its precise technique is safe and effective [30] while others are convinced that a form of "relaxation response" alone is quite sufficient.[39] Ironically, but not too surprisingly, the two scientists who originated the earliest scientific research on TM now sit on opposite sides of the theoretical fence.

At a more important level, none of the studies on blood pressure has applied a meaningful control for the time, interest, or mystique of meditation. In this regard, it is relevant to reflect on the impact of nonspecific variables on some patients who experience problems in coping with stress. In 1930, Ayman [40] conducted a review of over thirty studies on the therapeutic effects of the many nostrums used to treat hypertension before modern drugs became available. Treatments such as dilute hydrochloric acid and liver extract often produced marked relief of symptoms such as headache or lassitude that are commonly regarded as "psychosomatic." This led Ayman to conclude his review as follows: "On the basis of these reports, it may therefore be concluded that the symptoms associated with hypertension are easily relieved; that they are more easily relieved than the blood pressures lowered, and that this may be obtained by the use on any of numerous drugs or methods." Somewhat similar conclusions were arrived at by Shapiro [41] following a detailed review of nonpharmacologic influences on blood pressure and methods of treating it.

ADVICE TO THE PATIENT

Treatment in medicine seldom waits on proof. The causes of hypertension are uncertain, the efficacy of drugs unproven in mild uncomplicated cases, and the validity of most risk factors remains in doubt. But preventative action in fatal diseases is wide at probability levels below five per cent, particularly if prophylaxis can be accomplished at low risk. TM is therefore one more therapy that deserves consideration as an adjunct in the management of hypertension.

The benefits of TM are real but sometimes temporary in duration and perhaps nonspecific in origin. TM is not for everybody. Those who value caretaking may prefer conventional treatment (which includes being prescribed drugs but not taking them). Hypertensives discovered as a result of illness behavior are more likely to behave this way than those found through screening programs who may value self-control procedures more highly. Our study indicates that compliance is also a problem for some people with meditation and that it can be rejected if it does not fit within the individual's life style, daily economy, and belief system.

Any patient who asks for advice about TM may already have taken an important step toward recognizing that stress and coping with it could be contributory factors in the disease. This alone deserves discussion and exploration of the individual's attitude toward health, caretaking, vulnerability, and medication. Such discussion may lead not necessarily or only to meditation but to modification of the life style and changes in personal behavior that may reduce one of the many risk factors in this complex disease and its fatal complications.

REFERENCES

1. Cannon WB: The emergency function of the adrenal medulla in pain and the major emotions. Am J Physiol 33:356-372, 1914.
2. Selye H: The Stress of Life. New York, McGraw Hill, 1956.
3. Lacey JI, Bateman DE, Van Lehn R: Autonomic response specificity: an experimental study. Psychosom Med 15:8-21, 1953.
4. Engel BT, Bickford AF: Response specificity: stimulus-response and individual response in essential hypertensives. Arch Gen Psychiat 5:478-489, 1961.
5. Gutmann MC, Benson H: Interaction of environmental factors and systemic arterial blood pressure: a review. Medicine 50:543-553, 1971.
6. Dohrenwend BS, Dohrenwend BP: Stressful Life Events. New York, Wiley, 1974.
7. Edwards MK: Life Crisis and Myocardial Infarction. Master of Nursing Thesis. University of Washington, Seattle, 1971.
8. Rahe RH, Lind E: Psychosocial factors and sudden cardiac death: a pilot study. J Psychosom Res 15:19-24, 1971.
9. Rahe RH, Paasikivi J: Psychosocial factors and myocardial infarction: II. An outpatient study in Sweden. J Psychosom Res 15:33-39, 1971.
10. Theorell T, Rahe RH: Psychosocial factors and myocardial infarction: I. An inpatient study in Sweden. J Psychosom Res 15:25-31, 1971.
11. Holmes TH, Masuda M: Life change and illness susceptibility. In BS Dohrenwend, BP Dohrenwend (eds): Stressful Life Events. New York, Wiley, 1974.
12. Cobb S, Rose RM: Hypertension, peptic ulcer and diabetes in air traffic controllers. JAMA 224:489-521, 1973.
13. Liljefors L, Rahe RH: An identical twin study of psychosocial factors in coronary heart disease in Sweden. Psychosom Med 32:523-543, 1970.
14. Alexander F: Psychosomatic Medicine. New York, Norton, 1950, pp 143-153.
15. Friedman M, Roseman RH: Type A Behavior and Your Heart. Greenwich, Fawcett, 1974.
16. Theorell T: Life events before and after the outset of a premature myocardial infarction. In Dohrenwend BS, Dohrenwend BP (eds): Stressful Life Events. New York, Wiley, 1974.
17. Mechanic D: Discussion of research programs on relations between stressful life events and episodes of physical illness. In Dohrenwend BS, Dohrenwend BP (eds): Stressful Life Events. New York, Wiley, 1974.
18. Wooley SC, Blackwell B: A behavioral probe into social contingencies on a psychosomatics ward. J App Behav Analy 8:337, 1975.
19. Cochrane R: Hostility and neuroticism among unselected essential hypertensives. J Psychosom Res 17:215-218, 1973.
20. Veterans Administration Cooperative Study Group on Antihypertensive Agents: effects of treatment on morbidity in hypertension. Circulation 45:991-1003, 1972.
21. Blackwell B: Minor tranquilizers: use, misuse or overuse? Psychosomatics 16:28-31, 1975.

22. Blackwell B, Whitehead W, Robinson A: Benzodiazepine use in hypertension: a phase IV study. Unpublished data.

23. Blackwell B: Drug therapy: patient compliance. N Engl J Med 289:249, 1973.

24. Blackwell B: Enhancing Compliance with Therapeutic Regimens. Paper presented at the First International Congress on Patient Counseling. Amsterdam, 1976.

25. Manheimer DI, Davidson ST, Balter BB, Mellinger GD, Cisin IH, Parry HJ: Popular attitudes and beliefs about tranquilizers. Am J Psychiat 130:1246, 1973.

26. Joubert P, Lasagna L: Patient package inserts: II. Towards a rational patient package insert. Clin Pharmacol Ther 18:663-669.

27. Leventhal H: Fear appeals and persuasion: the differentiation of a motivational construct. Am J Public Health 61:1208-1224, 1971.

28. Briggs WA, Lowenthal DT, Cirksena WJ et al: Propranolol in hypertensive patients: efficacy and compliance. Clin Pharmacol Ther 18:606-612, 1975.

29. Mechanic D, Volkart EH: Stress, illness behavior and the sick role. Am Social Rev 26:51-58, 1961.

30. Bloomfield H, Cain M, Jaffe D, Kory R: TM Discovering Inner Energy and Overcoming Stress. New York, Dell, 1975.

31. Allison J: Respiration changes during transcendental meditation. Lancet 1:833-834, 1970.

32. Wallace RK: Physiological effects of transcendental meditation. Science 167:1751-1754, 1970.

33. Woolford RH: Psychophysiological correlates of meditation. Arch Gen Psychiat 32:1326-1333, 1975.

34. Patel C: Twelve month follow-up of yoga and biofeedback in the management of hypertension. Lancet: 62-64, 1975.

35. Stove RA, DeLeo J: Psychotherapeutic control of hypertension. New Engl J Med 294:80-84, 1976.

36. Benson H, Rosner BA, Marzetta BR, Klemchuk HP: Decreased blood pressure in borderline hypertensive subjects who practiced meditation. J Chronic Dis 27:163-169, 1974.

37. Benson H, Rosner BA, Marzetta BR, Klemchuk HP: Decreased blood pressure in pharmacologically treated hypertensive patients who regularly elicited the relaxation response. Lancet 1:289-291, 1975.

38. Blackwell B, Homenson I, Bloomfield S, Magenheim G, Gartside P, Nidich S, Robinson A, Zigler R: Transcendental meditation in hypertension: individual response patterns. Lancet 1:223, 1976.

39. Benson H: The Relaxation Response. New York, W Morrow and Company, 1975.

40. Ayman D: An evaluation of therapeutic results in hypertension. JAMA 95:246-249, 1930.

41. Shapiro AP: Consideration of multiple variables in evaluation of hypertensive drugs. JAMA 160:30-39, 1956.

Contracts as a Means of Improving Patient Compliance*

CHARLES E. LEWIS
MARIE MICHNICH

Department of Medicine
University of California
Los Angeles, California

HISTORY

The concept of a "contract" has permeated the literature of Western civilization for centuries. For example, there has been considerable debate regarding the relation of a legal contract to the social contract described by Locke, Hume, Montesquieu, and Rousseau.[1] These seventeenth and eighteenth century scholars saw the development of a democratic form of government as deriving from the natural needs for a social contract between men. However, historians have pointed out that English common law preceded their concept of a social contract, and that the latter represents an *ad hoc* explanation or justification of an ideology. Regardless of the historical associations between legal and social contracts, both imply an agreement between individuals that states in explicit terms what is to be exchanged for what, and the consequences to be imposed if either of the parties default on their obligations.

BEHAVIORISM

Rewards and punishments have been associated with the exchange of services and goods throughout history. However, only in the past century has this phenomenon been developed into a field of science through the basic work of Pavlov.[2] The demonstration of the operant conditioning of behavior was further

Supported in part by the National High Blood Pressure Education Program.

explored by several individuals. Perhaps the best known was B.F. Skinner, who suggested that all behavior is contingent upon stimuli in the environment that are reinforced or not reinforced.[3]

Reinforcement can occur in a variety of ways: (1) presentation of positive reinforcement or a direct reward, e.g., money, praise, food, in association with a desired act or behavior; (2) the presentation of a negative reinforcement, e.g., pain, scolding, for a behavior other than that desired; (3) the removal of a positive reinforcement such as withholding privileges, love or praise, or denying food, when the desired act does not occur; and (4) the removal of a negative reinforcement, e.g., cessation of pain, fear, threat, when the desired act is performed.

At this point specific differences between a legal contract and a social contract between provider and consumer which has been applied in the treatment of individuals must be reviewed. The term *contract* may be perhaps inappropriate since the negative sanctions associated with failure to execute one's obligations in a legal contract (forfeiture of deposit, loss of funds, potential imprisonment, etc.) are not enforceable in agreements between providers and consumers of health services. These "contracts" represent pledges of a consumer to a provider and vice versa, or, depending upon the terms, *negotiated agreements* between the parties as to the relative and absolute authority and responsibility of each in achieving a defined goal or objective that is mutually decided upon by both. "Contracts" between therapist and client (physician and patient) have the following characteristics:

1. An objective or goal is specified. This objective *may* represent the results of negotiations between the provider and consumer (this depends primarily upon the orientation or attitudes of the provider).
2. Specific responsibilities of both parties in achieving that objective or goal are set forth. The consumer is provided information that describes what is expected of him/her (and the more specific, in behavioral terms, these are, the better). This constitutes the educational or informational aspect of the "treatment."
3. A specific time limit for this agreement is usually stipulated, i.e., a date when the goal must be achieved. The contract may or may not be signed by both provider and consumer.

CONTRACTS AND MENTAL HEALTH SERVICES

By the early 1950s behavioral conditioning principles were being applied by behavioral psychologists and psychiatrists to modify the behavior of their clients.[4] These techniques were/are employed frequently to deal with "deviant" behaviors, i.e., alcoholism, hyperactivity, overeating, etc. The predominant approach was the direct reward and/or punishment for certain behaviors delivered in a reasonably controlled environment.

By 1960, the word *contract* began to appear more commonly in the literature describing psychological counseling/intervention.[5] Sulzer discussed the "therapeutic contract" as a means for introducing guidelines for the relations between therapist and patient.[6] A portion of the assumptions explicit in his approach are as follows:

> Unless clearly explicated otherwise, the therapist is the agent of the patient and undertakes to teach only what is specifically determined jointly by the patient and therapist...there is a period of interaction between therapist and patient before therapy, per se, takes place that is oriented toward establishing the psychotherapeutic contract between them. The contract is always modifiable by joint agreement, and is as explicit as possible so as to prevent future misunderstanding and to state clearly what is the nature of the dyadic relationship, and what other relationships may be necessary."

Pratt and Tooley further developed an approach in which the therapist provides predetermined reinforcements decided upon by deliberate negotiations between therapist and patient.[7]

CONTRACTS IN EDUCATION

The rewarding of "good performances" with gold or silver stars, or smiling faces on spelling or arithmetic papers is an ubiquitous manifestation of the application of reinforcement theory. (Perhaps more of us remember the negative reinforcements or sanctions applied for unacceptable classroom behavior.) However, only during the past two decades, with increased stress on "accountability in education," have contingent management techniques received specific attention.

The techniques currently employed to assure maximum performance of an educational system depend to a large degree on "incentives" for the learner as well as technological innovations. In 1966, Homme discussed written and formally negotiated contracts between learner and teacher.[8] Later the term *performance contract* became common in the language of education. These contracts were defined as "agreements by a firm or individual to produce specified results by a certain date using acceptable methods for a set fee." Even though this form was meant to be a binding contract of a legal nature between school systems and the funding agencies, the development of contracts between teachers and students drew greater interest, and several trials, although lacking in rigorous study design, have suggested the utility of this method for enhancing student performance.

CONTRACTS AND MEDICAL CARE

Aside from the field of psychotherapy and certain areas of rehabilitation, behavior modification techniques of a formal nature have been utilized minimally in *medical* care,[7] although nursing has advocated the use of these approaches.[9] However, the concept of a contract between consumer and provider as a means of enhancing the therapeutic relationship and fostering patient

FIGURE 1

TREATMENT PLAN

Patient Name _____   Date Effective:

Phone Number _____   From _____

Problem/Diagnosis _____   To _____

Physician _____   Renewed to _____

RECOMMENDATIONS:

   Medicine(s) _____

              _____

       Diet _____

              _____

     Activity _____

              _____

    Follow-up _____

              _____

              _____

              _____

              _____

              _____

AGREEMENT

The above recommendations for my treatment have been explained to me by my doctor. I have been told that only I can assure that these treatments are carried out completely. I understand that this part of my care is my responsibility and I agree to follow these recommendations to the best of my ability.

Signed _____

Doctor _____

FIGURE 1

TREATMENT PLAN

Patient Name _Mrs. Mary A. Smith_   Date Effective:

Phone Number _262 - 1234_   From _6/17_

Problem/Diagnosis _Essential hypertension_ To _7/7_

Physician _William Andrews, M.D._   Renewed to _____

RECOMMENDATIONS:

Medicine(s) _Diuretic - hydrochlorothiazide 50 mg 1 tablet in morning and afternoon_

Diet _Low Sodium (SALT) Diet - see diet sheet add High Potassium foods (bananas, tomato juice, raisins)_

Activity _Increase activity - at least 2 long walks a day._

Follow-up _Return to office in 3 weeks_

AGREEMENT

The above recommendations for my treatment have been explained to me by my doctor. I have been told that only I can assure that these treatments are carried out completely. I understand that this part of my care is my responsibility and I agree to follow these recommendations to the best of my ability.

Signed _Mrs. Mary A. Smith_

Doctor _William Andrews, M.D._

adherence to therapeutic regimens has received increasing attention in recent literature.[10,11]

An example of a contract involving a treatment planned for a patient with hypertension is shown in Figure 1. Additional examples of contracts are available through other sources.

RESEARCH AND EVALUATION

While there has been considerable discussion regarding the potential value of contracts in improving patient compliance as of early 1975, there have been no well-designed controlled trials of the effects of such interventions. Perhaps this vacuum has been related to the absence of a conceptual framework to explain their effect on health and illness behaviors. A variety of articles appeared in the counseling literature in the 1950s and 1960s discussing the importance of the expectations of the client or patient in the counseling process,[12,13] and more recent studies have suggested the role of thee expectancies in shaping health-related behaviors.

It might be hypothesized that the nature of the intervention represented by a contract is twofold: (1) clarification of the relative responsibilities of both provider and consumer in achieving an agreed-upon goal by explicit exchange of *information* about what is required in the act of treatment by the patient; and (2) a perceived (or real) transfer of power from provider to consumer that affects certain health-related expectancies.

In the example shown in the figure, the explicit information relates to the dosage and time of taking medications, diet, and activity. This example could be altered to provide more detailed information or content referring to a specific diet outline and the definition of terms, such as "afternoon" or "long walks." The transfer of power is implied in the agreement as signed by both patient and physician.

This area begs for thoughtful and well-conducted research to examine the effects of contracts on variables such as (1) level of information, and (2) locus of control and/or cognitive style and various elements of the models of illness behavior as explicated by Hochbaum,[14] Rosenstock,[15] and Becker,[16] as well as the behavior of the consumer.

To this end, the example "treatment plan" provided is not intended as a prescription of a therapeutic technique known to be efficacious, but primarily to illustrate a type of "experimental agent" that should be administered under well-controlled circumstances.

SUMMARY

At this point, the state of the art may be summarized as follows:
1. There is a great deal of enthusiastic speculation about the value of contracts in modifying the behavior of individuals with chronic illness (either biological or nonbiological in nature);

2. The nature of the intervention in a "contract"/negotiation/pledge has not been clearly defined in terms of its point(s) of impact in the models of health and illness behavior that have been proposed;

3. There have been no well-designed experimental studies to assess the impact of such an intervention.

If the contract has more than one site of action in the model, then a factorial experimental design will be needed to provide some insight into the relative importance of cognitive and affective variables that may be influenced by contracts. Clearly, in the treatment of a disease such as hypertension, where the efficacy of treatment is clearly demonstrable, such interventions *must* be examined by further descriptive and analytical studies, if we will ever be able to prescribe comprehensive "therapy" that will improve the outcomes of care.

REFERENCES

1. Rousseau JJ: The Social Contract. New York, Hafner, 1962. (originally published in 1962).
2. Pavlov IP: Conditioned Reflexes. London, Oxford Univ Press, 1927.
3. Skinner BF: Science and Human Behavior. New York, Macmillan, 1953.
4. Lindsley OR: Operant conditioning methods applied to research in chronic schizophrenia. Psychiat Res Rep No. 5:11-139, 1956.
5. Severinsen KN: Client expectations and preparation of the counselor's role and their relationship to client satisfaction. J Counseling Psychol 3:109-112, 1966.
6. Sulzer ES: Reinforcement and the therapeutic contract. J Counseling Psychol 9:271-275, 1962.
7. Pratt S, Tolley J: Contract psychology: some methodological considerations and the research contract. Mimeo, Wichita State University, 1964.
8. Homme LE: Contiguity theory and contingency management. Psychol Rec: 16:223-241, 1966.
9. Berni R, Fordyce WE: Behavior Modification and the Nursing Process. St. Louis, Missouri, CV Mosby, 1973.
10. Etzweiler DD: The contract for health care. JAMA 224:1034, 1973.
11. Etzweiler DD: Why not put your patients under contract? Prism 2:26-28, 1974.
12. Grasz RD: Effect of client expectations on the counseling relationship. Pers Guid J: 46:797-800, 1968.
13. Krause MS: Clients' expectation of the value of treatment. Mental Hyg 51:359-365, 1967.
14. Hochbaum GM: Public participation in medical screening programs: a sociological psychological study. Washington, US Ptg Off, Publ Health Serv, Publ No 573, 1958.
15. Rosenstock IM: Why people use health services. Milbank Mem Fund Q: 44:94-127, 1966.
16. Becker MH, Drachman RH, Kirscht JP: A new approach to explaining sick role behavior in low income populations. Am J Public Health 64:205-216, 1974.

Patient Self-Management of Hypertension Medication*

STEVEN M. ZIFFERBLATT

National Heart and Lung Institute
National Institutes of Health
Bethesda, Maryland

PAMELA J. CURRY

Stanford University
School of Medicine
Stanford, California

WHY SHOULD PATIENTS TAKE HIGH BLOOD PRESSURE MEDICATION?

High blood pressure or hypertension is a major cause of death or illness in our country. According to the National High Blood Pressure Program Task Force II Report of 1973 it is "the primary cause of 60,000 deaths and a contributing factor in the 1,500,000 heart attacks and strokes that occur each year." Scientific data presented by the American Medical Association Committee on Hypertension point out that the 20-year death rate for men between the ages of 35 and 45 is *five times higher* for individuals whose blood pressure is above 160/100 mm Hg than for individuals below 140/90 mm Hg.

Supported in part by the National High Blood Pressure Education Program.

Yet an optimistic note should be sounded regarding its treatment. High blood pressure can be effectively treated with several drugs. Today the evidence is conclusive regarding the benefits of drug therapy for hypertension. Can high blood pressure be controlled? The answer is an overwhelming *YES!*

Consider the following physician/patient sequence with a hypertensive patient: (1) the physician detects the problem and diagnoses it as hypertension; (2) the physician routinely initiates a medication regimen with the intent to subsequently modify the regimen; (3) the physician tells the patient what to do or provides an educational pamphlet; (4) the patient leaves; and (5) the patient is expected, upon going home, to behave as instructed. *The probability that the patient will comply with the prescribed regimen is poor.* Reviews of the literature on medication compliance suggest that patients comply with only forty per cent of their regimen.[1,2]

This patient is dependent upon physician-based decisions to alter some aspect of his environment (*i.e.,* take medication). Yet, on close inspection the events which largely influence whether or not prescribed behaviors are successfully implemented are everyday behaviors. These behaviors are most subject to influence *by the patient* — not by the physician.

Recent work in the field of behavioral science has produced self-management strategies that enable both the patient and physician to play a major role in solving their mutual problem: establishing a new, habitual therapeutic behavior on the part of the patient.[3-9] Such strategies of behavioral self-management include: (1) self observation, (2) setting goals, and (3) determining realistic means to achieve the goals. They can be used to enable the patient to assume responsibility for implementing a self-managed medication compliance program. They also allow the physician to act as a resource to provide the skills and continual support necessary to help the patient achieve a high degree of adherence to an important regimen (in this case, antihypertension therapy).

This paper is designed to provide the physician/practitioner with conceptual and specific materials to assist a patient in acquiring techniques of behavioral self-control. These techniques can enhance the patient's ability to adhere to a regimen of hypertension medication. Specific sections for patient use are built into the text. The reader may adopt all or any aspect of the four self-management steps discussed.

SELF-CONTROL

Historically man has incorporated a wide variety of explanations to aid him in understanding the world around him. The Greeks believed that thunder and lightning were the expression of anger by the gods. Aristotle held that physical illness was a function of the state of imbalance among four body components: blood, phlegm, choler, and melancholy. These archaic notions have not held up over the centuries, in light of current scientifically based techniques.

Yet, even today vague metaphysical notions of mystical powers pervade explanations of man's ability to control or direct his behavior to more healthy ways of living. We all know some individuals who, in the face of the very same obstacles we experience, have been able to direct their own behavior.

> Jim has not smoked a cigarette in six weeks, but we all knew he had more will power than the rest of us and that's why he was able to do it.

We attribute such sterling qualities to "will power" or other underlying and mysterious personality traits such as perseverance, stubbornness, or luck. These are clearly inappropriate rationalizations to explain why one person can stick to his medication consistently and another cannot. Medication adherence is best understood in terms of the "here and now" events around taking one's medication.

DEBUNKING SELF-CONTROL

The development of self-control techniques have contributed greatly to the debunking of the will-power model. Science has demonstrated that people can actually learn to control behaviors related to personal problems. We now have available simple techniques to enable patients to assume command over their hypertension medication regimens. You and your patients have been intuitively employing self-control techniques in your everyday lives. A few simple descriptions might help bring these procedures to light.

Picture yourself on a harried schedule at the hospital. A person that you absolutely detest approaches you and puts his arm around your shoulder, calls you "buddy" or "honey," and asks for a few minutes of your time. You smile back, chat pleasantly, and patiently give him the minimum amount of time possible.

Consider those cold and dark wintry mornings when you rise at a ridiculously early hour, shiver, and trudge off to work — certainly not a behavior that comes "naturally." You exercise self-control also, when you come home after work and instead of grumbling and complaining about what a terrible day it has been, you smile pleasantly and greet your family as if you have not seen them for two years.

Successful instances of self-control require that an unobtrusive and routine habit be formed which is specific to the situation. Reliable cues or reminders come naturally to such situations. Taking medication at a predictable and routine time is just such a habit, but it must fit exactly and unobtrusively into the patient's life.

Another critical aspect of self-control is that the act must result in a satisfying consequence. Successful self-control habits have become "successful" and "habits" because they were useful to us or they had pleasant consequences for us from the beginning. Typically, we continuously experiment with many new behaviors and those that "get us what we want" (recognition, money, compliments, etc.) tend to become strong and fixed responses. Antihypertensive medication regimens present a problem in relation to this aspect of self-control,

however, since immediate rewards to pill-taking are not automatically
forthcoming. But we will return to this issue in a moment.

As we have seen, then, most behaviors depicting self-control have two common
aspects: (1) either they occur routinely — unobtrusively — in one's life (such as
getting up in the morning, washing, shaving, cooking breakfast, etc.); or (2) they
offer some important consequences or personal gain (such as preservation of
family harmony, job security, the status quo, etc.). It is important, therefore, to
be guided by these components, cues or reminders, and positive consequences
when assisting patients in planning to acquire new, more effective habits for
taking antihypertensive medication.

WHY THE PROBLEM?

Effective medication is available — all one has to do is take it! Adhering or
sticking to hypertension medication sounds simple. However, taking medication
regularly is not that simple — just ask those that are taking it.

> Mrs. Phillips, a 38-year-old perfectly healthy homemaker, was surprised when
> her doctor told her she had high blood pressure. Diuril, twice a day, was
> prescribed for her condition. Mrs. Phillips stopped taking the medication after
> three days. She said that, being healthy all her life, she did not like the idea of
> being a sick person and found it difficult to take the medication on a regular
> basis.

In a recent panel discussion among patients with diagnosed hypertension, five
of the seven patients revealed that their hypertension was diagnosed "years
before" they actually committed themselves to taking their medication
regularly.[10] Several patients did start taking medication, but soon dropped it. All
the panelists agreed that the absence of any symptoms of high blood pressure
diminished the advice their physicians had given them. In addition many of the
panelists began experiencing side effects such as drowsiness, when attempting to
remain on the medication.

> Mr. Williams, a 42-year-old industrial foreman, was put on Adlomet
> medication. He began, for the first time in his life, to experience drowsiness and
> dizziness. It affected his work performance. Finally he just could not seem to
> "remember" to take it. Today he is not taking his medication.

PATIENT POWER — HANDLING
THE HYPERTENSION HASSLE

What actions can your patients personally take to control medication-taking
behavior and commence a comfortable, effective daily medication regimen?
There are several simple steps which you can help patients initiate in order to
solve this problem.

The following sections will be interspersed with four specific *Steps* for the patient to employ in acquiring the necessary self-control skills to increase hypertension medication adherence. Physicians are encouraged to abstract these self-instructional steps and provide the opportunity for patients to employ them.

Identifying the observable "here and now" and manipulable events related to medication adherence is the physician's main concern. Behavioral self-control techniques define medication problems in terms of the current immediate behaviors of patients and related events antecedent and consequent to taking medication. Antecedents suggest that behavior is usually preceded by observable events. For these reasons the physician and the patient must identify the antecedents of behavior. The patient may attempt to take his medication in the context of incompatible cues, antecedent events, or obtrusive schedules. The patient may be trying to take his medication at the latest possible moment as he is running out of the door to get to work. Such a cue would be incompatible to the performance of the behavior. In order for a behavior to occur easily it must have a compatible and highly reliable cue, one which clearly tells the patient, "This is the occasion to take my medication." The proper combination of a timing and a situational cue is suggested to facilitate the occurrence of a behavior. A clear self-portrayal of the patient's routines, regimen, and life style provides important information and creates a heightened awareness of the relationship between one's activities and taking medication.

SPECIFYING EXACTLY WHAT THE PROBLEM IS

Self-control of behavior stresses the importance of teaching the patient systematically to observe antecedents and consequences of taking medication. The physician must know what is happening before any change program is initiated. Therefore the physician should have the patient observe and record events and thoughts preceding and subsequent to taking medication in a behavior record prepared by the physician. Observation techniques have already been employed to enhance patient charting and recording of medication,[11] imipramine therapy,[12] and general pharmacological tracking.[13]

A medication behavior record accurately represents all environmental events coming before and after taking medication. It might reveal that the patient has a fairly stable routine in the morning and very late in the evening. Many individual behavioral regimens clearly do not fit neatly prescribed *b.i.d* or *t.i.d* regimens. But adherence can be increased in any case by tailoring medication regimens to the patient's routine: *e.g.,* including the more stable environments in the medication regimen. If the patient's morning routine is quite reliable, taking medication at this time seems appropriate. Perhaps a stable cue (antecedent) such as "taking vitamins" can be transplanted to a given evening hour so as to produce a predictable and motivating situation.

The observations taken by the patient also reveal awareness of the effectiveness of cues (antecedents) to trigger taking medication, *e.g.* "put pills on kitchen counter where I can see them.....maybe I can make this easier....."

STEP 1

BECOMING OBJECTIVE: WHAT DO YOU LOOK LIKE?

In order to see what you look like in terms of taking medication try to "step outside of yourself" for a few moments. Observe and jot down your everyday habits and routines. This will help you tailor a medication-taking program to your own very special needs. On the following pages write out your typical (1) daily workday schedule, (2) usual weekend schedule.(Appendices 1 and 2)

Daily Workday Schedule

Time	Activity
7:30 A.M.	_____
8:00 A.M.	_____
9:00 A.M.	_____
10:00 A.M.	_____
11:00 A.M.	_____
12:00 Noon	_____
1:00 P.M.	_____
2:00 P.M.	_____
3:00 P.M.	_____
4:00 P.M.	_____
5:00 P.M.	_____
6:00 P.M.	_____
7:00 P.M.	_____
8:00 P.M.	_____
9:00 P.M.	_____
10:00 P.M.	_____
11:00 P.M.	_____
Midnight	_____

Weekend Schedule

Time	Activity
7:30 A.M.	_____
8:00 A.M.	_____
9:00 A.M.	_____

10:00 A.M.	_____
11:00 A.M.	_____
12:00 Noon	_____
1:00 P.M.	_____
2:00 P.M.	_____
3:00 P.M.	_____
4:00 P.M.	_____
5:00 P.M.	_____
6:00 P.M.	_____
7:00 P.M.	_____
8:00 P.M.	_____
9:00 P.M.	_____
10:00 P.M.	_____
11:00 P.M.	_____
Midnight	_____

What about the amount of travel you do in your work? This could easily interfere with a well-developed drug-taking routine. How much travel do you do a month? What would each travel day be like in terms of a routine?

(1) Day you leave from house   _____

(return)   _____

(2) Daily travel routine   _____

_____

Is there anything about your daily travel routine which would make it difficult for you to schedule drug-taking? Make some suggestions below and we will discuss them.

_____

_____

_____

Do you think your spouse could be helpful in assisting you to stick to taking your drugs as prescribed?

In what way?
reminding you . . . . . preparing the drug . . . . . setting your medication on the table . . . . . placing the drug in your briefcase . . . . . keeping a record of your medication-taking . . . . . providing special incentives to motivate you . . . . .

Medication-Taking Record

	Time	Occasion	People	Behavior	Thoughts	What happens after
Day 1						
Day 2						
Day 3						

Beside numbers 1-3 write the (1) time, (2) occasion, (3) and people.

Sample Medication-Taking Record

	Time	Occasion	People	Behavior	Thoughts	What happens after
Day 1	9:00 A.M. 9:00 P.M.	breakfast orange juice TV	Helen Helen	take medication	glad I remembered hope it decreases my appetite	ate breakfast nothing special
Day 2	9:40 A.M. 9:30 P.M.	reminded by Helen as I was leaving for work reading a book	 Helen	take medication	I don't care if I remember this will make me drowsy this is too difficult	nothing special went to work nothing, went to bed
Day 3	8:30 A.M. 10:00 P.M.	brushing teeth reminded by Helen getting into bed	 Helen	take medication	Helen is a nag makes me too sleepy can't seem to remember	had breakfast went to bed

Develop your own system of codes, but make sure you put it on the back of the record so you don't forget it and can understand your recording.

Here the record reveals the effects which salient antecedents may exert on behavior. The diary might also reveal the patient's attempt to direct behavior in constructive ways. Under careful physician direction this patient can capitalize on extant self-control capabilities and thus increase compliance.

Our language is full of vague words and phrases such as *forget, will power, motivation,* and *independent.* For purposes of self-control, words of this kind pose two dangers: they do not specify the situations in which taking medication did or did not occur and they do not specify exactly what the patient's actions were. Thus, in order to assume control over taking medication the patient must be able to identify all observable actions and environmental events that relate to the act of actually taking the medication.

DEVELOPING AWARENESS

The second step in developing self-control skills with a patient is to teach him to become an objective and accurate observer of his medication-taking activities. While it is true that the patient "knows" he is having difficulties it is important to identify in *observable terms* exactly what is meant when the patient says, "I am having problems taking my medication." The patient needs to become an observer of himself. His perceptions of the difficulties will become much more clear and useful when he actually begins to observe himself in the problem situation. It is something we all intuitively practice. We will remember becoming more "aware" of our actions when someone criticizes us.

> Susie came home from school, looked her mother squarely in the eye, and said, "Mother, I am leading an unfulfilled bourgeoise life." Mrs. Dayton said in exasperation, "What do you mean by that? Tell me exactly what situations or aspects of your life trouble you."

Self-observation requires that you not only observe your actions, but that you record their occurrence for purposes of analysis and evaluation. This activity is perhaps the most obtrusive aspect of self-control. Few of us are in the habit of carefully recording our behavior. However, the patient who records his own behavior can become more aware of the actions and those environmental events related to the problem of taking medication. Step II guides patients through this experience. It is useful to provide patients with a pocket-sized notebook as a medication record.

The third step assists patients in identifying their problems and developing an intervention strategy. The patient's everyday environment and routines must be harnessed to support taking medication. Patients are now able to identify cues or reminders that are present in their routines which can be attached to the act of taking medication. They must now think of the act of taking medication in combination with the situation in which the actions occur. *The goal is to identify routine and powerful cues already existing in one's environment and harness them to taking medication.* Another way of accomplishing this is to select new

STEP II

HOW TO OBSERVE AND RECORD TAKING MEDICATION

First

Let us try to identify some actions related to difficulties in trying to adhere to prescribed medication routine. Look carefully at all routines related to taking medication.

(1) What observable actions do you like?

(a) _____

(b) _____

(2) What actions would you like to change?

(a) _____

(b) _____

(c) _____

(If you are having any difficulty trying to think of "actions," just pretend you are looking at a motion picture of yourself around medication-taking time. WHAT DO YOU SEE?)

MAKE SURE YOU CAN SEE THE ACTIONS!

If you cannot see the actions listed above rework them below:

(1) Like

(a) _____

(b) _____

(c) _____

(2) Like to change

(a) _____

(b) _____

(c) _____

It is important to observe these actions and the circumstances under which they occur. If you do a good job on observing then you have a good chance at improving your medication-taking behavior. We are going to provide you with a pocket-sized medication record to help you keep track of your actions that are related to taking medication.

The reason it is pocket-sized is that we would like it to be handy when you are actually taking your medication. Take it along when you go out. Keep it handy when you are home.

In the record we'd like you to jot down the:
  (1) time . . . (9:00 A.M.)
  (2) occasion . . . (just before juice)
  (3) people . . . (with my wife)
  (4) dates . . . (August 4)
  (5) thoughts . . . ("This is a pain in the neck!")
  (6) what happens after . . . ("I got nauseous.")

Open the record and get acquainted

Notice there are 6 columns that correspond to the items above (the date is missing because you just have to jot it down at the top of the page)

The first page is filled in as a sample page to give you an idea of how to do it.

You now have
          (1) a medication record;
          (2) an idea of how to use it;
          (3) some actions for you to observe;
          (4) a place to put down other actions also as they naturally occur.

REMEMBER . . . . .

The record is a place for you to record everything that occurs around the time you take your medication.

Start tonight—JUMP right in the water and fill in the medication record.

Identifying the "here and now" events related to taking your medication is most important.

IDENTIFYING PROBLEMS AND
CHANGING MEDICATION ROUTINES

The medication record has helped you to *observe, identify,* and *implement* cues and consequences for taking medication. You are on the way to controlling your medication routine. Let's again take a brief look at Mr. Phillips' medication record (page 84). The medication record accurately represents all the events coming before and after taking his medication. Notice the irregularity with regard to scheduling the medication. A very consistent schedule should be decided upon—one to which you can readily adhere. We are all slaves to routines and habits and this is one time when you might capitalize upon this. Select a convenient event which occurs at the same time every day and can serve to remind you to take medication. Notice that Mr. Phillips' wife started to remind him to take his medication. After he experienced some side effects "reminding" became "nagging." If you choose to have your spouse cue you about taking medication don't punish her or him for doing it! The record also indicates that there were no pleasant consequences for taking medication. There were, in fact, some unpleasant consequences in the form of side effects. Experiencing unpleasant consequences leads to an avoidance of your medication. Select some rewards or pleasant consequences which you can obtain after taking your medication as prescribed *for a period of 2 or 3 days!* Perhaps a special food, dessert, or a movie. You can, along with your spouse, identify many events or experiences. These rewarding events should be obtained *only* if your medication-taking is on schedule. After a few months you will form a comfortable routine or habit will be developed and you may dispense with rewards.

Take a look at your medication record now. Inspect it and see which events are important and select some specific actions to improve taking medication.

Look through all the pages.

Do you see any trends?

Do you see any generalities?

Are some days better than others and why?

Are some days poorer than others and why?

Are there any people, or time of the day that is related to better, or poorer, medication routines?

Is medication taking better before or after meals, with certain foods?

Now take a look at the daily routines listed previously.

Is there anything you need to add based upon your actual observations of your actions?

1. Specify exactly what time taking medication must occur in order for it to be done effectively and easily.
2. Under *routine,* specify the occasion (dinner, TV, breakfast, etc.) which must occur in order for it to be done effectively and easily.
3. Under *routine,* specify the people, if any, that will assist you, or be present when it occurs in order for it to be done effectively and easily.

DURING THE WORKING WEEK

Time	Setting, Routine, People, Reminders
(1)	
(2)	
(3)	

Time	Setting, Routine, People, Reminders

(1)

(2)

(3)

DURING TRAVEL

Time	Setting, Routine, People, Reminders

(1)

(2)

(3)

Let's look through the record again for the presence of any rewards to strengthen taking medication.

What Happens After refers to some of the events, action or happenings that come after taking your medication. Usually the targeted action is very closely associated with taking your medication.

Sometimes *what happens after* is a natural and ***positive*** event!

For instance: Picking up a glass is followed by drinking what is in it.

Picking up a fork is followed by eating what is on it.

Sitting down at the table is followed by eating.

The *IMPORTANT POINT* is that the event be *POSITIVE*.

Sometimes nothing positive happens after a TARGETED ACTION.

For instance: Putting your medication on the kitchen counter.

Placing your medication by the alarm clock.

Putting your medication in your briefcase.

Taking your medication.

If *what happens after* taking your medication is *POSITIVE* then there is better chance that you will perform the TARGETED ACTION!

SO . . . ARRANGE IT!!

You can insure that something happens afterwards which is POSITIVE by. . . .

ARRANGING IT YOURSELF!!

Identify some experiences, or activities that you like *and* . . . occur *every day* . . . and that YOU have some control over their occurrence.

(continued on reverse side)

For example: dessert
              TV   reading the newspaper
              music   snacks
              wine   sporting events
              relaxing outside in the backyard   shopping trips

Prepare your own list below:

(1) _____

(2) _____

(3) _____

(4) _____

(5) _____

(6) _____

Select one or more of these events as rewards (be generous with yourself!)

(1) _____

(2) _____

(3) _____

Fill in the chart below with your medication plan.

WORKING DAY ROUTINE

Time(s)	Setting, Routine, People, Reminders	Rewards

WEEKEND ROUTINE

Time(s)	Setting, Routine, People, Reminders	Rewards

STEP IV

WRITING A MEDICATION CONTRACT
TO ENHANCE "COMMITMENT CHANGE"

Formalizing your actions with yourself or others is another self-control technique to foster commitment and motivation. We all seem to be more comfortable and effective when we know exactly what to do and the conditions under which it should occur. A medication-taking contract provides such a vehicle. Approach your contract seriously. If possible, obtain the assistance of your physician and spouse to help you with its management. Clarify and summarize what you are going to do by actually writing a medication contract with yourself or your spouse.

Medication Contract

In order to improve taking my medication as prescribed I agree to take my medication under the following conditions:

	Time	Setting, Routine, People, Reminders	Rewards
1. Workdays			
2. Weekends			
3. Holidays or Vacations			

If, at any time, I have any problems with carrying out these actions, I will call, or consult with _____ *immediately!*

This agreement is implemented in alliance with _____who readily recognizes some of the normal everyday difficulties in taking medication. _____ is very willing to provide whatever assistance is necessary to help me.

_____
Physician

Signed: _____   _____
             Patient   Spouse

Date: _____

If you experience side effects do not hesitate to ask your doctor about them. Your dosage might have to be adjusted. Your doctor is aware that anyone taking high blood pressure medication may experience temporary side effects. He will know what to do. Present your medication record to your physician. He will value its precision and accuracy. Your documented reactions to your medication may aid him in selecting a more comfortable drug and schedule for you.

Employing self-control techniques with your antihypertensive drug regimen is employing skills which you have lived with all of your life. The suggestions given in this article merely make them public and more usable for your specific problem. Self-control merely exploits your own power to be a healthy person.

powerful cues which have the potential to be integrated into a routine and employ them for medication. Patients may be trying to take medication at inopportune times: while leaving for work, or at a hectic time of the day. An unobtrusive, reliable, and powerful cue enhances the probability that taking medication will occur on time. The cue selected must clearly say, "This is the occasion to take medication."

Taking medication is more likely to occur when it is followed by pleasant consequences. Taking an aspirin for a headache has pleasant consequences in that it relieves the headache. Brushing one's teeth or swishing with mouthwash has pleasant consequences in that it gives one's mouth a fresh, clean taste. However, medication may be preventive in nature and thus have no pleasant natural consequences. Patients in fact experience unpleasant consequences — in the form of side effects! *Another goal is to identify extrinsic consequences, or rewards that will motivate patients to take medication.* This will further ensure its proper occurrence.

EMPLOYING BEHAVIOR CONTRACTS

One method by which physicians can encourage self-change is through the use of an adherence contract, such that the exact sequence of actions which optimize adherence are specified and agreed to by the patient. While contracts have not been used for promoting drug adherence, they have been useful in eliciting other types of behaviors [14-16] and offer several advantages. The contract provides a written outline of behavioral expectations for the patient. A contract reduces ambiguity and results in less confusion among patient behaviors than the customary general instruction. Thus, a contract circumvents the "remembering" problems. The development of a contract provides an opportunity to discuss means to achieve adherence. It encourages a reciprocal interaction between the physician, spouse, and patient and involves the patient in decision-making about his regimen. Informing another person about one's intentions (making a commitment) should increase the probability of success. Promises and intentions may themselves determine the execution of self-control. Thus self-management of the regimen is enhanced. Finally, the contract itself has incentive value for patients who are reinforced by attainment of a self-established goal.

Thus, the contract technique involves the patient in planning, serves as a medium by which self-management of the drug regimen can be taught, and maximizes the probability of reinforcement for adherence from the health worker or others. Additionally, it minimizes ambiguity in instructions and elicits a formal commitment to adhere.

CONCLUSION

Patients employ self-management techniques every day of their lives. They do not walk in front of cars, they eat certain foods, they decide what movie to see, they "control their tempers," and they exercise restraint in social situations. Several studies point to the process of fitting treatment into a patient's existing routine. This technique is termed **tailoring** and attempts to make dose schedules, doctor visits, and other health-seeking behaviors as tolerable, convenient, and self-determined as possible.[1, 14, 17] All these situations suggest conscious consensual manipulation of environmental events and behaviors to achieve a predetermined goal. Medication compliance is an exercise in self-control: a conscious and deliberate attempt to self-direct one's medication-taking behavior. Patient self-management technologies offer the physician and patient an opportunity to engage in a more mutually satisfying role in enhancing compliance. For the physician it suggests that behavioral problems in compliance are not to be taken lightly or dismissed with terminal statements: *e.g.,* "He is not motivated." To the contrary, the physician and his patient now have access to an effective self-management technique. The patient can now assume a major role to play in identifying compliance-related events and achieving a sense of instrumentality and responsibility in pursuing matters related to health.[18]

REFERENCES

1. Blackwell B: The drug defaulter. Clinical Pharmacol Ther 13:841-848, 1972.
2. Blackwell B: Drug therapy: patient compliance. New Engl J Med 289:249-252, 1973.
3. Benson H et al: Decreased blood pressure in pharmacologically treated hypertensive patients who regularly elicited the relaxation response. Lancet 289, 1974.
4. Bernstein D, McAlister A: The modification of smoking behavior: progress and problems. Addictive Behaviors (in press).
5. Mahoney MJ: Self-reward and self-monitoring techniques for weight control. Behav Ther 5:48-57, 1974.
6. Nash J: The self-mod method of body conditioning. Stanford University, Heart Disease Prevention Program, 1974.
7. Stuart RB, Davis B: Slim Chance in a Fat World: Behavioral Control of Obesity. Champaign, Illinois, Research Press, 1972.
8. Thoresen C, Coates T: Behavioral self-control: some clinical concerns *In* Hersen M et al (eds): Progress in Behavior Modification. New York, Academic Press, 1975.
9. Thoresen C, Mahoney M: Behavioral Self-control. New York, Holt, Rinehart Winston, 1974.
10. Why treat a disease that doesn't hurt? Patient Care 18-103, 1973.
11. Liberman P, Schwartz AJ: Prescription dispensing to the problem patient. Am J Hosp Pharm 29:163-166, 1972.
12. Moulding T: Preliminary study of the pill calendar as a method of improving the self-administration of drugs. Am Rev Respir Dis 84:284-287, 1961.
13. Park LC, Lipman RS: A comparison of patient dosage deviation reports and pill counts. Psychopharmacol 6:299-302, 1964.
14. Fink D, Malloy MJ, Gohen M et al: Effective patient care in the pediatric ambulatory setting: a study of the acute care clinic. Pediatrics 43:927-935, 1969.
15. Homme L, Csany AP, Gonzoles MA et al: How To Use Contingency Contracting in the Classroom. Champaign, Illinois, Research Press, 1969.
16. Kanfer FH, Cox LE, Greiner JM et al: Contract, demand characteristics and self-control. J Pers Social Psychol 30:605-619, 1974.
17. Anderson FP, Roew DS, Dean VD et al: An approach to the problem of non-compliance in a pediatric O.P.D. Am J Dis Chil 122:142-143, 1971.
18. Zifferblatt SM: Increasing medication compliance through the applied analysis of behavior. Preventive Med (in press).

The Patient
Package Insert
as Drug Education

LOUIS A. MORRIS
VINCENT J. GAGLIARDI

Bureau of Drugs
Food and Drug Administration
Washington, D.C.

The Food and Drug Administration (FDA) is the federal agency responsible for the labeling of prescription drugs. Unlike the labeling of nonprescription drugs, prescription drug information is primarily directed toward the health professionals who prescribe or dispense medicines. However, with certain drugs, such as the oral contraceptives, FDA requires that patients receive written information. For the oral contraceptives, this regulated information is a boxed warning (Figure 1) which tells consumers about serious side effects and directions for use, notifies them of the existence of a brochure or leaflet on this subject, warns that the pill cannot prevent or treat venereal disease, and asks patients to notify their doctor in case of any unusual discomfort or disturbance.

The rationale for FDA's requirement of this written information is one of "patient consent."[1] Oral contraceptives are usually given to young healthy women for nontherapeutic purposes. There is a definite risk of delayed side effects and there are alternative, nonchemical means of contraception. In order for patients to make a rational decision about their therapy, they must be informed.

FIGURE 1

ORAL CONTRACEPTIVES
(Birth Control Pills)

**Do Not Take This Drug Without Your
Doctor's Continued Supervision.**

The oral contraceptives are powerful and effective drugs which can cause side effects in some users and should not be used at all by some women. The most serious known side effect is abnormal blood clotting which can be fatal.

Safe use of this drug requires a careful discussion with your doctor. To assist him in providing you with the necessary information, _____ has prepared a booklet written in a style understandable to you as the drug user. This provides information on the effects and who should not use it. Your doctor will give you the booklet if you ask for it and he will answer any questions you may have about the use of this drug.

Notify your doctor if you notice any unusual physical disturbance or discomfort.

Caution: Oral contraceptives are of no value in the prevention or treatment of venereal disease.

Although patient package inserts are currently required for only a few prescription drugs, it seems likely that FDA will require these type of documents for additional drugs. There are several reasons for this trend. Risk-benefit decisions about drug use are becoming increasingly complex. Individual preferences, rather than pure scientific judgments, may serve as a basis for deciding whether a drug should be taken. There is a movement toward involving patients in decisions about their own health. The consumerism movement has also fostered rulemaking which requires disclosure of greater amounts of information to patients. Recently, FDA was petitioned by several consumer interest groups to require more adequate labeling for prescription drugs. On December 16, 1975, an FDA advisory committee recommended that a patient package insert be included for the conjugated estrogens to warn women of an increased risk of cancer.

In addition to helping patients make risk-benefit decisions on whether to take specific drugs, patient information has also been suggested as a means of preventing adverse drug reactions.[2] The Pharmaceutical Society in England issues "treatment cards" which warn patients taking coumarin anticoagulants, oral antidiabetic drugs, and methotrexate that they should not take aspirin at the same time.[3] Similarly, patient package inserts could contain a list of precautions that would warn patients to avoid certain foods and drugs, and to tell their doctor if they have certain pre-existing medical conditions.

Patient-oriented drug information could, therefore, serve several uses. Perhaps the most widely mentioned purpose of patient information is that it is a means of increasing medication compliance. Written drug information in the form of brochures, leaflets, stickers, and booklets have been produced by both commercial firms and private health care groups. In addition, several experimental or observational studies have assessed the usefulness of these documents in increasing compliance rates.

The results of these studies are conflicting and difficult to interpret since written information is often confounded with additional verbal or audiovisual instructions, or special materials (such as unit-dose packaging or medication calendars) which would tend to influence medication adherence. However, three recent studies indicate that, at least for antibiotic therapy, written instructions can help decrease regimen deviations.[4-6] The Sharp and Mikeal study [6] is particularly encouraging because their methodological rigor allows one to specifically identify written instructions as causing increased compliance.

Therefore, the patient package insert, which historically has been used as a vehicle for informing patients about risks of drug therapy, may help increase patients' adherence to medication regimens. Unfortunately, the opposite may be true. Patient-oriented drug information, rather than educating patients, may thoroughly confuse them. Documents which stress potential side effects may unduly and overly frighten patients. They may decide not to take drugs that are objectively needed.

If regulated patient-oriented drug information documents are to become more common in the future, several questions should be addressed. The remainder of this chapter will concentrate on two of these questions: "What types of prescription drug information do consumers desire?" and "What approaches have been taken to provide this type of information to consumers?"

WHAT TYPE OF PRESCRIPTION DRUG INFORMATION DO CONSUMERS DESIRE?

In an FDA-sponsored survey,[7] a national sample of 1,321 consumers was asked the question, "In addition to the information you presently get, do you believe that more information should be made available to you regarding prescription medicines?" About half (49 per cent) of the respondents said *yes.* The people surveyed who desired more information tended to be younger and better educated. Those saying *yes* to this question were also asked, "How do you think this additional information should be made available?" Eighty-four per cent wanted "written information that comes with the medicine but in a way you can understand"; 17 per cent wanted oral information given by the pharmacist; 26 per cent wanted oral information given by the physician; and 6 per cent preferred it "on TV, in magazines and newspapers." Therefore, the great majority of people who wanted additional prescription drug information wanted it in the form of a specially prepared package insert.

The FDA survey suggests that a large segment of the population desires additional prescription drug information. However, a patient package insert cannot replace the doctor as the main source of guidance and advice. In this same FDA-sponsored survey,[7] a national sample of 2,005 adults was asked to compare the safety of prescription drugs to over-the-counter (OTC) drugs. Twenty per cent replied there was no difference, 8 per cent said that nonprescription drugs were safer, and 68 per cent said prescription drugs were safer. Although there is no way of knowing why consumers felt that prescription drugs were safer, answers to other questions enable one to infer that consumers feel safer about taking drugs that doctors prescribe.

Joubert and Lasagna [8] have presented data which support the role of the doctor as a main desired source of drug information. The authors surveyed three groups of people: orthopedic inpatients, people attending a general medical outpatient clinic, and people entering two pharmacies to fill prescriptions. Of the 207 people asked to complete questionnaires, 137 were returned. The preferred main source of prescription drug information was clearly the doctor (chosen by 78 per cent of the respondents). A package insert was preferred as the main source of prescription drug information by 7 per cent of the respondents. All other sources (such as the pharmacist, medicine labels, or medical reference books) were preferred by fewer people.

Joubert and Lasagna [8] also asked their respondents how detailed a patient package insert should be. Most respondents (60 per cent) wanted both a short summary and more detailed information. Therefore, consumers seem to want a good deal of information about their drugs. A recent FDA-sponsored survey of oral contraceptive users supports this notion.[9] A national probability (cluster) sample of 1,700 current users of the oral contraceptive (OC) were asked if they would prefer a patient package insert or a longer booklet included with additional drugs. Sixty-seven per cent preferred a booklet and 20 per cent preferred an insert. Only 7 per cent said both, and 5 per cent said there was no difference.

The survey of OC users also suggests that individuals who have had experience with a package insert feel it is important to include this type of document with other drugs. In response to questions that asked respondents to rate the importance of including inserts with other prescription drugs, 93 per cent stated it was important to include it with antibiotics, 88 per cent said it was important to include it with cough and cold preparations, and about 97 per cent said it was important to include it with tranquilizers.

Although people may say that they want a good deal of information about the prescription drugs they take, perhaps an equally important issue is what form of written information will maximally communicate important details to consumers. Data from the OC users survey indicate that individuals may better remember information which is concisely presented. Respondents were shown a "dummy" copy of the insert (the information in the box warning was blacked out). They were asked, "What does the information in the box say about side effects?" Fifty-four per cent of the current OC users who said they read the insert remembered that blood clots were the most serious side effect. Users who said they had read the AMA or manufacturer's booklet on the pill were asked to recall what was said in the booklet. Only 32 per cent mentioned blood clots.

When these respondents were specifically asked about the blood clots, only 27 per cent recalled what was mentioned in the booklet.

Unfortunately, surveys which rely on retrospective opinions cannot determine what is the best way to communicate important information. However, they are suggestive. People may say that they want longer and more detailed information about drugs. However, important information about serious side effects must be stressed in order for it to be communicated properly. If the information is buried in the middle of a long brochure, it is likely to be missed. It is impossible to know from the survey whether brochure information about blood clots was forgotten, denied, incorrectly measured, or never communicated in the first place.

WHAT APPROACHES HAVE BEEN TAKEN TOWARD PROVIDING PRESCRIPTION DRUG INFORMATION TO CONSUMERS?

The remainder of this chapter will focus on different approaches that have been taken to provide patients with written information on prescription drugs. For the most part, these alternative techniques have not been evaluated. Therefore, the information presented will primarily be descriptive in nature. This section will cite a few examples of the type of information provided to patients.

Written prescription drug information for patients comes in many styles and contents. Patients may receive stickers, checklists, short handouts, one-page descriptions, folded leaflets, multipaneled brochures, or multipage booklets.

Stickers which can be directly affixed to medication bottles are perhaps the simplest way of warning patients about certain precautions or side effects. Several drug companies provide pharmacists with stickers for some of their drugs (e.g., Parke Davis and Co. for Povan suspension and Burroughs Wellcome for Leukeran). In addition, some commercial firms produce stickers stating some of the more common warnings (such as "the medicine may cause drowsiness" or "shake well and keep refrigerated") (e.g., Pictorial Package, Aurora, Illinois, and Drug Package, Inc., O'Fallon, Missouri). Stickers have the advantage of remaining on the medication bottle. Even if the individual purchasing the medicine is not the same person taking it, important instructions will not be lost. Therefore, the warning placed on the bottle is a constant reminder to the patient.

A second way in which common precautions can be communicated to patients is by the use of a checklist (United Mine Workers Health and Retirement Fund). The checklist contains a series of warnings and precautions. The pharmacist checks off the relevant items prior to dispensing the medication. The checklist affords a slightly greater degree of flexibility than stickers, since the pharmacist can also write special instructions on the sheet. However, the checklist may be lost, whereas the stickers will not. Although stickers and checklists are simple and convenient ways of communicating prescription drug information to consumers, their major drawback is space limitation. Furthermore, since there are a limited number of available messages, each warning must be short and to the point. There is no space for explanations, nor can there be "full disclosure" of all the relevant information about the drug. (*Full disclosure* may operationally and legalistically be defined as all the consumer-relevant information which is contained in the official drug labeling.)

In order to achieve a greater degree of disclosure and specificity, several pharmacy groups, government agencies, colleges, and commercial enterprises have prepared drug information documents on specific drugs (or drug classes). These documents are usually in the form of leaflets, one-page handouts, or brochures.

Recently, a book has been published which contains instructions for patients.[10] The book is in the form of a looseleaf notebook and contains page-long directions for patients on several prescription drugs. Physicians can photocopy the desired pages for patients as they become needed. Each page contains instructions, precautions, and directions on when to notify the doctor. Sheets are available for several drug classes such as anticonvulsants, tranquilizers, antitussives, etc.

Several pharmacy groups have also produced written documents on prescription drugs (*e.g.,* University of Virginia, Minnesota State Pharmaceutical Association, University of Miami, and many others).

FDA occasionally produces special material on specific drugs to alert the general public of the dangers that can be caused by the use of certain drugs. The National High Blood Pressure Educational Program produces and coordinates material relating to high blood pressure medication.

It would be impossible to list and describe all the relevant features of these leaflets, brochures and booklets. In order to illustrate important aspects of a prescription drug information document for patients, an FDA-produced document will be discussed in detail. Figures 2 and 3 display the contents of two brochures produced by FDA. These brochures are currently being tested in an experiment to determine their relative utility at communicating drug information and their effectiveness in producing increased adherence to medication schedules.

The information is presented to patients in a six-panel, well-illustrated folded brochure. The contents of these brochures are the result of input from several medical, social science, educational, and consumer-interest authorities.

These documents are longer than most other consumer-oriented drug information materials. Their sections are clearly identifiable and they are written at below ninth grade level reading. The first section is a general *introduction* which names the drug (phonetically). Patients are asked to follow their latest health instructions. Some non-FDA brochures allow health professionals to write in the dosage instructions. This was not done for the present brochure because of constraints in the experimental situation.

The second section highlights *precautions.* Patients were asked to tell their doctor if they have certain problems. One of the reasons for overall length of the documents is that, wherever possible, patients are told the reasons for a particular statement or request.

The third section of the document discusses the *uses* of the drug. This section corresponds to the benefits of drug therapy. During the drafting of the brochure,

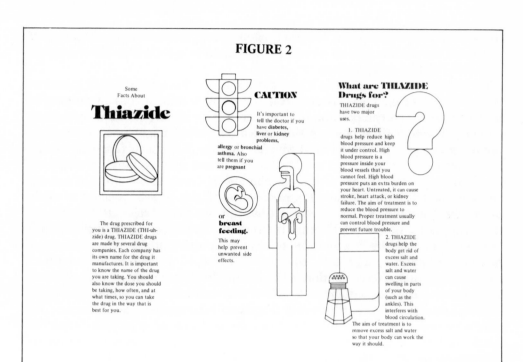

FIGURE 2

Some Facts About

Thiazide

The drug prescribed for you is a THIAZIDE (THI-uh-zide) drug. THIAZIDE drugs are made by several drug companies. Each company has its own name for the drug it manufactures. It is important to know the name of the drug you are taking. You should also know the dose you should be taking, how often, and at what times, so you can take the drug in the way that is best for you.

CAUTION

It's important to tell the doctor if you have **diabetes, liver or kidney problems, allergy** or **bronchial asthma.** Also tell them if you are **pregnant** or **breast feeding.** This may help prevent unwanted side effects.

What are THIAZIDE Drugs for?

THIAZIDE drugs have two major uses.

1. THIAZIDE drugs help reduce high blood pressure and keep it under control. High blood pressure is a pressure inside your blood vessels that you cannot feel. High blood pressure puts an extra burden on your heart. Untreated, it can cause stroke, heart attack, or kidney failure. The aim of treatment is to reduce the blood pressure to normal. Proper treatment usually can control blood pressure and prevent future trouble.

2. THIAZIDE drugs help the body get rid of excess salt and water. Excess salt and water can cause swelling in parts of your body (such as the ankles). This interferes with blood circulation. The aim of treatment is to remove excess salt and water so that your body can work the way it should.

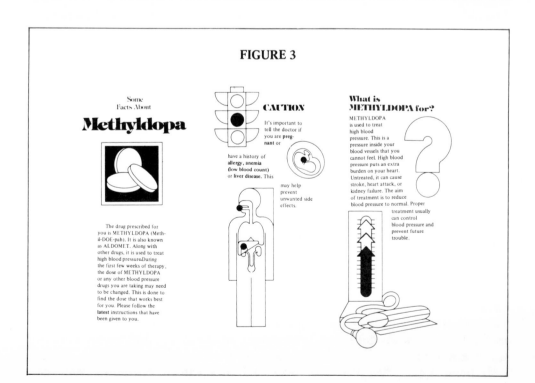

FIGURE 3

Some Facts About

Methyldopa

The drug prescribed for you is METHYLDOPA (Meth-il-DOE-pah). It is also known as ALDOMET. Along with other drugs, it is used to treat high blood pressure. During the first few weeks of therapy, the dose of METHYLDOPA or any other blood pressure drugs you are taking may need to be changed. This is done to find the dose that works best for you. Please follow the **latest** instructions that have been given to you.

CAUTION

It's important to tell the doctor if you are **preg-nant** or have a history of **allergy, anemia (low blood count)** or **liver disease.** This may help prevent unwanted side effects.

What is METHYLDOPA for?

METHYLDOPA is used to treat high blood pressure. This is a pressure inside your blood vessels that you cannot feel. High blood pressure puts an extra burden on your heart. Untreated, it can cause stroke, heart attack, or kidney failure. The aim of treatment is to reduce blood pressure to normal. Proper treatment usually can control blood pressure and prevent future trouble.

this section had been deleted. However, upon review, it was reinstated because of the belief that a balanced document is preferable to a document that mentions only the risks of drug therapy.

The fourth section is the longest of the document. It states the *side effects* of the particular drug. This section serves the major informed consent purpose of the document. The composition of this section also presented major problems.

Simply listing all the possible side effects of a drug might possibly frighten people rather than inform them. It was felt that the side effects of a drug should be introduced in a way that was truthful, yet put into explanatory context.

A second problem is that of the placebo effect. One possible effect of patient package inserts is to increase the experience of side effects because of their suggestion potential. Although recent literature on the placebo effect indicates that there is no simple relationship between the suggestion of drug effects and their production,[11] the potential for increased reporting of side effects exists. A second mechanism, other than suggestion, which may lead to an increased reporting of side effects, is that of "labeling."[12] The brochure may provide convenient "labels" to patients with which they can interpret and describe their reactions to the drug. Furthermore, they may become more sensitive to drug effects because the insert may lead people to focus on particular types of reactions. Normal symptoms, which may have been otherwise unnoticed, may be interpreted as side effects and "labeled" with the words mentioned in the brochure.

In order to try to minimize the potential for the "suggestion" and "labeling" effects, several approaches were taken. First, patients were told that most people get few or no side effects and that these tend to go away with time. Second, some side effects were introduced as "signs that the drug is working." For example, the experience of a dry mouth and needing to urinate is a sign that a diuretic drug is helping the body get rid of excess water. An experiment by Kast and Loesch [13] supports the idea that a "therapeutic side effect interpretation" can lead to beneficial results. Unfortunately, another experiment by Lipman, Park, and Rickels [14] casts doubt that this technique can work and suggests it may be worse than saying nothing at all about side effects.

A third approach taken was to tell patients how to handle side effects if they do occur. For example, if patients feel faint in the morning, they are told to sit at the side of the bed before standing up. It is hoped that if patients know what to do if a side effect occurs, they will not be frightened.

Fourth, a large number of side effects are mentioned. On the one hand, this might increase the potential for suggestion effects. On the other hand, a "fuller disclosure" of side effects may serve to better prepare patients for side effects if they do occur.

Finally, one problem of administering medicines is that naturally occurring reactions are attributed to the drug when they are due to other factors. In the brochure, patients are told that, sometimes, symptoms can occur even without taking any drugs.

All these approaches are theoretical and they cannot guarantee that the mentioning of side effects will not alarm and frighten patients. One purpose of the experimental study is to test whether these approaches will be successful.

The final two sections of the brochures are answers to commonly asked questions. They are intended to help patients deal with experience or fear of side effects in a way that will maximize beneficial effects and minimize adverse effects.

The consumerism movement has made the advent of patient package inserts for prescription drugs much more likely. These inserts will serve legal and ethical requirements to inform patients of serious side effects. However, in order to be fully effective, they should be of assistance to both the physician and the patient in the adjustment and management of drug therapy.

REFERENCES

1. Schmidt A: Dimension of change in the FDA. Paper presented at the Pharm Advert Seminar, Chicago, Illinois, Sept 13, 1973.
2. Seward R, Finger K: Adverse drug reactions: an educational tool in patient-oriented pharmacy program. Am J Pharm Educ 38:23-29, 1974.
3. Editorial: Society issues aspirin warning cards. Pharm J 28:409, 1972.
4. Colcher I, Bass J: Penicillin treatment of streptcoccal pharyngitis. JAMA 222:657-659, 1972.
5. Linkewich J, Catalano R, Flack J: The effect of packaging and instructions on outpatient compliance with medication regimens. Drug Intel Clin Pharm 8:10-15, 1974.
6. Sharpe T, Mikeal R: Patient compliance with antibiotic regimens. Am J Hosp Pharm 31:479-483, 1974.
7. Knapp DE: Consumers and medication. NTIS report PB-232-172, 1974.
8. Joubert P, Lasagna L: Patient package inserts: I. Nature, notions, and needs. Clin Pharmacol Ther 18:507-5-13, 1975.
9. FDA: Final report: Survey of consumers perceptions of patient package inserts for oral contraceptives. Contract No. 223-74-8058, Sept, 1975.
10. Griffith H: Instructions for patients. Philadelphia, Pennsylvania, WB Saunders, 1975.
11. Shapiro A: Placebo effects in medicine, psychotherapy and psychoanalysis. In Bergin A, Garfield S (eds): Handbook of Psychotherapy and Behavior Change. New York, John Wiley, 1971, pp 439-473.
12. Schachter S, Singer J: Cognitive, social and psychological determinant of emotional states. Psychol Rev 69:379-399, 1962.
13. Kast E, Loesch J: Influence of the doctor-patient relationship on drug action. Ill Med 119:390-393, 1961.
14. Lipman R, Park L, Rickel K: Paradoxical influence of a therapeutic side effect interpretation. Arch Gen Psychiat 15:462-474, 1966.

Patient Self-care in Hypertension: A Physician's Perspective*

R.L. GRISSOM

Division of Cardiovascular Medicine
The University of Nebraska Medical Center
Omaha, Nebraska

A doctor is a *teacher* in the ancient meaning of the word *doctor*. Likewise all our patients can be considered to function, at times, as students. To be sure, the level of competence will vary with education, age, and motivation, but every encounter we have with patients should be considered an educational experience, for better or for worse. Certainly, patients with hypertension learn more from their physicians than they would have a few years ago, when it was customary not even to reveal their blood pressure levels. A survey among physicians in our clinics failed to uncover a single recollection of harm produced by education of the patient about his hypertension problem. Thus, the adverse consequences of such patient education appears minimal, although many physicians still hesitate to provide the patient with the information required for adequate self-care. The purpose of this paper is to examine, from a physician's perspective, the hazards and benefits of encouraging patient self-care and to discuss methods for implementing such a program.†

Sponsored in part by the National High Blood Pressure Education Program.
†*This paper has been written with both the physician and patient in mind so that the physician may find it useful to have his patient read this chapter and discuss it later with him.*

SOME TYPICAL PATIENTS

E.H., an intelligent 40-year-old rancher in western Nebraska, lives in a county where there are many more cows than people. His doctor's office is 25 minutes away, in good weather. He has diabetes, requiring insulin, which he adjusts himself within the limits outlined by his physician. He is taking ten blood pressure tablets daily plus some liquid potassium chloride. How much freedom will you allow him in adjusting medications?

Mrs. B., a black urban woman social worker, age 36, travels over the state part of nearly every week. She has had hypertension for 12 years, first noted when she finished college. She is well aware of the propensity for problems with hypertension in blacks, and her own family's incidence of strokes. She readily learned to take her own blood pressure and owns her own sphygmomanometer. She requires enough guanethidine that sometimes she has some postural hypotension. How much can she do to help control her blood pressure?

Joe College, a white sophomore college student, has labile hypertension involving mainly his systolic level, which frequently will be 172/94-96 mm Hg. He loves a good time and college life, and sometimes indulges in a "few beers" on weekends. Despite strong advice he continues to smoke cigarettes. His family background shows some coronary artery disease in middle life. How much leeway will you give him in his blood pressure management?

Clearly the rancher and the social worker have problems that merit considerable self-care which they seem emotionally and intellectually capable of handling. The college student, on the other hand, is intellectually, but not psychologically, ready to care for his hypertension. The physician had best keep frequent appointments with him in an effort to obtain good adherence to the program, and consider the possibility of using propranolol and a diuretic, along with correction of "risk" factors. Thus each patient must be individually assessed as to his potential for adequate self-care. This assessment must include determining not only the patient's potential for self-care but also whether certain critical incidences occurred (e.g., side effects from a medication) that would compromise any such self-care efforts.

What hazards may trap the patient given the chance to help care for himself?
1. He may become neglectful of his control without the authoritative doctor to remind him of his good intentions.
2. He may fail to consult his physician on a regular basis: "Why should I spend $15.00 to see my doctor just to be told I'm doing fine?"
3. He may become neurotically obsessive about his blood pressure.
4. He may take an unbalanced view toward his total health needs.

In short, he may exemplify the old adage: "A little knowledge is a dangerous thing."

But what are the possible benefits to the patient in this partnership of care?

1. Understanding of medications and their potential ill-effects as well as benefits should give him an early warning sensibility.
2. He learns "the language," so that it becomes easier to discuss problems with him.
3. He needs to see the physician less often, saving time and money (for him).
4. He has the chance to see that hypertension is *his* problem, not his doctor's, and that hypertension is usually only *part* of a total health problem.

THE BALANCE SHEET

I believe that most patients are helped by being partners in patient care. The basic education that every patient ought to achieve has the following specific goals. He must know what high and normal blood pressures are, the significance of the systolic and diastolic readings, something of the variability from time to time of the blood pressure, and the target organs for damage. On at least one occasion he ought to learn how to record the blood pressure by palpation at his wrist so that he will feel how the pulse comes through as the cuff is deflated. Finally, he should have reliable records of his blood pressure. Such record-keeping is an important feedback to self-care.

More advanced knowledge is to be sought at varying degrees for perhaps half of our patients. This calls for knowledge of the drugs, their main complications and their interactions; knowledge of the role of salt in high blood pressure control; and more detailed knowledge of the long-term ill effects of elevated blood pressure. This patient ought also learn how to use a stethoscope and to hear the difference between the systolic and diastolic pressure as the sphygmomanometer is used. For these persons, a quiz may be given which will ensure their learning certain critical facts (Figure 1).

The advent of physician's assistants and nurse managers of hypertension, as in some of our veterans hospitals, has greatly increased the amount of staff time for patient teaching. Everywhere hypertensive patients waste potentially valuable periods of time: waiting in our offices, waiting for laboratory tests, and waiting for medications at the pharmacy. Each of these intervals represents a time period of high motivation. It is a truism to say that, for the most part, we who are in health care are not using this time properly. Nor is it only the doctors who are the educators; the nurses, the dieticians, the pharmacists, all have the opportunity to help teach our patients. In addition to what they learn by direct contact, there are now a variety of education tapes, of pamphlets, and of patient-related articles to make available to them.

How can the physician help the hypertensive patient to know what hypertension is?

The patient should understand the disease in that it is mainly one of regulation, with the cause or causes generally unknown. Hypertension will last

FIGURE 1

What have you learned from what you have just read?

1. In general I will be able to tell if my blood pressure is high by the way I feel. True or False.

   Answer: *False.* If a patient is tense or anxious the blood pressure may rise for that reason, but otherwise the patient under treatment may feel worse with too much reduction of his pressure than with too little reduction.

2. The basic drug offered most patients with hypertension is:
   a. a nerve blocker.
   b. a sedative or tranquilizer.
   c. a diuretic.
   d. a tablet to slow the heart.

   Answer: Although any of these may be correct in some instances, the diuretic is chosen mainly because it may be sufficient in itself for control in half or more of patients, is simple to take, inexpensive, and relative safe.

3. The *main* reason to restrict salt in the diet is:
   a. to reduce potassium loss.
   b. to make the diuretic action on the blood pressure more effective.
   c. to make the patient drink less water.

   Answer: Although (*a*) is also true, the diuretic effectiveness is enhanced by moderate salt restriction. Thirst and urinary frequency are frequently noted but relatively unimportant. Best choice is (*b*).

4. Is my systolic blood pressure more important, or my diastolic blood pressure?

   Answer: Depending on their relative levels, either may be "more" important to your health. Although moderate diastolic elevation is in general of greater concern, either elevation may be associated with reduced life expectancy.

5. Suppose I go on a long auto trip in which I will do much of the driving. What hazards are increased for me by reason of my hypertension and the medicines I am taking, which are hydrochlorothiazide, methyl dopa, and hydralazine? Check those applicable.
   a. heart irregularity.
   b. venous thrombosis or phlebitis.
   c. sleepiness while driving.
   d. blackout from prolonged quiet sitting.
   e. headache.
   f. urgency to stop at rest stops.

   Answer: *b,c,f.* The diuretic produces a slight fluid deficiency and when added to prolonged sitting and dependency of the legs can increase the likelihood of phlebitis. Because of the diuretic, you may need to urinate more, depending on when you take the diuretic. Methyl dopa causes sleepiness primarily in the first four days of taking it, but individuals vary in this.

6. I am a man in my mid-thirties. Since taking medicine for my blood pressure, I have a problem sexually. I am taking hydrochlorothiazide, reserpine and guanethidine. Which of these is causing this?

Answer: You should discuss this with your physician. Perhaps none of the medicines is. However, both the diuretic and guanethidine have been found to affect sexual activities in previous studies.

7. My doctor seems quite concerned about my potassium blood level. I take thiazide, digitalis, and aspirin, along with an occasional laxative. Which of these may be involved with potassium?
   a. diuretic.
   b. digitalis.
   c. aspirin.
   d. laxative.

Answer: *a,b,d*. Both diuretics and laxatives produce a loss of potassium. Ordinarily this produces no problem in the patient but if he also takes digitalis, toxicity, especially in the form of an arrhythmia, is more apt to occur.

8. I am a diabetic and have heard that the blood sugar goes up after taking some medicines for hypertension. Which one of these is most apt to be at fault?
   a. reserpine.
   b. spironolactone.
   c. thiazide diuretic.
   d. clonidine.
   e. guanethidine.

Answer: *c*. The blood sugar may rise after the diuretic but in most cases this is only slight and is easily corrected with your diabetic medication. You should discuss this with your doctor.

9. Why must I take so many kinds of pills? What is possibly harmful about combining them in a single tablet or capsule?
   a. The absorption may be affected by the combination.
   b. The relative amounts of the two drugs in a single form may not be ideal for you, as contrasted with the "average" person.
   c. The combination probably would cost more.
   d. The intervals when you should take the individual drugs may not be the same for the various drugs in the combination form.

Answer: If you marked (*b*) and (*d*), you are well informed and perceptive. In some instances, absorption may be affected adversely but no such problems exist now among antihypertensive medications. If it is determined by your doctor that a combination is similar to your current medicines on an individual drug basis, then probably it will be satisfactory to use such a combination.

10. Where may I volunteer to help others with hypertension?

Answer: Ask your doctor or ask your local Heart Association.

his lifetime and as a rule must be treated during the whole of his lifetime. The disease causes damage mainly to the heart, through heart attacks and heart failure, but to a lesser extent may cause fatal complications in the brain, through a stroke, or the kidneys through kidney failure. It is mainly asymptomatic and progressively worsens over the years, though this process may accelerate over a very few months. There is no clear dividing line separating normal blood pressure from an elevated blood pressure which is damaging to tissues.

Control is achieved by drugs which lower the blood pressure by a variety of mechanisms. In the majority of persons with high blood pressure this drug program can be as simple as one tablet a day if the blood pressure elevation is found and treated early.

The major reasons for taking drugs are to protect the heart, brain, and kidneys from damage. Regardless of cause, the goal is to bring the blood pressure as near to normal as possible, which for most persons is less than 140/90 mm Hg.

Compliance (adherence) to the schedule is essential. The patient can help by understanding the need for drugs, what side effects may be expected, and by taking the drugs at the best "reminder time," usually with a meal. If possible he should get someone else to help him "keep track" of the drugs. He should leave the pills in their regular containers with labels on them, and bring them to his physician each visit for verification of proper dosage, for a pill count, and for future guidance.

The doctor can help by keeping the regimen simple. He must see the patient frequently, especially in the beginning. He must keep close tab on the patient, and contact him if he misses an appointment.

What should we tell the patient we "watch for" with each of the major drugs? Thiazides and thiazide-like drugs: higher blood sugar, blood urea nitrogen (BUN) concentrations, uric acid values, and lower potassium levels. Reserpine: nasal stuffiness, drowsiness, and occasionally depression. Methyl dopa: a hemolytic state, depression, sleepiness, and that alcohol may accentuate drowsiness. Clonidine: dry mouth, and sometimes blood pressure worsening if the drug is stopped suddenly; again alcohol may accentuate drowsiness. Hydralazine: a fast pulse; and, with larger doses, rheumatism and a positive antinuclear antibody. Guanethidine: loose stools and, in the male, sometimes sexual problems. Interactions can be major problems: *e.g.,* diuretics, especially with digitalis; mood-changing drugs and guanethidine; estrogens and blood pressure control; furosemide and chloral hydrate.

To what extent can the patient adjust his own medicine? Only if the physician allows him to do so. In general, an effective regimen once established remains quite constant for months and tampering with the dosage when all is going well is discouraged.

How is the diet important? For three reasons: weight control; to reduce salt; to assure adequate potassium concentrations.

Should the patient purchase a blood pressure unit? It has been shown generally to have more advantages than disadvantages to take home blood pressures providing there is someone who can do it with regularity and who is trustworthy.

In most instances it is better that someone other than the patient take the blood pressure reading, but there are exceptions to this. The major problem to be avoided in this circumstance is that the spouse must be taught the hazards of nagging, and of a lack of accuracy.

Which type unit should be obtained? On the whole, one should avoid the "cheapies." The mercury manometer is the standard, is durable and accurate, but is a little bulky. The aneroid manometer is easier to handle but it can be inaccurate and no one may know it without recalibration; it also has to be repaired at the factory. A useful change in the stethoscope is the modification of the sound pick-up diaphragm added to the inexpensive type used in anesthesia, held with an elastic band around the arm. Some newer though expensive semiautomatic units, now becoming available, may make them attractive to some hypertensive patients. Although expensive (approximately $1,000) such a unit with flashing red lights can be fun to operate and even a conversation piece at a party. There is an element of chance one can wage a bet on. Besides, to the owner of a Cadillac, a thousand dollars extra is not all that much. Figure 2 summarizes some commercially available sphygmomanometers.

What advantage is there to exercise and physical fitness to lower the blood pressure? These measures are good for the general health and are recommended but will accomplish very little for the blood pressure.

How about more rest? Relaxation and rest periods can be quite important, especially if the patient has been driving himself to nervous exhaustion. For example, the blood pressure often will drop to near normal just with bed rest in a hospital after two or three days. Worry and anxiety will make the blood pressure more difficult to control; equanimity is helpful. Some persons have had remarkable results with bio-feedback by using meditation and emotional control of blood pressure and pulse responses.

Is there a uniform guide to self-care?

Many physicians hesitate involving their patients in self-care because they worry that no simple rules can be given patients, so that patients almost always need the skill of a physician to adjust elements of the therapeutic regimen. Is this so? For ongoing monitoring of blood pressure, the answer is *No*. Properly taught, patients can take blood pressures in typical daily activities which are more informative than those taken in the artificial situation of a doctor's office.

For self-management, the answer can be *Yes* but I use a "qualified" uniform guide for self-care to avoid problems. At the start, the patient, with my concurrence, may vary the dose of his diuretic. Thus, if invited to a dinner with ham and beans, he may double his diuretic dose. Or in hot weather with heavy sweating, he may reduce his dose of diuretic. Additionally, I allow some patients to modify doses of some other drugs on their own: if on a long auto trip where there is a danger of sleeping while driving, to reduce or stop methyl dopa; if there is a nasal obstruction in hay fever season or during a respiratory infection, to stop reserpine; if expecting to take a highball or two at a party, to stop methyl dopa; if sexual potency is a problem, to experiment with 24-hour omission of

FIGURE 2

COMMERCIALLY AVAILABLE SPHYGMOMANOMETERS

Home Care Deluxe Aneroid Sphygmomanometer
(standard with stethoscope)
Mfg. for Abco Dealers, Inc.
Milwaukee, Wisconsin 53217
About $35.00

Tycos Sphygmomanometer—Aneroid
HR1 8104-5098-02
No stethoscope
About $80.00

Arden Kit Aneroid Sphygmomanometer
Taylor Consumer Products Co. (includes stethoscope)
Arden, NC 28704
HR1 8104-705201
About $50.00

Baumanometer, mercury
(No stethoscope)
WA Baum Co., Inc.
Copiague, NY 11726
Wall unit *L* 33
About $58.00

Hi/Lo Baumanometer
0661-0620 (with stethoscope)
About $45.00

Electronic Blood Pressure
(uses Doppler effect)
Filac Corp.
1259 Reamwood Ave.
Sunnyvale, California 94086
About $1,000.00

BPI—Blood Pressure Indicator
Model 2200
Parke-Davis Medical Electronics Div.
180 Bear Hill Road
Waltham, Massachusetts 02154
About $165.00

diuretic, or methyl dopa, or guanethidine. I insist he discuss these changes with me, but make such self-management a part of the patient's education program.

It has been said that knowledge is power; now we are saying that self-knowledge is a means of providing patients with the power to "control" their risk of illness. The value of such an activity in dealing with compliance seems obvious.

ACHIEVEMENT RECOGNITION

Aside from the foregoing levels of knowledge it is useful to have an "achievement award" in terms of blood pressure control. It is well known that despite a patient's frequently coming back for visits to the physician, the level of successful control of the blood pressure is often incomplete. Similarly this has been true for the diabetic patient and for the obese patient. But the hypertensive patient should have greater success than either the diabetic or the obese patient, because the management is so much simpler.

I set four goals: normalization of the blood pressure; relative freedom from side effects of fatigue, nausea, dry mouth, depression, etc.; control of salt intake; and elimination of other controllable risk factors for coronary heart disease and strokes since these are his major hazards through the years. Two other elements may be added to grace the achievement award. One of these is the ability to take a blood pressure reading on himself or on another person, with accuracy. Certification of this sort is similar to the American Heart Association's certification for skill in cardiopulmonary resuscitation. A further achievement is the volunteer activity of the patient to help others in detecting high blood pressure and encouraging their compliance. We are told that only 10 per cent of persons with hypertension in our country are "under control." This evangelistic fervor to help detect hypertension in others and to get them under treatment will go a long way toward ensuring that the individual himself adheres to his program. Moreover, it gives him a sense of belonging to the health team and, because he himself becomes an example and a teacher, it behooves him to improve his own performance.

SUMMARY

For the Patient:

Welcome to the club! You have *not* been punished for your past misdeeds by getting high blood pressure! But from now on, you are one who has a problem with it. Care for it properly with your physician's help and you can enjoy nearly a normal life and life expectancy.

For the Doctor:

What has proved so successful for so many diabetic patients is proving successful also for hypertension patients. Understanding the disease and the drugs gives the patient an extra advantage. Make the patient a knowledgeable partner. Allow him to help make some judgments, but please don't let him get away from your continuing care!

B. Focus on the Practitioner

Probably the two health care practitioners who receive the least formal training in patient-care procedures are the physician and pharmacist. Hingson and Sharpe describe how both may become more involved in patient care and thereby contribute to the management of medication noncompliance. Marston, on the other hand, reviews for us the variety of ways that nurses can expand their contributions to a patient's self-care.

The Physician's Problems in Identifying Potentially Non-compliant Patients

R.W. HINGSON

Department of Socio-Medical Sciences
Boston University School of Medicine
Boston, Massachusetts

PROBLEMS PRESENTED BY NONCOMPLIANCE

After a physician examines a patient, conducts laboratory tests, and reaches a medical diagnosis, a critical moment in medical care is reached. A treatment regimen is developed and offered to the patient. From the standpoint of the medical profession, all the efforts of medical education, medical research, and medical technology to diagnose, understand, and determine a therapy are finally offered to the patient; and much of the extent to which these processes will be efficacious is not largely in the hands of the patient.

From the patient's point of view, he has now gone through a number of behaviors which may include having (1) recognized physiologic symptoms or an altered body state; (2) consulted with relatives and friends; (3) considered his own past experience with illness, especially his interaction with health personnel; (4) obtained an appointment with a physician; (5) spent considerable time in a waiting room; and (6) submitted to physical examination and probably a wide variety of auxiliary lab and X-ray tests. He now awaits the climax of all this activity: diagnosis and treatment. All these efforts offer testimony of the patient's feeling of *need* on the one hand, and *trust* in medicine and his own physician, on the other.

It is at this critical juncture that the ultimate benefits of these two highly complex forces (medical and patient behavior) interact to produce either (1) agreement, cooperation and "successful" treatment; (2) disagreement, noncooperation, and unsuccessful treatment; or (3) something in between.

All too often the illogical occurs and the patient who needed and trusted the physician fails to comply with the medical regimen which so many people, visible and not visible to the patient, worked hard to produce. According to Marston, while some published reports claim 100 per cent compliance by patients with medical regimens, other studies have indicated that as few as 4 per cent of patients comply.[1] Although the exact proportion of patients who comply is still being debated, the reported variability in compliance has caused many physicians to recognize that they cannot merely tell patients to follow a regimen and expect that they will.

This problem is exacerbated because many physicians have considerable difficulty in ascertaining which patients comply and which patients do not. Berkowitz, in a study of physicians in 55 clinics,[2] and Caron, in a study of 27 physicians and 525 patients,[3] reported that over three-quarters of the physicians studied overestimated the degree to which their patients comply. Caron also reported that physicians in his study were unable to distinguish which patients were good compliers and which patients were poor compliers. Inability of physicians to distinguish between patients who comply and those who do not and inability to assess the extent to which patients comply pose a serious problem in the management of patients. Without such knowledge physicians cannot assess the value of specific therapies for a noncompliant patient's recovery. On a broader scale, the value of specific regimens for patient recovery in general may be called into question if those assessing the treatments do not know which persons treated, in fact, followed the regimen as prescribed.

In this paper, I would like to focus on how physicians as well as other health professionals, such as pharmacists, nurses, social workers can identify noncompliant patients in clinical practice. Let us begin by noting that a number of techniques have been employed to identify noncompliance in medical research. These include patient reports, pill counts and bottle counts, drug excretion tests, blood assays, appointments records, direct observation, and a variety of composite indices. At first glance these measures might appear useful for the physician in practice. But just as these measures have varying validity from a research viewpoint, they also have varying utility from a clinician's viewpoint. Furthermore, the correspondence is not direct. Some of the measures which are most valid from a research viewpoint are not particularly useful from a clinician's point of view. First, many of the measures are difficult and expensive to to implement. Second, most of the methods which have been used in research are not useful to clinicians because they identify noncompliance only after it has already occurred, or after a pattern of noncompliance has already begun. The problem for physicians in practice differs from that of researchers in that clinicians need to identify noncompliance or a potentially noncompliant patient *before* his noncompliance begins.

If the problem for physicians in clinical practice is to identify the potential noncomplier before noncompliance begins, then the initial physician-patient interaction appears to be the logical time to identify noncompliance. Zola (*see* chapter 1) has already wisely pointed out that physician-patient interactions are usually poor learning situations for patients. The problems some physicians have exhibited in identifying which patients comply and which do not suggest that to date physician-patient interactions can also be a poor learning situation for the physician. This chapter shall therefore explore ways to improve physician learning during physician-patient interaction. Moreover, to fully identify and understand noncompliance, physicians need to recognize that compliance is not a single act, but the outcome of a series of behaviors and events. Many of the factors which may influence compliance do not suddenly materialize when a patient first receives a regimen to follow. Characteristics present in a patient or events experienced by a patient even before he contacts a physician may affect how well he complies. Furthermore, compliance does not have a tightly defined end point. While for some individuals compliance may entail following a regimen for a limited period of time, for others, like diabetics, the need to comply is a life-long proposition. For such persons compliance is not a single behavior at one point in time. Rather, it is a continued succession of action, assessment, reaction, and reassessment. In short, compliance occurs over time, and behavior at one point in time may have an impact on subsequent behavior.

Consequently, the practicing physician faces the problem of having to identify potential noncompliance in a patient not only when he first arrives for treatment, but also after a regimen has been recommended. The remainder of this paper examines factors that some have hypothesized to affect compliance which can be identified by a physician: (1) when a patient first arrives for treatment and interacts with a physician, and (2) subsequent to the initial physician-patient interaction. It is my argument that if physicians can identify and understand the factors which are predictive of noncompliance in patients, they may be better able to identify which patients are likely to be noncompliant. In the identification process insights into the reasons for noncompliance will undoubtedly arise, thus increasing the ability of physicians to forestall noncompliance in individual patients.

FACTORS IDENTIFIABLE WHEN A PATIENT FIRST RECEIVES HIS REGIMEN

Research on compliance has examined a number of factors which could be identified by a physician when a regimen is prescribed. These include:
1. factors which the patient brings to the physician:
   a. the nature of his disorder,
   b. the patient's social status and demographic characteristics,
   c. patient psychological predispositions or beliefs about the disorder or treatment;

2. factors over which the physician exerts some controls:
    a. the nature of the regimen prescribed,
    b. the physician's interaction with the patient.

The next section will briefly review some recent research on these factors and compliance.

Factors the Patient
Brings to the Physician

The Nature of the Disorder: The factor most visible to a physician which might affect compliance is the nature of a person's medical disorder. One would logically expect that persons with more severe and disabling disorders would be more likely than persons with asymptomatic or less disabling disorders to perceive the necessity for compliance. But, does the nature of a disorder influence compliance?

It appears from a review of compliance studies that there is no consistent direct relation between the severity of a disorder and compliance. This inconsistency can be found within the same disease and when comparing different diseases. Donabedian, in a study of heart disease, diabetic and arthritis patients, reported a direct relation between severity and compliance.[4] Heinzelman's study of college students with histories of rheumatic heart disease [5] and Ludwig's study of patients with a variety of chronic disabling diseases [6] concurred with this finding. However, the studies which indicate a direct relation between severity of illness and compliance appear to be outnumbered by those which do not. Watkin's study of diabetic patients uncovered no relation between management, i.e., compliance and control of the disease.[7] Charney and MacDonald, in separate studies, likewise found that patients with severe streptococcal sore throat were no more likely to comply than those with milder cases.[8, 9] Lendrum and Kobrin, in a study of 100 children with previous history of rheumatic fever, found that those with heart trouble were no more likely to maintain penicillin prophylaxis than those with no heart complications.[10] Davis, in a survey of cardiac patients, even reported that patients who had another cardiac episode after initiating compliance were more likely to discontinue compliance. Those who had an initial coronary episode did not initially comply but those who had no subsequent recurrence were more likely to begin compliance after a period of time than those who did not comply at first, but had a subsequent episode.[11] In other words, several studies reported no relation of severity to compliance, and Davis even suggested an inverse relation.[12]

Davis furthermore conducted a survey of 154 patients who presented with a variety of complaints. Based on physician assessments, he found that patients with more severe problems were less likely to comply than patients with less severe disorders. Patients who were physically disabled were less likely to comply than patients not so disabled.[13]

Several explanations for such behavior can be hypothesized. First, a more severe disorder may require more complex and difficult regimens than a less severe disorder. Second, persons with more severe disorders may, because of limitations imposed by their illnesses, have more difficulty complying even with relatively simple regimens. Third, persons with severe disorders may have experienced prior lack of success with the regimens offered to deal with their disorders. Unfortunately, most studies examining the relationships between the severity of a disorder and compliance have not controlled for the difficulty or complexity of a regimen. Also, no studies have explored the past history of a patient's compliance and attempted to relate that experience to present compliance.

Thus, previous work has suggested that the severity of a disorder may not always affect the extent to which patients are compliant, but the reasons why there is no effect are unclear. Given these findings and the still unanswered questions, one must conclude that compliance may be a potential problem for all disorders, regardless of the severity of those disorders in terms of painfulness, disability, or threat to life.

Demographic Variables: Demographic variables, especially those which determine socioeconomic status, have rather consistently been related to morbidity and mortality,[14] preventive health behavior [15] and seeking medical care.[16] Women, whites, and persons with higher levels of education, higher income, and more skilled occupations in general are more likely to engage in preventive measures, such as immunization or diagnostic screening, are more likely to seek medical care and seek it promptly when needed, and experience less illness and greater longevity. Consequently, it would seem probable that persons with such characteristics are more likely to follow physician suggestions when they are sick.

However, persons who ultimately obtain medical care from physicians and thereby reach the point that compliance is important may not be a cross section of the general population, or even a cross section of the population with any given medical disorders. Between the time individuals first notice an unusual body state or first consider obtaining a preventive checkup and the time a regimen is suggested, many individuals drop out of the seeking care process by adjusting to the disorder without treatment, recovering without treatment, or dying. Thus, one can hypothesize that some of the individuals undergoing medical treatment for a specific disorder may not be representative of the population with that disorder. If true then the subjects of some compliance studies may not be representative of all individuals in the population with those characteristics who have the same type and degree of disorder.

This in part may explain why these demographic characteristics do not consistently operate to the same extent or in the same fashion as they do in predicting preventive health behavior or decisions to seek care.

The effects of social class variables on compliance illustrate this phenomenon. For a variety of reasons, various aspects of socioeconomic status, such as education, income, and occupation, influence whether or not an individual will participate in screening programs or will seek medical treatment. Generally, persons of lower social classes are less likely to obtain screening and treatment. Those individuals of lower classes who manage to obtain care may be more like their middle-class counterparts and more likely to comply with physician regimens than their lower-class counterparts who do not receive care. Thus one can predict that the measures of socioeconomic status will have less predictive power in determining compliance behavior than in determining whether or not a person will participate in a preventive screening program or decide to seek care.

This hypothesis seems to be verified by the literature in the field. Davis, in an early literature review,[17] and Caldwell,[18] Hardy,[5] Schwartz,[19] and Stine,[20] in separate articles, reported relations between measures of compliance and measures of social class, especially education. But numerous other studies have reported that various measures of social class are not related to compliance. Davis, in his empirical studies, was unable to find a relation between education, income, and compliance.[11-13] In a study of rheumatic college students, Heinzelman found no relation between compliance and the income and the occupation of patients before hospital admission and compliance.[21] Elling reported that neither family income nor social class position related to the level of participation in a pediatric clinic.[22] Francis et al failed to find any relation between education, social class, and compliance.[23] Similarly, Hoenig and Ragg [24] found no difference between the social class of 150 psychiatric outpatients who followed up on clinic referral and 150 outpatients who failed to keep referral appointments.

In fact, Marston, in her literature review, concluded that not only social class, but age, sex, education, occupation, income, and marital status were seldom found related to compliance.[1] It appears that studies which have reported no observed relation outnumber those which have reported relations almost three to one.[25]

The credibility of these reports is enhanced because the lack of relation between demographic characteristics and compliance has been observed for a variety of disorders in a variety of settings with a variety of techniques. For example, studies reporting no observed relation between social class measures and compliance have examined short-term acute illnesses,[23] chronic illnesses,[4,26] and asymptomatic problems, such as past history of rheumatic fever.[21,27] Moreover, compliance measures employed have been in home, hospital, and clinic settings and have included such measures as physician interviews and medical records,[13] bottle counts and appointment records,[23] interviews of patients,[4,13,21] and tracers in urine samples.[27]

Thus, although it might still be unwarranted at this point to conclude that demographic factors never have any impact on compliance, those studies which have noted a relationship between social status and compliance indicate a need to conduct additional research to clarify exactly when social status can be important. Even so, at present one can anticipate that compliance can be a problem for a patient regardless of his demographic and social status characteristics.

In sum, the two factors physicians can most easily identify in a patient have been explored and have been shown to be poor predictors of compliance. Neither a person's medical disorder nor his demographic or social status characteristics affect compliance consistently. Consequently, physicians cannot employ such highly visible characteristics of patients to identify those less likely to comply. Moreover, those physicians who have used such criteria to identify noncompliers may have erred in their assessments of patients. Such error may in part account for physician inability to distinguish compliant and noncompliant patients. Noncompliance is not a problem restricted to persons with certain medical disorders or social status. Rather, it is a potential problem regardless of disease severity and the social status or demographic characteristics of patients.

Psychological Predisposition Toward the Disorder and Compliance: Because the factors just discussed have not helped physicians identify noncompliers or understand noncompliance, physicians need to examine motivations and beliefs patients bring to the medical setting to identify potential noncomplying patients. The way people perceive an illness or its treatment often differs markedly from the actual characteristics of the disease or treatment. Consequently, some studies have explored the relationship of how sick persons regard their illnesses and/or the nature of their regimen with compliance. By looking at *beliefs* of patients about disease and treatment it is hypothesized that patient compliance can be more accurately predicted. Heinzelman,[21] Becker, Brachman and Kirscht,[27] and Gordis et al [28] have looked at the psychological predispositions which Hochbaum, Rosenstock [29] and others proposed to explain preventive health behavior. Heinzelman took a group of college students with a history of rheumatic fever and examined their prophylactic drug taking to prevent future streptococcal infection. Although Heinzelman referred to this as prophylaxis behavior, it can be considered compliance behavior in the sense that patients were asked by physicians to follow a medical regimen. His study reported that following the medical regimen was significantly related to (1) beliefs concerning perceived susceptibility to a recurrent attack of rheumatic fever, (2) beliefs concerning self-defined seriousness of the disease, and (3) knowledge and beliefs concerning the effectiveness of various treatments in avoiding future attacks. When Heinzelman examined whether the respondent actually had rheumatic fever and whether he had contracted it more than once, he found a direct significant relation between these indices of severity and compliance. But he also found that the number of attacks experienced by an individual was related to following the prescribed regimen only among persons who believed their attacks to be serious. Moreover, he found the recency of an attack was related to such behavior only for persons who believed they were susceptible to another attack. He reported that hospitalization was related to following the regimen only among persons who believed their attack was serious.

These findings led Heinzelman to conclude that medical factors are mediated by various psychological perceptions in relation to following prescribed regimens. "In short, it is not the rheumatic fever experiences themselves which appear to be important in determining prophylaxis behavior, but the individual's reactions to these experiences in terms of the particular meaning they have for them."[21]

In a study by Gordis, Markowitz and Lillenfeld [27] on 136 children with a past history of rheumatic fever in Baltimore, urine tests were obtained on a randomized schedule by school nurses to detect whether the children were taking prescribed penicillin, and mothers of compliant children were interviewed. Interviews, however, were taken after, not before, patients had an opportunity to comply. Supporting the model, mothers of noncompliant children also reported that the consequences of rheumatic fever if contracted would be less serious as compared to mothers of compliant children. Moreover, mothers of noncompliant children were more likely than other mothers to report that they felt their children could acquire rheumatic fever no matter what the child did.

Becker, Drachman and Kirscht [27] sought to augment the model proposed by Hochbaum [30] and Rosenstock.[29] In addition to looking at a person's perceived effectiveness of various actions to reduce the threat of the disease, Becker et al explicitly introduced the concept of health motivation. *Health motivation* means that there exists some differential degree of readiness which does not pertain to a specific illness, but to health in general. Some dimensions of the concept include arousal evoked by thoughts of suffering from a variety of disorders, feelings of ability to control health matters, willingness to be directed by health personnel, and concern with and tendency to act toward maintenance of general good health.

Studying mothers of children suffering from otitis media, the authors reported that: (1) mothers who felt their children contract illnesses easily and often and who perceive illness as an important threat to children in general were more likely to comply than those who did not feel this way; (2) feelings of control over health matters were not related to compliance; (3) mothers' willingness to defer to medical advice and intervention was related to compliance; and (4) measures of general health concern consistently predict compliance.

Looking at the more traditional aspects of the Hochbaum-Rosenstock model, the authors also reported that: (1) mothers who felt their children were resusceptible to ear infection were more likely to comply; (2) perceived severity as measured by intensity, probable duration, and sequellae also related to most measures of compliance; and (3) perceived effectiveness of physicians as measured by accuracy of diagnosis and efficacy of medications was partially related to degree of compliance.

These three studies suggest that the health belief model of Hochbaum and Rosenstock may well prove useful in explaining compliance behavior. In addition, the health motivation concept offered by Becker et al may well offer an additional refinement to the predictive power of the model (*see* Barofsky pages 29-44).

Factors the Physician Influences

Characteristics of the Regimen: A set of factors over which the physician has some control, which can affect compliance, is the characteristics of the medical regimen recommended to patients. For example, the more complex the regimen, the less likely it is to be followed. Francis et al found that when physicians prescribe more than one medication, patients are less likely to comply.[23] Schwartz [19] and Davis [12] confirmed this finding. Unfortunately, none of these reports indicated whether complexity of regimens reduced patients' attempts to comply or instead confused them to the point that they complied incorrectly.

Johannsen [26] and Davis [12] found that prescriptions were less difficult for patients to follow than proscriptions. In their studies of heart disease patients, respondents were more likely to comply with medical aspects of their regimens than to change their work habits. Apparently, the more likely a regimen is to disrupt the normal behavior patterns of a patient, the less likely a patient is to comply. The implications of Johannsen's finding are clear. Patients often bring competing priorities to a medical setting. Not only do patients desire good health, many also have monetary needs and psychological needs which outweigh the desire for good health. It may be unrealistic for physicians to alter those priorities for the patient, especially when the efficacy of such regimens are disputed within the medical profession.

Patient Interaction with Physicians and Others: The importance of physician interaction with patients was pointed out by Zola (*see* pages 3-8) and can be seen from variables already examined. Findings which show less compliance with more complex regimens suggest that compliance may be increased if physicians can simplify their regimens or make them appear less complex. In addition, findings which show a direct relation between beliefs about illness and treatment regimens indicate that if physicians can create appropriate beliefs among patients compliance may be increased. Thus, one can hypothesize that if physicians can give patients appropriate instructions about how to comply and what creates the need to comply, levels of compliance will be increased.

While giving appropriate instruction and molding beliefs of patients do not sound like difficult tasks, many physicians have found that obtaining these objectives in practice is quite difficult. Perhaps one reason is that there often is considerable misunderstanding and even mistrust between patients and physicians.

Moreover, some misunderstanding and mistrust may come from physicians. For example, when Davis asked over 100 physician faculty members at a major medical school in New York why patients fail to comply with medical regimens, over two thirds of those responding blamed noncompliance on the uncooperative personalities of patients.[17] In a more recent article McKinley cites a number of studies which suggest that many physicians have difficulty accurately estimating how much medical information patients are capable of comprehending.[31]

Pratt and her colleagues [32] sought to examine the impact on patient behavior of physicians underestimating their knowledge. They compared the physician-patient interactions in situations where physicians underestimated patient knowledge and where physicians made efforts to give their patients full information about their disorders. They reported that:

> When a doctor perceives the patient as rather poorly informed, he considers the tremendous difficulties of translating his knowledge into language the patient can understand, along with dangers of frightening the patient; the patient in turn reacts dully to this limited information, either asking uninspired questions or

refraining from questioning the doctor at all, thus reinforcing the doctor's view that the patient is ill-equipped to comprehend his problem. Lacking guidance the patient performs at a low level; hence the doctor rates his capacities as even lower than they are.

This description contrasts with that for patients who are given more thorough explanations.

Patients who were given more thorough explanations were found to participate somewhat more effectively with the physician and were more likely to accept completely the doctor's formulation than were patients who received very little explanation.[32]

The effect of negative evaluations of patients made by physicians was further explored in a study of compliance by mothers with children having rheumatic fever. In this study, Elling introduced the idea of *reflexive self concept*.[22] Reflexive self concept refers to how mothers felt physicians view them. It was found that mothers who felt physicians had negative perceptions of them were significantly less likely to have complied with physician recommendations for the child.

Taken together, these studies imply that some physicians may have unrealistic perceptions and expectations of patients. In addition, when physicians underestimate the knowledge or competence of patients, the compliance behavior of the patient is altered. When the physician makes a personal judgment about a patient's knowledge or behavior, the judgment is frequently inaccurate. Moreover, if the physician's assessments of patients are negative, compliance may be reduced either by the physician failing to fully explain to patients the nature and reasons of a regimen, or the consequence of such an assessment: the patient's losing interest in satisfying the expectations of the physician.

Milton Davis also conducted a study to identify what causes physician-patient rapport to deteriorate to the point where compliance is jeopardized.[17] Davis studied 154 new patients in a general medical clinic who were seen by 76 senior medical students and 78 physicians. Using the Bales interaction scale to analyze tape-recorded interaction, he found that noncompliant behavior was in part explained by increased difficulty in communication and attempts by physicians and patients to control each other. He specifically reported:

1. Revisits between an authoritative patient and a physician who passively accepts such patient participation may promote patient noncompliance.
2. Effective communication between physicians and patients is impeded when doctors and patients evidence tension in their relationships. Unless released, the tension may result in noncompliance.
3. When the doctor confines his activity to analysis of the situation and expression of his opinions noncompliance is likely. In particular when the doctor seeks information from a patient without giving him feedback the patient is unlikely to follow the physician's orders.

In sum, research findings on physician-patient interaction illustrate that to focus the entire blame for noncompliance on physicians is just as unwarranted as to focus the blame on patients. One can conclude that some physician-patient communication problems stem from physicians, and others stem from patients. However, in the medical setting, under the pressures of illness, one cannot expect all patients to behave in a fully rational manner. For realistic progress to be made, initiatives to identify and resolve those problems in physician-patient interaction which might affect compliance, clearly are the responsibility of professional medical personnel, not patients.

FACTORS IDENTIFIABLE AFTER A
PATIENT'S REGIMEN HAS BEEN PRESCRIBED

Finally, after a patient is given a regimen to follow he must decide whether or not he should comply. At this point the patient's predispositions towards his illness will have been altered or reinforced by his interaction with the physician. Some patients may be thoroughly committed to accepting the regimen. Others may adopt a willingness merely to try out the regimen, and some patients may decide not to comply. The extent of physician follow-up, the effects of the regimen, and the influence of friends may constitute new factors which may arise at this point in time to alter compliance.

Physician Follow-up

One obvious factor which might influence patient compliance is the extent to which medical professionals overtly follow up on their patients. Studies have shown that even procedures as simple as mailing reminder postcards and/or telephone reminders about clinic appointments can significantly reduce missed follow-up appointment keeping by patients.[33,34]

Effects of the Regimen

In addition, after a period of time many patients will try to evaluate the appropriateness of their decision by the effects of compliance or noncompliance on their physical well-being. Marston in her review of the literature concluded that some evidence has been found to support the notion that drug regimens with unpleasant side effects are likely to be discontinued by patients.[6] Davis also reported that cardiac patients following a physician's regimen, who succumb to a new cardiac episode while on the regimen, are likely to stop compliance. Unfortunately, there are only a few studies of patient reactions over time to regimens which seem to have beneficial effects. Some studies do suggest that the patient for whom a regimen has beneficial effects may stop compliance prematurely, simply because he feels well.[18,35]

Influence of Other Persons

Some patients, as they evaluate the effects of their decision to comply or not, may seek to discuss their regimens with other persons or their physicians. Davis, in his study of physician-patient interaction, determined that a patient's initial visit and interaction with a physician was usually not as important for long-term compliance behavior as his subsequent interactions.[12] In the same study, Davis also observed that patients with influential family members were more likely to continue compliance over time.

On the other hand, a study by McKinlay [36] illustrates how friends and relatives can have a negative impact on seeking and continuing health care. In a study of 87 working-class families in Scotland, McKinlay observed that women classified as underutilizers of prenatal and postpartum medical care were less likely to discuss their health with others before seeing a physician, and if they did discuss their health with others, they were more likely than adequate utilizers of health care to have discussed their health with members of their immediate family, not friends or distant relatives. Many of the underutilizers indicated that their own mothers discouraged them from using health services. Thus, friends and especially family members can exert an influence over compliance. At times their views may support compliance while at other times they may discourage compliance. Consequently physicians need to be alert to the impact family and friends may have on their patients.

WHAT CAN BE DONE?

We have found thus far that there are a number of factors known to be related to compliance which clinicians can identify as they initially interact with patients and after a medical regimen has been offered. If physicians focus attention on identifying factors which might impede compliance among their patients, not only will they be better able to identify potentially noncomplying patients, the information gathered in the process may prove useful in reducing noncompliance.

The question then becomes, how to identify these factors. Let us start by considering the feedback from physicians to patients when they interact. It is my contention that some physicians neither provide adequate feedback to patients about their health nor elicit adequate feedback and information from patients. In our review of compliance studies, we observed that the beliefs a patient brings to a physician-patient interaction about his illness, the effectiveness, and difficulties in treatment, can affect the extent to which he follows the physician's recommendations. Therefore, we recommend that to identify potential noncomplying patients and forestall noncompliance, physicians need to systematically undertake the task of exploring the beliefs and motivations of each patient with regards to his illness and treatment. At a minimum each patient should be asked:

1. Have you been taking anything for this problem already?
2. Does anything worry you about the illness?
3. What can happen if the recommended regimen is not followed?
4. How likely is that to occur?

5. How effective do you feel the regimen will be in treating the disorder?
6. Can you think of any problems you might have in following the regimen?
7. Do you have any questions about the regimen or how to follow it?

It is also useful to have the patient verbally repeat the regimen and to request that the patient contact the physician if any problems or unpleasant side effects emerge from treatment.

In asking these questions it is of great importance for the physician not to rush his patient's answers. We can learn from psychiatry in this regard. Psychiatrists point out that all of us have a tendency to be frightened by silence during conversations, and physicians are no exception. If a physician starts to fill in information for the patient or cuts the patient off before he has an opportunity to voice his real opinions, or musters the courage to tell the physician how he feels, that physician may close off valuable information which later could be used to foster compliance or reduce barriers to compliance.

One can hypothesize that merely by routinely asking this series of questions about patient beliefs concerning illness and treatment, and allowing the patient time to answer these questions adequately, (1) physician-patient interaction will be improved, and (2) information will come to the physician's attention which can be used to more adequately encourage or foster compliance. First, by attempting to determine salient beliefs, the physician can gain fuller insight into exactly what patients understand or do not understand about their illnesses and their treatment. Consequently, underestimation of patient knowledge as noted by Pratt [32] et al will be less likely to occur. By earnestly seeking to understand patient concerns regarding illness and treatment, the physician may also reduce feelings among some patients that they are not respected by their physician, which Elling et al [22] reported inhibits compliance. If patients feel the physician respects and is concerned about their feelings, they may be less likely to think that the physician has negative perceptions of them. By discussing patient concerns, some of the tensions which impede physician-patient interactions may be reduced. Most probably, if patients can voice their concerns, fewer will feel that they have given information to the physician about their 'illnesses' without receiving feedback concerning the worries their illnesses produce.

Second, the information gleaned by these questions can be helpful to physicians in adjusting regimens or encouraging compliance. A number of examples come to mind. Patients may not be aware of the potential ramifications of noncompliance. Patients may not understand the seriousness of their disorders or exactly how to comply. Missing information can be supplied by the physician and incorrect beliefs addressed. Moreover, the physician may not be aware of the potential difficulties some patients encounter in compliance. Efforts to accommodate or simplify regimens may be the result of the physician actively attempting to uncover patient-perceived obstacles to compliance. Finally, when compliance may eliminate or reduce the source of patient worries about their illnesses, that fact can be underscored by the physician in an effort to encourage compliance. In short, if the physician has more information with which to work during his initial patient interaction as a regimen is recommended, it is logical to believe that as a reasonable, intelligent person, he will use that information to more adequately foster compliance.

Furthermore, our review of compliance studies suggests that gathering information after the initial interaction with patients may also prove useful. After a regimen is prescribed, patients decide whether or not to begin compliance and they subsequently assess the merit of their decision. Some patients fail to comply initially but begin after their symptoms become worse. Other comply initially, but discontinue after symptoms subside or unanticipated negative side effects of their regimens make compliance unacceptable from the patient point of view. The problems of negative side effects often are not uncovered by physicians, because patients are reluctant to bother a physician about themselves, or to describe effects which the patients may perceive as embarrassing.

Thus, many patients need an *overt* invitation to express their impression of treatment to a physician rapidly if problems arise. Others frequently need an additional stimulus to continue compliance if symptoms subside. Physicians need to openly ask patients to indicate their response to a regimen, either through a telephone call or a postcard reminding the patient of his/her regimen while requesting the patient to report noncompliance, or difficulties in compliance to the physician. Efforts to request that *significant others*, such as family members or friends, notify a physician if the patient is noncompliant or is experiencing difficulties in compliance can also be attempted.

The point to be noted is that once compliance with a therapeutic regimen has begun or has been rejected, that does not mean that such behavior will continue. While we have learned a great deal about why some patients initially comply with regimens, we know much less about why compliance is abandoned, sustained, or adopted initially by some only after a period of noncompliance. As suggested earlier, compliance is not a single behavior at one point in time, but a continual process of action, assessment, reaction, and reassessment over time by the patient of his disorder, his physician, and his regimen. Just as some regimens have only marginal utility unless followed over time, so, too, our analyses of compliance behavior have only marginal usefulness unless compliance is monitored over long periods.

In summary, I am arguing that if physicians attempt to gather information about patient worries and concerns regarding illness and treatment, they may be better able to promote patient compliance. Certainly such an approach is both more humane and effective than the commonly used fear arousal strategies, in which physicians try to scare patients into "appropriate behavior" by underlining the potential hazards of noncompliance. The literature on such fear arousal approaches indicates only mixed success at best.[37]

By attempting to identify potential noncompliers and making the effort to explore their beliefs about their illness and treatment, physicians may be better able to understand the reasons for noncompliance and avoid such barriers to compliance. Simultaneously, rapport with patients may improve and physicians may help patients to reduce or cope with their illness-associated anxieties. In short, "when patient recovery requires patient compliance, it is as important to know what patient has the disease as what disease the patient has."[8]

REFERENCES

1. Marston MV: Compliance with medical regimens: a review of the literature. Nurs Res 19:312-323, 1970.
2. Berkowitz N: Patient follow through in the outpatient department. Nurs Res 12:16-22, 1963.
3. Caron H, Roth H: Patient cooperation with a medical regimen. JAMA 203:922-926, 1968.
4. Donabedian A, Rosenfeld L: Follow-up study of chronically ill patients discharged from hospital. J Chronic Dis 17:847-862, 1964.
5. Hardy M: Patient resistance to need for remedial and preventive services. Pediatrics 48:104-114, 1956.
6. Ludwig E, Adams SD: Patient cooperation as a rehabilitation center: assumption of the client role. J Health Soc Behav 9:328-336, 1968.
7. Watkins J, Williams FT, Marlin DA, Hogon MD, Anderson E: A study of diabetic patients at home. Am J Public Health 57:452-459, 1967.
8. Charney E, Bynom R, Eldredge D, Frank D, MacWhinney J, McNabb N, Scheiner A, Sumpter EA, Iker H: How well do patients take oral penicillin: a collaborative study in private practice. Pediatrics 40:188-195, 1967.
9. McDonald M, Hagber K, Grossman B: Social factors in relation to participation in follow-up care of rheumatic fever. J Pediatrics 62:503-513, 1963.
10. Lendrum B, Kobrin C: Prevention of recurrent attacks of rheumatic fever. JAMA 162:13-16, 1956.
11. Davis M, Eichorn R: Compliance with medical regimens: a panel study. J Health Hum Behav 4:240-249, 1963.
12. Davis M: Variations in compliance with doctor's advice: an empirical analysis of patterns of communications. Am J Public Health 58:274-288, 1968.
13. Davis M: Physiologic, psychological and demographic factors in patient compliance with doctor's orders. Med Care 6:112-115, 1968.
14. Antonovsky A: Social class, life expectancy and overall mortality. Milbank Mem Fund Q 45:31-73, 1967.
15. Douglas CW: A social psychological view of health behavior for health services research. Health Ser Res 6:10, 1971.
16. Anderson O, Anderson R: Medical care use in Sweden and the United States. Chicago Center Health Admin Studies 27, 1970.
17. Davis M: Variations in patients' compliance with doctor's orders: analysis of congruence between survey responses and results of empirical investigations. J Med Educ 41:1037-1040, 1966.
18. Caldwell J, Cobb S, Dowling M, DeJongh D: The drop-out problem in antihypertensive treatment. J Chron Dis 22:579-592, 1970.
19. Schwartz D: Medication errors made by elderly chronically ill patients. Am J Public Health 52:2018-2029, 1962.
20. Stine O, Chuaqui C, Jiminez C, Appel WC: Broken appointments at a comprehensive clinic for children. Med Care 6:332-339, 1968.
21. Heinzelman F: Factors in prophylaxis behavior in treating rheumatic fever. Health Hum Behav 3:73-81, 1962.
22. Elling R: Patient participation in a pediatric program. Health Hum Behav 1:183-191, 1960.
23. Francis V, Korsch B, Moris M: Gaps in doctor-patient communication. N Engl J Med 289:535-540, 1967.
24. Hoenig J, Ragg N: The non-attending psychiatric outpatient: an administrative problem. Med Care 4:96-100, 1966.
25. Mitchell J: Compliance with medical regimens: an annotated bibliography. Health Educ Monogr 2:75-87, 1974.

26. Johannsen W, Hellmuth G, Sorauf T: On accepting medical recommendations. Arch Environ Health 12:63-69, 1966.
27. Becker M, Drachman R, Kirscht J: Mothers' Perceptions and Compliance with Medical Regimens. Presented before the Joint Session of the Am Pharm Assoc and the Medical Care Section of the Am Public Health Assoc at the 99th annual meeting in Minneapolis, Minnesota, October 14, 1971.
28. Gordis L, Markowitz, Lillienfeld A: Why patients don't follow medical advice: a study of children on long-term anti-streptococcal prophylaxis. Pediatrics 75:957-968, 1969.
29. Rosenstock I: Why people use health services. Milbank Mem Fund Q 44:94-127, 1956.
30. Hochbaum G: Public participation in medical screening programs: a socio-psychological study. Public Health Services Publication No. 572, Washington, D.C., U.S. Government Printing Office, 1958.
31. McKinley J: Who is really ignorant? J Health Soc Behav 16:3-12, 1975.
32. Pratt I, Seligman A, Reader G: Physician views on the level of medical information among patients. Am J Public Health 47:1277-1283, 1957.
33. Fletcher S, Appel F, Bourgois M: Improving emergency room patient follow-up in a metropolitan teaching hospital. N Engl J Med 291:385-388, 1974.
34. Nazarion L, Mechaber J, Charney E, Coulter N: Effect of mailed appointment reminder on appointment keeping. Pediatrics 53:349-352, 1974.
35. Mohler D, Wallin D, Dryfus E: Studies in home treatment of streptococcal disease. N Engl J Med 252:111-117, 1955.
36. McKinlay JB: Social networks, lay consultation and help-seeking behavior. Soci Forces 51:275-292, 1973.
37. Higbee K: Fifteen years of fear arousal: research on threat appeals, 1953-68. Psychol Bull 72(6):426-444, 1969.

The Pharmacist's Potential Role as a Factor in Increasing Compliance

THOMAS R. SHARPE

Research Institutes of Pharmaceutical Sciences
School of Pharmacy
University of Mississippi
University, Mississippi

Hypertension, the most common adult chronic disease in the United States, is a staggering public health problem. According to the National Health Survey [1] the disease affects over 20 million Americans. In 1974, there were over 53 million patient visits for hypertension and hypertensive heart disease, representing the largest number of visits for any disease. Hypertensive individuals have a shortened life-expectancy, with an increased prevalence of such complications as stroke, congestive heart failure, renal damage and failure, and accelerated atherosclerosis.[2, 3]

Much progress has been made in the ability to control this disease, especially when the therapy of forty to fifty years ago is considered. At that time medical science offered such remedies as extract of watermelon and cucumber seeds, misteltoe and garlic, and ovarian gland preparations. Treatment later included psychotherapy, careful regulation of life-style, well-balanced diet, clear gastrointestinal tracts, low-salt diets, and surgical sympathectomies.[4]

Only recently have pharmacological agents of proven efficacy become available for the treatment of hypertension. Fortunately, the results have been very favorable. Support for the efficacy of modern pharmacological therapy exists in demonstrated outcome measures of lowered systolic and diastolic blood pressures, and more importantly, in significant decreases in morbidity and mortality.[5-8] Well-designed studies have shown that through proper control programs the morbid and fatal effects of untreated hypertension can be *drastically* reduced.[9],[10]

Our enthusiasm must be mitigated, however, by reports that a majority of hypertensive individuals are undiagnosed, untreated, or inadequately treated.[11-13]

Wilber and Barrow [14] found that in a random sample of persons in a Georgia community 42 per cent of the 630 patients in the sample had elevated blood pressures but were unaware of it. Furthermore, only 30 per cent of those patients who were aware of their conditions were under treatment, and only about half of the treated group were judged to be under good control. After an intensive follow-up program was instituted the percentage judged to be under good control was raised dramatically to 80 per cent. Two years after the intensive follow-up program was discontinued, however, only 24 per cent remained under good control. The investigators concluded that the patients lacked a proper understanding of their disease state, and that the primary factor contributing to their failure to remain under good control was their failure to take their medications.

The last study illustrates several needs which pharmacist intervention might help to satisfy:

1. There is a need for identification of previously undiagnosed hypertensive patients.
2. Once identified, treatment of these newly diagnosed hypertensive patients is needed.
3. There is a need for continuous follow-up care once the patient is diagnosed and stabilized.
4. Education of the patient concerning his disease state is needed.
5. Continuous monitoring of the patient's drug therapy regimen is necessary.

The community pharmacist is in a unique position to aid both the patient and his physician in maintaining the patient on a normotensive status through increased compliance.

Before discussing the pharmacist's potential role in this regard, I would like to briefly discuss what I mean by the term *compliance.* Compliance results from an encounter between the patient and his physician. The likely outcome of the encounter is that the physician prescribes a therapy and expects the patient to adhere to it. The therapy may require one or more forms of behavior. The patient may be required to obtain a drug from a pharmacy and consume it on a given schedule, adjust his eating habits to conform to a therapeutic diet, discontinue use of tobacco or alcohol, restrict or increase his physical activity, present himself for diagnostic tests, or keep an appointment for follow-up care. Any one or all of these may be included in the therapy regimen of the hypertensive patient.

When drug therapy is involved, the outcome of the physician-patient encounter typically involves a prescription. The physician, through the medium of the prescription, requests the pharmacist to dispense to the patient a specified number of units of a specific drug in a specific dosage form at a specific dose. He further requests the pharmacist to provide written instructions, through the medium of the prescription label, directing the patient to consume the drug according to the prescribed schedule. The patient is then expected to consume the medication as directed; he is expected to comply with his prescribed drug therapy regimen.

From this it can be seen that patient compliance with a prescription drug regimen is a two-stage process. First, the patient must take the prescription to the pharmacist (often the physician completes this act by telephoning the prescription to the pharmacist) and have it dispensed. At the second stage, the patient must consume the drug at the *rate* and for the *duration* prescribed. Although it occurs in only about three per cent of the cases, the patient may choose not to have his prescription dispensed. If he chooses not to comply with this prerequisite first stage of the process, he cannot be compliant with the second stage.

The specification of both rate and duration of therapy is usually made because in most cases the efficacy of drug therapy depends upon the presence of the drug exceeding a minimal blood or tissue concentration for some minimal continuous time period. Thus patient compliance to prescribed drug therapy is a *longitudinal* process occurring over contiguous time segments. The patient must consume the drug at the rate and for the duration prescribed. Deviation from that rate or duration or the consumption of the drug over noncontiguous time segments constitutes noncompliance.

The emphasis on both rate and duration is particularly important in the case of the hypertensive patient for two reasons. First, the duration of his drug therapy, although it may be periodically modified, is likely to be for the rest of his life. Second, many hypotensive agents are characterized by a therapeutic onset of several days; such a patient could conceivably take his medication so sporadically that he would never achieve therapeutic levels!

For the most part, three methods are used to measure compliance. One method is a urinalysis for the excreted drug, its metabolite, or a tracer included in the dosage form. A second method is a physical count of the remaining medication. Patient self-reports constitute a third method for determing compliance. It should be pointed out, however, that self-reports have been shown to be inaccurate by several investigators.[15-19] Patients generally report a higher degree of compliance than can be verified by the other, more objective, measurement procedures.

This does not mean that self-reports are totally without value, however. Certain information is accessible *only* through patient self-reports. For example, patients' perceptions of the reasons why they did not take their medications as prescribed are often most easily and accurately accessible from self-reports once we know from the more objective methods that noncompliance has actually occurred.

I see basically three mechanisms by which the pharmacist can play an important role in increasing patient compliance:

1. Pharmacist monitoring of blood pressures;
2. Pharmacist monitoring of drug regimens and drug-taking behavior;

3. Pharmacist provision of health-related information to the patient, particularly information on the effect of legend and over-the-counter medications on blood pressure.

Through pharmacist monitoring of blood pressures, previously undiagnosed potential hypertensives may be identified and referred to the proper medical agency for diagnostic and treatment procedures. While this activity by the pharmacist does not really fit into the compliance model, nevertheless, it is an important service which the pharmacist can provide for the hypertensive patient. The pharmacist, by virtue of his easy accessibility to the patient, is in an excellent position within the communication system to screen potential hypertensive patients and to aid their entry into what medical sociologists call the professional referral system.

Once the patient is identified, diagnosed, and placed on a stabilized treatment regimen, the pharmacist can serve to continuously monitor blood pressure at the times when the patient returns to the pharmacy for prescription refills. In this way, the pharmacist can regularly monitor blood pressure extremes and, when indicated, report them to the physician. Furthermore, this mechanism can be utilized to effectively counsel the patient as to the importance of his compliant behavior. The patient can actually see the beneficial effect of his medical therapy, as well as the consequences of his noncompliant behavior.

A second mechanism by which the pharmacist might contribute toward increasing patient compliance involves the use of patient drug profiles. Through proper utilization of these profiles the pharmacist can screen the patient's drug regimen for unintended drug interactions — particularly when multiple physicians (but a single pharmacy) are involved. In this way the pharmacist can prevent potential serious effects resulting from certain of these interactions. Furthermore, the pharmacist may prevent potential patient-initiated discontinuance of drug therapy precipitated by manifest adverse effects.

Pharmacists can also use profile information to estimate the adherence of the patient to his drug regimen. This is done by examining the frequency at which the patient returns for refills of his prescription and comparing that frequency to the theoretical one. The theoretical frequency, of course, is based upon the number of dosage units dispensed to the patient and the frequency at which the patient is instructed to take the medication.

A profile system based upon duplicate prescription labels has been developed by Srnka at University of Tennessee.[20] The original label is placed on the prescription container for the patient, and a duplicate copy is kept as a permanent record on the profile. All information necessary for refilling the prescription is on the label, so that the pharmacist can refill the prescription directly from the profile. This system might be modified to include a second carbon copy which the pharmacist could mail to the physician for his medical record. This, then, would provide the physician also with a rough measure of the patient's compliance through frequency-of-refill data.

The third area of pharmacist involvement, as I see it, is in providing to the patient general health information and specific counseling as to the importance of his compliant behavior. A study which we conducted at the University of Mississippi revealed that provision of written information in the form of auxiliary information sheets and auxiliary labels cautioning the patient to consume his medication according to the prescribed schedule resulted in a significant increase in patient compliance among patients on antibiotic therapy.[21] Similar techniques have been successful with patients taking chronic medications.

An often overlooked, but extremely important, contribution of the pharmacist lies in advising the patient about over-the-counter medications. Several classes of over-the-counter medications contain ingredients which may exert an effect on blood pressures. The APhA *Handbook of Non-Prescription Drugs* [22] lists over seventy cough/cold products and over forty antitussive products which contain sympathomimetics or antihistamines. Both sympathomimetics and antihistamines may elevate blood pressures.

Antacids are another potentially serious offender, especially since many patients are chronic users. The high sodium content, particularly of the sodium bicarbonate-containing products, can contribute significantly to increased blood pressure.

I picture the pharmacist actually walking the newly diagnosed hypertensive patient through the over-the-counter medication section of the pharmacy and pointing out to the patient those products, or at least those classes of products, which may affect blood pressure. In this manner the pharmacist can alert the patient to be certain to consult the pharmacist before purchasing one of those types of products for self-medication.

In conclusion, the community pharmacist is in a unique position to contribute to increased patient compliance, by virtue of his expertise in the field of drug therapy and by virtue of the fact that he, more than any other health professional, has frequent, continuous contact with the patient. Through more aggressive participation in his traditional role as advisor on over-the-counter medications, through broader use of pharmacy patient profiles, and through the hopefully traditional role in the future of monitoring blood pressures, the pharmacist can play an important role in the total therapy of the hypertensive patient.

REFERENCES

1. National Center for Health Statistics: Heart Disease in Adults: United States 1960-1962. Vital Health Stat, Series 11-No. 2, Washington, D.C., U.S. Govt Ptg Off, 1964.
2. Beeson PB, McDermott W (eds): Cecil-Loeb Textbook of Medicine. Philadelphia, W.B. Saunders, 1971, pp 1050-1062.
3. Holvey DN (ed): The Merck Manual, 12th ed. Rahway, New Jersey, Merck, Sharp and Dohme Laboratories, 1973, pp 465-471.
4. Page IH: Drug treatment of hypertension. In Gross F (ed): Antihypertensive Therapy: Principles and Practice. New York, Springer-Verlag, 1965, pp 602-614.
5. Hamilton M: Selection of patients for hypertensive therapy. In Gross F (ed): Antihypertensive Therapy: Principles and Practice. New York, Springer-Verlag, 1965, pp 196-206.
6. Harrington M et al: Results of treatment in malignant hypertension. Br Med J 2:969-980, 1959.

7. Perry HM, Schroeder HA: The effect of treatment on mortality rates in severe hypertension. Arch Intern Med 102:418-425, 1958.
8. Sokolow M, Perloff D: Five-year survival of consecutive patients with malignant hypertension treated with antihypertensive agents. Am J Cardiol 6:858-863, 1960.
9. Veterans Administration Cooperative Study Group on Antihypertensive Agents: Effect of treatment on morbidity in hypertension: results in patients with diastolic blood pressures averaging 115 through 129 mm Hg. JAMA 202:1028-1034, 1967.
10. Veterans Administration Cooperative Study Group on Antihypertensive Agents: Effects of treatment on morbidity in hypertension: II. Results in patients with diastolic blood pressures averaging 90 through 114 mm Hg. JAMA 213:1143-1152, 1970.
11. AMA Committee on Hypertension: Drug treatment of ambulatory patients with hypertension. JAMA 225:1647-1653, 1973.
12. Frohlich ED et al: Evaluation of initial care of hypertensive patients. JAMA 218:1036-1038, 1971.
13. Schoonberger JA et al: Current statistics of hypertension control in an industrial population. JAMA 222:559-562, 1972.
14. Wilber JA, Barrow JG: Reducing elevated blood pressure. Minn Med 52:1303-1305, 1969.
15. Gordis L et al: The inaccuracy of using interviews to estimate patient reliability in taking medications at home. Med Care 7:49-54, 1969.
16. McInnes JK: Do patients take their antituberculosis drugs? Am J Nurs 70:2152-2153, 1970.
17. Park LC, Lipman RS: A comparison of patient dosage and deviation reports with pill counts. Psychopharmacol 6:299-302, 1964.
18. Preston DF, Miller FL: The tuberculosis outpatient's defection from therapy. Am J Med Sci 247:21-25, 1964.
19. Simpson J McD: Simple tests for the detection of urinary P.A.S. Tubercle 37:333-340, 1956.
20. Srnka QM et al: Evaluation of a patient medication profile based on the use of duplicate labels. Am J Hosp Pharm 31:79-83, 1974.
21. Sharpe TR, Mikeal RL: Patient compliance with antibiotic regimens. Am J Hosp Pharm 31:479-84, 1974.
22. Griffenhagen GB, Hawkins LL (eds): Handbook of Non-Prescription Drugs, 1973 ed. Washington, D.C., Am Pharm Assoc, 1973.

Nursing Management of Compliance with Medication Regimens

MARY-'VESTA MARSTON

School of Nursing
Boston University
Boston, Massachusetts

CHANGING PHILOSOPHY OF THE NURSING PROFESSION WITH RESPECT TO MANAGING PATIENT HEALTH BEHAVIOR

Nurses, by virtue of their numbers and amount of patient contact, have the greatest potential of any group of health professionals for exerting an impact on patient health behavior. Until recently, however, nurses have not taken advantage of the opportunities available to them.

This paper will address the role of nurses in managing patient health behavior. Major events in the historical development of the nursing profession which have paved the way for nurses to assume an active role in patient management will be reviewed. These include the trend toward education of increased numbers of professional nurses at the baccalaureate, master's and doctoral levels, recruitment of students from diverse socioeconomic and cultural backgrounds, and professional and consumer acceptance of extended roles in nursing practice. The primary purpose of this paper are to sensitize nurses to their opportunities and obligations to help patients improve their health; to present some theoretical approaches and techniques which nurses may use to assist patients to reach this goal; and to identify areas in need of applied nursing research.

TRADITIONAL ORIENTATION OF NURSING

Until fairly recently the majority of young women recruited into nursing were from lower socioeconomic levels. Nursing was a route by which a woman could advance socially and economically.

With rare exceptions, the education of nurses in the past was considered a function of the hospital. Training programs consisted of some formal didactic input, along with an apprenticeship system for providing practice. Much of the didactic input was provided by physicians, and was disease-oriented. Many of the hospital-based programs existed primarily for the purpose of providing service to the hospital, with education of nurses a secondary concern. The net effect of this policy was that it produced a narrowly educated nurse.

Public health nurses were the first group to recognize that nurses working in community settings needed more formal preparation than that being provided by hospital training programs. About 1920, nurses began trying to place nursing education in institutions of higher learning, and baccalaureate programs in nursing began to be developed.

In 1965, the American Nurses' Association issued the *Position Paper on Education for Nursing,*[1] which proposed that all nursing education take place in institutions of higher learning. The *Position Paper* distinguished between "professional" and "technical" nursing. Professional nursing practice encompasses *caring, curing,* and *coordination* functions. *Caring* denotes dealing with patients under stress; the *curative* aspect emphasizes promotion of health and healing; and *coordination* implies a sharing of responsibility with other health professionals for the promotion of health and prevention of illness. *Professional nursing practice* places priority on the need for a theoretical basis for practice, and requires knowledge in depth and a high degree of skill. *Technical nursing practice* involves the carrying out of nursing measures and medically delegated techniques, and requires supervision by professional nurses. Emphasis is placed on a technical orientation rather than a theoretical orientation. The *Position Paper* recommended that minimal preparation for beginning professional nursing practice should be a baccalaureate degree in nursing, and minimal preparation for technical nursing practice should be an associate degree in nursing. The National League for Nursing (NLN), the professional organization which accredits educational programs in nursing, has reaffirmed the baccalaureate degree with an upper division major in nursing as the first professional degree in nursing. In March 1976, the NLN's Council of Baccalaureate and Higher Degree Programs passed a resolution supporting the concept that by 1985 all candidates for licensure meet this educational criterion.

The majority of registered nurses continue to be prepared in diploma programs. Many diploma programs have closed, however, or affiliated with junior colleges or four-year colleges and universities, and there has been a proliferation of associate degree programs offered by junior colleges. According to the most recent *Facts About Nursing,*[2] 71.1 percent (801,780) of all registered nurses were prepared in hospital diploma programs, 4.3 percent (48,918) in associate degree programs, and 11.8 percent (133,085) in baccalaureate programs in nursing. Only 1.9 percent (21,527) held master's degrees in nursing, and 0.1 percent (1,539) held earned doctorates.* Such diversity in levels of preparation has inevitably resulted in variability in scope of practice among nurses.

THE EXTENDED ROLE OF THE NURSE

During the last ten years the number of physicians being prepared has been insufficient to meet patient needs for care. The medical profession's response to this dilemma was the development of physician assistant programs.[3] Men who had had some experience as medical corpsmen during the war, young men and women who probably would not have had the intellectual and/or financial resources to complete medical school, and nurses were recruited into physician assistant programs. The possibility of nurses taking over more physician functions was an attractive option to some. Also, salaries of graduates of physician assistant programs usually could not be matched by organizations employing nurses without this special preparation.

Nursing's response to the physician assistant programs was to develop programs to prepare nurse practitioners. The American Nurses' Association's definition of a nurse practitioner [4] is a nurse with at least diploma preparation who has completed a program equipping her with history-taking and physical-assessment skills. The majority of nurse practitioner programs have been offered through continuing education programs, along with on-the-job experience. Some, however, have been developed at the baccalaureate and master's levels. Master's level programs prepare nurse clinicians with knowledge and experience in depth in a clinical nursing specialty.[4] Master's programs in nursing do not necessarily include the so-called "practitioner skills." However, increased numbers of master's as well as baccalaureate programs, are including history-taking and physical-assessment content and practice as an integral part of the curriculum, but *without* placing major emphasis on this aspect of the educational program.

The focus of physician assistant programs has been on preparation of physician extenders who can take medical histories, perform physical examinations, possess some diagnostic knowledges and skills, and assume responsibility for ongoing supervision of selected patients. The focus of nurse practitioner programs, especially those associated with universities, has been primarily on the acquisition by nurses of assessment knowledges and skills to provide a data base for nursing interventions *vs.* preparation of nurses as physician extenders.

The Secretary of Health, Education and Welfare appointed an expert committee consisting of representatives from nursing, medicine, hospital administration, and allied health for the purpose of clarifying the responsibilities of nurses in

---

*The most recent year for which statistics are available is 1972. The percentages reported do not add up to 100%, because some nurses hold degrees in fields other than nursing, and data regarding level of preparation are not available for some. Also, most nurses holding doctorates earned their degrees in education, the behavioral sciences, the biological sciences, or in public health, because of the paucity of doctoral programs in nursing, per se.

expanded roles. Although the nursing profession had already delineated some of their independent, interdependent, and dependent functions, the *Secretary's Report,*[5] issued in 1971, spelled out, more clearly than ever before, nurses' functions in expanded roles in primary care, acute care and long-term care.

Primary care was defined by the *Secretary's Report* as a person's first contact with the health care system, in any given illness episode leading to evaluation, symptom management, referral, and could include continuing surveillance and health supervision. Nurses functioning in extended roles in primary care need preparation to take health histories; perform physical and psychosocial assessments; assess family relationships and home, school, and work environments; interpret common laboratory findings; make tentative diagnoses and select therapies; assess resources; provide emergency care; and teach the patient and/or his family about diagnoses and care plans.

The *Secretary's Report* defined *acute care* as services which treat the acute phase of illness or disability, and are aimed at restoration of function. Nurses practicing in extended roles in acute care need the kinds of preparation enumerated above. In addition, they need to be able to initiate actions in line with protocols developed jointly by physicians and nurses (*e.g.,* adjust medication dosages, order laboratory tests, and prescribe rehabilitative and restorative measures).

According to the *Secretary's Report, long-term care* includes services designed to provide symptomatic treatment, maintenance and rehabilitative services for patients in all age groups and health care settings. Such care should be an outgrowth of mutual agreements between physicians and nurses, and based on needs and resources of patient and/or family to participate in implementation of care. In addition to the expanded functions outlined for primary and acute care, nurses involved in long-term care conduct nurse clinics for long-term care of patients with relatively stable chronic illnesses, and conduct community clinics for purposes of case finding and early detection of incipient health problems.

The *Secretary's Report* provided nurses with official recognition of latitude and responsibility for health surveillance of patients at all points on the health-illness continuum, and for making independent nursing interventions to promote the health of patients. In the past, nurses have taken a relatively passive role in working with patients to change their health behavior. Clearly, nurses can and must take a more aggressive role in intervening to help patients achieve optimal health.

INCREASED EMPHASIS ON ACCOUNTABILITY
OF NURSE TO PATIENT

Nurses employed by bureaucratic institutions — hospitals, community health nursing agencies, schools, industry — usually have been delegated administrative authority and accountability by the institution.[6,7] However, until the concept of primary care gained prominence, rarely have nurses been granted responsibility for their own patients over extended periods of time. Traditionally, nurses have been responsible to their superiors, rather than to their patients, for their actions. One major exception to this generalization has been New York's Loeb Center, where nurses have had freedom to plan and execute nursing care without the traditional constraints.[8] Along with the assumption of greater responsibility and autonomy in the provision of care goes the obligation of greater accountability of the nurse to the patients she serves rather than to the employing institution or to the physician in solo or group practice.

In summary, the development of physician assistant and nurse practitioner programs accelerated explication of independent, interdependent, and dependent practice in nursing. The scope of nursing practice is defined by the nurse practice acts in the individual states, and these are revised and updated continuously in accordance with the needs of people for nursing and other health care services.[9] No nurse is a truly independent practitioner. Dependent functions remain, where the physician is the only health professional with sufficient knowledge and license, in the legal sense, to make decisions which the nurse will implement. Interdependent functions also remain, where physicians, nurse, and other health professionals bring together their individual knowledge and expertise to work collaboratively in the patient's behalf. Making independent nursing functions explicit has increased the importance of accountability of the nurse to the individual patient.

RESPONSIBILITIES OF THE NURSE WITH RESPECT TO COMPLIANCE WITH MEDICATION REGIMENS

Nurses should place the highest priority on activities directed toward helping patients to undertake behaviors designed to promote health. Although the primary focus of this paper is on compliance with medication regimens, in actual nursing practice, compliance with a medication regimen would be addressed in the context of the patient's entire self-care regimen.

Definition of Compliance

For purposes of the present paper, compliance with a medication regimen, or more broadly with the whole self-care regimen, connotes those health behaviors which the patient undertakes:

1. To improve present health status.
2. To determine state of health (whether, indeed, some heretofore unknown health problem is present, and in need of medical treatment).
3. To recover from a diagnosed and reversible medical condition.
4. To control and prevent deterioration due to a chronic and/or progressive medically diagnosed illness.
5. To regain temporarily lost physical or psychological functions.
6. To compensate for functions which have been lost permanently (rehabilitation).

The goals of compliance which have just been outlined are synonymous with Leavell and Clark's levels of prevention.[10]

Kelman [11] provides an approach to the definition of compliance, in terms of social influence. Kelman identifies three stages of the influence process: *compliance, identification,* and *internalization.*

According to Kelman, **compliance** occurs when an individual changes his behavior in the hope of gaining the approval of another person or group. For example, the patient may take his medication because he wants to please the nurse.

Identification occurs when (health) behavior is associated with an important relationship with another person. Identification may be with one individual or with a group of patients with similar health problems. Examples of the latter are health-related behaviors embraced by members of self-help groups for patients with diagnoses such as carcinoma, end-stage kidney disease, etc.

Internalization occurs when an individual exhibits a particular behavior because it is congruent with his value system. Internalization as a basis for compliance implies that the patient is persuaded that a particular behavior is effective in bringing about improved health status. Internalization, as defined by Kelman and as applied to compliance with medication regimens, is similar to the phenomenological principles underlying the Health Belief Model.[12]

The concepts of conformity and compliance are often confused with each other, and the implications for health behavior of the two are very different. Kiesler and Kiesler [13] distinguish between conformity as compliance, and conformity as private acceptance. These authors define compliance as outward actions which may not be congruent with the individual's private convictions concerning the behavior in question. An individual may exhibit the behavior desired by others without actually believing in what he is doing. This definition appears to be synonymous with Kelman's definition of compliance.[11] For example, a health professional may be successful in persuading a diabetic patient to test his urine regularly, and to keep a written record. The legitimate purpose for such a request should be to determine whether the patient's diabetes appears to be under increasingly better control. Usually conformity with the request per se is inappropriate, unless the health professional and patient have, as their agreed-upon aim, the improved control of the patient's diabetes.

Among health educators, there is an unresolved dilemma surrounding the issue of changing *behavior* first, in the anticipation that changes in attitude will follow, or changing *attitude* first, in the hope there will be subsequent change in (health) behavior. In some instances nurses may, with justifiable reasons, direct their nursing interventions toward changing health behavior first vs. changing attitude toward health behavior first.

By defining conformity as private acceptance, Kiesler and Kiesler [13] mean that the individual changes his attitudes and beliefs as well as his behavior. Private acceptance may mean that a patient persists in a particular behavior long after there is any overt pressure for him to do so. Conformity as private acceptance is very similar to Kelman's definition of internalization. In some cases, private acceptance may *not* be accompanied by the appropriate action: A patient may be convinced that a particular medical recommendation is important, but be unable or unwilling for a variety of reasons to follow it. For example, a patient may be convinced that smoking is harmful, yet not be able to cease smoking.

Except in contrived laboratory-type situations, it is very difficult to determine whether both private acceptance *and* compliance are present. This is an especially sticky problem in attempting to persuade patients to follow medication regimens. All health professionals find it extremely difficult to predict whether a particular intervention will result in a desired health behavior. Some of the reasons for this state of affairs are:

1. The demand characteristics of the situation [14] or experimenter bias [15] may be such that the desired health behavior is elicited to please the nurse.
2. The desired health behavior may be due to the attention given by the nurse (*i.e.,* the so-called "Hawthorne" effect). The attention given may be motivating in its own right, and may be further contaminated by cues to action provided by the nurse.
3. There is a profound lack of adequate criteria for measuring compliance for most medical regimens except those having to do with medication-taking.[16] Techniques more sophisticated than the pill count and patient report are not available to most practicing nurses.

The net result of the difficulty in distinguishing between compliance and conformity is that it places health professionals in the ambiguous position of encouraging patients to engage in health behavior without evaluating the degree of internalization that the behavior reflects. For this reason, some health practitioners have sought other definitions of the self-care process we are discussing (*e.g.,* adherence to therapeutic regimens).‡

Variations in health behavior have been attributed to differences in how people cope with illness. Recently Twaddle [17] has suggested that variations in health behavior may be due to the way in which illness is defined. The determination of health status results from interaction between the individual and those who define his health status, *i.e.,* health professionals and significant others. There must be agreement by both parties. Decisions concerning health status are made according to the individual's capacities for present and future role and task performance. Except in extreme cases, deviations from normality are ambiguous, and the individual may have difficulty deciding for himself whether he is sick or well. If agreement between the patient and his significant others does not exist, there are few grounds for expecting the individual to undertake health behavior (*i.e.,* compliance behavior) which would lead to any improvement in health status.

Kasl and Cobb [18] have made distinctions between health behavior, illness behavior, and sick role behavior. ***Health behavior*** encompasses those activities synonymous with Leavell and Clark's primary and secondary prevention [19]; ***illness behavior*** is an activity undertaken by an individual who feels ill for the

---

‡*Barofsky discusses other definitions of compliance in the Summary Chapter.*

purpose of ascertaining whether he is, indeed, ill, and if so, what steps should be taken to remedy this state of affairs; *sick role behavior* is defined as any activity undertaken for purposes of getting out of this (undesirable) condition. Illness behavior and sick role behavior are roughly synonymous with Leavell and Clark's tertiary prevention.[10]† The distinctions which Kasl and Cobb, and others, have made between health behavior, illness behavior, and sick role behavior provided a useful framework for summarizing a large number of theoretical and research papers. Compliance with a medication regimen may be required when the patient is trying to enhance his health, detect early illness, or recover from illness or injury. The goal of compliance with medical regimens is improved health. For purposes of this paper, distinctions between levels of prevention and among health behavior, illness behavior, and sick role behavior will be subsumed under the term "health behavior" and compliance with a medication regimen will be treated as one of a class of health behaviors.

Significance of Nursing
Diagnosis of Noncompliance

Nurses must be alert to indications of noncompliance. They must be able to make a behavioral diagnosis or, as the phenomenon is termed in the nursing literature, a *nursing diagnosis.* A nursing diagnosis is any health problem which is amenable to nursing intervention. According to Roy,[19] a nursing diagnosis is a summary statement or judgment based on a nursing assessment. It is an outgrowth of application of the nursing process which includes assessment, planning, intervention, evaluation of established behavioral criteria of effectiveness of the nursing intervention, reassessment, etc. Roy sees the development of nursing diagnoses as proceeding in an orderly fashion out of implementation of the *Standards of Nursing Practice* [20] developed by the American Nurses Association. Mundinger and Jauron [21] point out that a nursing diagnosis should make clear any unhealthful response of a patient *and* state possible activities the nurse may carry out independently to change the response. Examples of nursing diagnoses include noncompliance and dependency. A nursing diagnosis is not a part of a medical diagnosis but rather an independent nursing function.[22] The aim of a nursing diagnosis is to diagnose and assist a patient to make an appropriate response to illness. In contrast, the aim of a medical diagnosis is to diagnose medical illness and prescribe treatment.[23] Nursing diagnoses are limited to areas of independent nursing actions.

The first level of theory building in any discipline is the development of a taxonomy. A taxonomy helps identify potential patient self-care problems, as well as point to alternative nursing interventions. The chief advantages of a

---

†*According to Leavell and Clark primary prevention encompasses activities undertaken to improve one's health and/or specific protective measures such as immunizations; secondary prevention includes activities leading to detection of asymptomatic illness; and tertiary prevention includes those activities undertaken by an individual with a diagnosed illness for the purpose of recovering, slowing down or controlling the disease process, or rehabilitation following permanent injury or illness, accompanied by residual loss of function.*

taxonomy are the efficiency that results from the organization of information, and the facilitation of communication among nurses providing care.

One of the potential pitfalls to use of a taxonomy or labeling system lies in its potential misuse. Some of the arguments against development of a taxonomy of nursing diagnoses are: (1) there may be premature closure of the diagnostic process, with failure to make continued and careful assessments of the patient and to consider alternative nursing interventions over time; (2) with the increased use of protocols for caring for patients with similar specific medical diagnoses, the patient stands at risk of not being treated with an adequate degree of individualization; and (3) some labels, if known to the patient's friends and associates, may result in specific demands being placed on the patient which others believe (erroneously) to be congruent with the label. A potential misuse of a nursing diagnosis of noncompliance might be that nurses with too little understanding and working knowledge of nursing interventions appropriate for decreasing or reversing noncompliance may fail to undertake *any* intervention.

Bircher [22] notes that the main criticisms which have been leveled against the development of a taxonomy of nursing diagnoses are more a function of the cognitive limitations of the nurse, rather than being inherent in the label per se. The main advantages of development of a taxonomy lie in providing the nurse with a concise list of identified patient problems which are amenable to nursing intervention.

Beisser [24] has identified six models which, historically, have been used by members of the helping professions to define what may be wrong with an individual. A clear definition of what is wrong *may* serve to identify the most appropriate interventions for promoting compliance. These are as follows:

The Evil or Bad Model: This model holds that deviant behavior is purposefully performed. An individual exhibiting such behavior may be regarded as being possessed by the devil.

The Sick Role: This model views the patient as a victim of forces beyond his control. The sick model is synonymous with the medical model, and is congruent with Parsons' conceptualization of the sick role.[25] According to Parsons, the sick role is accompanied by rights (*i.e.,* of the patient to be relieved of his usual responsibilities to family and work, and to be cared for during his sickness), and obligations (*i.e.,* to seek and follow competent medical advice, and to do everything in his power to get himself out of the undesirable state of "being sick"). Parsons' depiction of the sick role has been subjected to considerable criticism because it is not clearly applicable to patients with chronic illnesses, who may never be able to rid themselves of residual disability.[26] However, recently Parsons stated that he never intended the sick role concept to be restricted to acute and self-limiting illnesses.[27]

The Social Issues Model: This model assumes that the individual is a helpless victim of forces within society. The only route to change in the individual lies in societal changes which could result indirectly in benefit to the individual.

A patient's view of himself as a victim of forces beyond his control is similar to

Rotter's definition of the person with a belief in external control: *i.e.,* one who believes that for the most part what happens to him is due to forces beyond his control such as chance, luck, or the influence of powerful others.[28] There is a growing research literature which demonstrates that locus of control, or belief in personal control over what happens to the individual, is significantly related to actions patients are willing to take with respect to their health.

The Problem-Solving Model: This model assumes that the patient's health behavior is more rational than is probably the case, in reality.

The Crisis Model: This model follows Erikson and Lindemann's depictions of developmental and situational crises. Situational crises, especially those involving the impact of illness and injury, are of more relevance for compliance with medication regimens although "normal" developmental crises such as pregnancy and childbirth may be accompanied by the need for following specific medication regimens also.

Green [29] notes that compliance with medication regimens can be enhanced if home visits are made at critical periods following initiation of a particular regimen. For example, the critical period for the greatest number of patients to discontinue contraception is one month after they begin taking the pill. Green states that home visits made at the critical period for the medication (and diagnosis) under consideration can substantially influence compliance. If critical periods for other medications could be identified, nurses could intervene more effectively to promote compliance.

The Growth and Human Potential Model: This model is an outgrowth of the crisis model. A crisis is a critical period during which usual modes of coping are, for whatever reason, no longer effective. Hopefully, a crisis may provide opportunity for developing new and better ways of coping. If the crisis is an illness or an injury, the outcome of the insult may be dependent upon the patient's willingness to follow specific medical regimens indefinitely to enable him to attain and maintain the highest possible level of functioning.

Each of the six models reviewed represents a potential basis for either compliance or noncompliance. However, the measurement of compliance behavior is very complex. In an earlier paper Marston [16] summarized the difficulties involved in arriving at valid conclusions concerning patient compliance or noncompliance. Laboratory tests of blood or urine samples provide the most reliable indicators of compliance. The pill count is somewhat less reliable, and patient report is likely to be a grossly unreliable indicator. Depending upon the diagnosis of the patient and his medication regimen, other criteria such as weight loss, blood pressure, etc., may give additional clues to compliance.

Davis [30] was able to document that physicians are not able to predict compliance at better than chance level. A comparable study where nurses have tried to predict patient compliance, accompanied by comparison of nurse estimates with objective measures, has not been reported.

The present paper is concerned with the nursing diagnosis of noncompliance with medication regimens, and with approaches the nurse can use to increase compliance behavior. A nursing diagnosis consists of an assessment of an unhealthful response of a patient, and stated (or implied) activities the nurse may carry out independently to change the response.[21] The making of the nursing diagnosis of noncompliance assumes that the nurse must engage in specific activities to promote a more healthful response, i.e., compliance with the medication regimen. In keeping with the nurse's increased emphasis on accountability to the patient for her professional practice, the following points are emphasized:

1. The nurse must be able to make a thorough assessment of the patient's condition and needs.
2. The nurse must have a sound understanding of theoretical models of health behavior which have been developed thus far, and of how they may be operationalized to assist the patient to comply.
3. The nurse must have a working knowledge of a wide repertoire of specific procedures and interpersonal approaches which research has shown to be effective in facilitating compliance with medication regimens.
4. The nurse must possess a sound knowledge base with respect to what is known about the determinants of compliance with medication regimens. She must be cognizant of the fact that there is a consistent lack of correlation between compliance with medication regimens and compliance with other parts of the medical regimen, such as the following of special diets, use of alcohol and tobacco, exercise prescriptions and proscriptions, etc. This is especially important since the nurse is almost never in a position to work with patients on compliance with medication regimens to the exclusion of compliance with the rest of the patient's self-care regimen.
5. The nurse must have up-to-date working knowledge of the medications patients are taking, including their expected action, appropriate dosages, potential side effects, and interactions with other medications. She must assume responsibility for knowing where to find accurate information concerning new pharmaceutical preparations.

Because of the increased emphasis on preparation of nurses to carry out *independent* nursing functions, the nurse may easily lose her perspective with regard to the need for helping the patient to follow his medication regimen. After all, medications are, for the most part, prescribed by the physician, and implementation of the physician's orders is sometimes considered to be a *dependent* function of nursing. The dichotomy between independent and dependent functions of nursing, which are value laden, is less clear-cut if the entire patient care regimen is looked at as a whole, instead of singling out compliance with the medication regimen as a discrete entity.

The lack of recognition of the fact that patients may not be taking their medications as ordered may lead the physician to change medications to preparations which are less effective for the particular intended purpose,[31] or it may lead to increasing the recommended dosages to levels which, if taken as directed, could produce toxic side effects. Furthermore, discontinuance and resumption of medication taking can result in development of unnecessary drug sensitivities.[31] For certain medication regimens it is important that medications be taken concurrently to facilitate the desired action, or to offset the adverse effects of other medications. An example of the latter is the use of potassium preparations with patients taking certain diuretics. The nurse must also be aware that certain over-the-counter (nonprescription) drugs may be incompatible with medications prescribed by physicians as well as contraindicated with certain diagnoses.

6. There must be congruence between nurse and patient with respect to perceptions of what is wrong with the patient,[24] i.e., the antecedents of the health problem from which a nursing diagnosis is derived. How nurse and patient view antecedent causes may influence which nursing interventions, if any, have the greatest chance for success.

7. The nurse must be convinced of the appropriateness of what she is doing, and of her obligation to intervene. She must be willing to take an aggressive approach in her interventions rather than the traditional approach of presenting information to the patient and leaving it to the patient to "make up his own mind what he will do about the information."

8. The nurse must be constantly alert to novel approaches which may enhance compliance behavior, and she must have the freedom to try these out in a systematic fashion.

In summary, the beginning development of a taxonomy of nursing diagnoses should help to identify patients in need of nursing interventions directed toward specific target (compliance) behaviors. Noncompliance is one nursing diagnosis which lends itself to independent nursing interventions. Use of a nursing diagnosis should facilitate communication between nurses providing care in hospital settings, and better coordination between nurses in hospital settings and nurses providing care in home settings. An understanding of alternative assumptions concerning antecedents of noncompliance should aid nurses in planning the most effective nursing interventions to enhance compliance.

MAJOR NURSING APPROACHES
FOR ENHANCING COMPLIANCE

Health Education and
Attitude Change Strategies

Traditionally, nurses have placed a great deal of emphasis on patient education concerning self-care. However, naivete of belief in the rationality of patients' health behavior has led to a false sense of security that patients, if taught, will comply with their self-care regimens.

Before 1950 some of the major life insurance companies such as John Hancock and Aetna offered subscribers additional benefits of home visits by community health nurses. These benefits were introduced, partly, to demonstrate that the services of community health nurses would be effective in reducing maternal and infant morbidity and mortality rates; also, services were provided to other groups of patients for purposes of giving direct nursing care and teaching them how to take their insulin, follow special diets, test urines, etc. By 1950 there was a marked decline in maternal and infant morbidity and mortality rates, perhaps due in part to teaching by community health nurses, and perhaps in part to greater availability of specific protective measures against the major childhood killers, improved nutrition, and the discovery of antibiotics. The insurance companies concluded that they had demonstrated the value of home visiting services, and gradually withdrew these benefits from their policy holders.

In the mid-1950s the Division of Nursing of the United States Public Health Service anticipated the time, which is now upon us, when more accountability would be required. The Division of Nursing embarked on a series of intramural evaluation studies designed to document how various categories of nursing service personnel were being utilized in inpatient and ambulatory settings. A modified randomized work sampling method was developed for data collection in inpatient units. It was anticipated that these data could be utilized as bases for making changes in responsibilities assigned to different categories of workers, and to develop new staffing patterns to the end of improving patient care. Contrary to expectation, almost no evidence of patient teaching was found. The procedure for collecting data in ambulatory settings was modified to utilize continuous observations of nursing service personnel for one-hour blocks, in the anticipation that the improved opportunity for observations would be more sensitive in revealing the amount of patient teaching being done. Continued failure to document appreciable amounts of teaching, with presumably better sampling, was an unsettling finding, to say the least.

In some of the institutions studied, reassignment of responsibilities of nursing service personnel was undertaken in order to permit nurses to spend more time with patients, with high priority being placed on patient teaching. When these institutions were restudied after introduction of new and better staffing patterns, no significant changes were found in the way in which nurses used their time (with patients, and especially in teaching patients) *except* in those cases where reassignment was accompanied by active inservice education programs to point out to nurses how they might better use their time.

The absence of measurable amounts of patient education by nurses may be due to an attitude pervasive even today among beginning master's students in nursing, that nurses *may* present information, but *must not* "inflict" their own attitudes and values on the patient. Patients and families should have the option to "take or leave" information regarding their self care, including compliance with medication regimens. Recently, a graduate student was heard to argue that perhaps nurses should not urge patients to follow medical regimens because they are "medical," not nursing, and because the resulting impact on the patient's life style may be more stressful than allowing the morbidity process to run its course unaltered. There is no question that nurses or other health professionals cannot force patients to comply, *but* if they are committed to a philosophy of patients' having a right to exposure to the best medical and nursing approaches now available for prevention and treatment, then they have an obligation to utilize whatever theoretical frameworks and techniques are available to persuade patients and families to assume responsibility for their own self-care. Orlando [32] advocates taking what she calls a "deliberative" approach with patients in exploring indicators which she observes and interprets as stress, pain, noncompliance, etc. To take this kind of approach in eliciting patient or family cooperation in a high degree of compliance with a medical regimen *cannot* be construed as inflicting one's values on the patient or family.

The teaching of patients concerning their medication regimens is still the main approach taken by nurses in their attempts to enhance compliance. A comprehensive review of the literature on compliance with medical regimens,[16] based on research reported up to 1970, revealed little relationship between knowledge regarding diagnosis and treatment, and the following of medical regimens. It is unlikely that the mere presentation of information regarding the patient's diagnosis and treatment, by itself, will result in substantial increments in compliance.

In 1970 Green [33] published a paper entitled, "Should health education abandon attitude-change strategies?" Green recommends strongly that, for the time being, there must be direct efforts to change health behavior (*i.e.,* compliance) at the individual and family level as well as through the mass media.

It is not possible to draw any hard and fast conclusions as to whether it is more effective to change attitudes toward compliance in the hope that appropriate compliance behavior will follow, or to attempt to initiate compliance behavior and hope that change of attitude toward compliance will follow.

The Health Belief Model

The Health Belief Model is based on a phenomenological orientation which holds that "it is the world of the perceiver that determines what he will do and not the physical environment, except as the physical environment comes to be represented in the mind of the behaving individual."[12] According to Lewin's field theory, an individual's behavior is a function of his interaction with his environment. Behavior is dependent on the *value an individual places on a given outcome* and his *estimate of the likelihood that a given action will result in that outcome.* The way in which an individual perceives the world around him determines his behavior in any given situation. The three major concepts and assumptions of the Health Belief Model are as follows:

1. The individual must perceive that he is *susceptible* to the diagnosis under consideration (*e.g.,* cancer) or to a complication or relapse if he has a diagnosed illness (*e.g.,* breakdown of a healed tuberculosis lesion; recurrence of rheumatic fever in the presence of untreated streptococcal infection).

2. The individual must perceive that to contract the condition under consideration would be a *serious state of affairs (e.g.,* a threat to his life, or at least to his independence of movement, as in the case of a stroke).

3. The individual must perceive that the *treatment being recommended is efficacious* in preventing a particular disease from occurring, or in protecting the individual from further complications (*e.g.,* taking diphenylhydantoin to prevent seizures).

In addition to the concepts of perceived susceptibility, seriousness, and effectiveness of treatment, compliance is further enhanced if those professionals working with the patient *remove as many barriers as possible* (*i.e.,* misconceptions, financial obstacles, attitudinal behaviors, etc.) and at the same time *provide as many cues to action as possible* (*i.e.,* provision of specific and utilitarian information about how to achieve the goal of optimal health).

Most research to date using the Health Belief Model demonstrates that compliance is greatest when people subscribe to beliefs in perceived susceptibility, seriousness, and effectiveness of treatment and when there are cues to action and a relative absence of barriers. For the most part the fewer the variables subscribed to, or present in the situation, the lower the degree of compliance.

In recent papers, Becker and his coworkers [34-37] have begun to identify moderator variables which interact with the major concepts of the Model to facilitate or hinder desired health behaviors. The moderator variables fall into categories such as demographic, social-psychological, reference group influence, and knowledge of the disease and its treatment.

The major limitation of the Health Belief Model lies in the fact that most research has been done with preventive health behaviors such as the obtaining of immunizations (primary prevention) [38] or with case finding such as chest X-ray films for detection of tuberculosis or cancer (secondary prevention).[39] Work is just beginning to be done with patient populations in which a diagnosis exists and the patient needs to take one or more medications indefinitely (*e.g.,* diabetes, hypertension, epilepsy).[40]

Nurse researchers and practicing nurses, however, have not made the most of opportunities to intervene with patients or to manipulate the five major concepts of the Health Belief Model in a systematic fashion. Only within the last year has the first article on the Health Belief Model appeared in a nursing journal.[41] There is no simple "how-to-do-it" prescription for use of the Model. Many different approaches need to be tested in all of the settings in which nurses are practicing: hospitals, ambulatory care settings, neighborhood health centers, home settings, schools, and industry.

Locus of Control

An assumption implicit in the Health Belief Model is that the situation in which the individual finds himself is more important than his past history in determining his behavior. A patient's past history is important only insofar as it may influence his expectations that a given action on his part will result in a valued outcome.

If an individual has had the repeated experience that his own efforts have been effective in getting for him those things which were of value to him, he will develop an expectation that his own efforts will get for him what he wants in the future. According to Rotter's Social Learning Theory, such a person is said to have a *belief in internal control,* i.e., to believe that for the most part what happens to him is due to his own skills, efforts, and abilities. Thus experience with success which has been repeated in a wide variety of situations results in development of an attitude of being able to cope in a competent fashion.[28]

If, on the other hand, the individual's experience has been such that his efforts have brought him little in the way of things of value to him, he may develop an expectation that he is relatively powerless to change situations, or to control what happens to him. According to Rotter, an individual meeting this description is said to have a *belief in external control,* i.e., to believe that for the most part what happens to him is due to chance, fate, or the influence of powerful others.

Theoretically, belief in personal control or personal causation should influence the extent to which patients embrace the elements of perceived susceptibility, seriousness, and effectiveness of the Health Belief Model. The individual who has a belief in internal control and believes that he can cope competently *may* be more likely to comply since he would be persuaded that actions taken by him in behalf of his health are likely to be effective. However, this may not hold up if the health problem is such that there is no realistic hope of successful treatment.

A number of scales for measuring belief in personal control have been developed, but the most widely used has been Rotter's 29-item forced-choice scale.[28] Hundreds of studies have been done in the search for relationships between belief in personal control and every other kind of variable imaginable. Approximately 20 to 30 studies have been published in which belief in personal control was investigated in patient and quasi-patient populations. Some interesting findings have included statistically significant relationships between belief in personal control and successful weight loss,[42] cessation of smoking,[43] use of contraceptives,[44] taking of influenza immunizations,[45] delay of elective surgery,[46] and adherence to a self-care regimen in a tuberculosis hospital.[47] Recently Wallston and Wallston [48] have developed a Health Locus of Control Scale, which promises to be more useful than the (general) Rotter scale for use with patient populations. Phares [49] points out that a single general locus of control may not reflect the attitudes of individuals in every situation, and may lead to errors in prediction.

One of the existing things about the work which has come out of research on the locus of control variable has been the beginning development of techniques for changing the individual's orientation toward the amount of control which he is able to exert in real-life situations.[50] Changes in belief in personal control may be accompanied by behavioral changes as well.[49]

Two methods for modifying belief in personal control are reviewed briefly:

Masters [51] described a technique which he has called *reconstrual of stimuli.* Masters used this technique to help an adolescent gain more control of things of value to him, such as occasional use of the family car. The technique involved persuading the youth to exhibit behaviors which his parents ordinarily had a great deal of difficulty forcing him to do (*e.g.,* mowing the lawn, carrying out the trash, etc.). By completing these tasks prior to being asked, he so astonished and pleased the parents that they rewarded him by allowing use of the family car. In the case of compliance with a medication regimen the elements of the situation are not exactly the same; *i.e.,* taking one's medications may prevent complications, but seldom brings a tangible reward, unless avoidance of a dreaded complication can be considered rewarding (*e.g.,* control of seizures).

Among college students who presented themselves at a counseling service with expressed concern over inability to relate in interpersonal situations, Dua [52] compared the relationship between belief in personal control among those who were treated by a behaviorally oriented action program, and those treated by traditional psychotherapy. The locus of control scale (I-E) was administered at the beginning and end of an eight-week series of counseling sessions. Students exposed to the behaviorally oriented action program in which the counselor made specific suggestions concerning how to cope with interpersonal problem situations showed significantly greater increments in belief in personal control that did those students participating in traditional psychotherapy. Furthermore, the students who had been exposed to the behaviorally oriented action therapy were more satisfied with their real life interpersonal relationships at the conclusion of the sessions.

Nurses could use a similar approach in helping patients to cope with the mechanics of managing their medication regimens. This kind of approach is similar to some of the techniques used in behavior modification. For example, Sackett has described taping the antihypertensive medication vial to the dishwash detergent container of a housewife patient as a reminder that she should take her medication at the same time she usually washed the dishes. A creative nurse could certainly find other novel ways of helping patients to organize their activities of daily living to incorporate compliance with the taking of medications in an integral part. It must be recognized, however, that such a direct approach runs counter to the nondirective approaches to which most practicing nurses have been indoctrinated.

Use of Threat Communications

Another body of research which has grown out of the Health Belief Model is the use of threat or fear communications in motivating health behavior. Leventhal has spearheaded much of this research.[53] Fear communications are relevant to the Health Belief Model since threat is one technique for increasing the salience of the patient's susceptibility to a diagnosis as well as its seriousness.

One of the earliest studies of the effectiveness of fear communications in motivating health behavior was that of Janis and Feshbach.[54] This study examined whether high fear or low fear communications were more effective in persuading school children to brush their teeth. Low fear was found to be more effective. Probably the question posed in the Janis and Feshbach study was much too simple since there are moderating factors which interact with the fear to facilitate or impede an individual's undertaking recommended action. Also dental hygiene is of a low level of importance in the hierarchy of perceived seriousness of potential health problems.

For example, Leventhal, Singer and Jones [55] investigated three levels of fear communications to motivate college students to obtain tetanus immunizations. Part of each of three groups was given specific instructions concerning the location of the student health facility where the immunizations could be obtained, the hours the health facility was open, etc. The students most likely to obtain the immunization were those in the high fear group who had specific instructions as to how to reduce the fear which has been aroused. This finding lends support, of course, to the Health Belief Model, two stipulations of which were that there be a relative absence of barriers and the presence of specific cues to action.

The use of fear communications can be effective in motivating health behavior. A note of caution is in order, since we do not yet understand all of the moderating variables which may be involved in bringing about desired health behaviors. Most nurses feel that caution should be exercised relative to this issue because too high a level of threat may result in the patient completely denying the content of the communication, and becoming more fixed in his noncompliance. However, this technique should not be dismissed until more research has been done to identify under what conditions the technique is successful or unsuccessful in real life, as opposed to the above related laboratory-type studies.††

Reference Groups

A more thorough understanding of the relevance of perceived attitudes of *significant others* and of important reference groups would assist nurses as well as other health professionals in their attempts to elicit compliance. For example, an early study by Gray, Kesler and Moody [56] demonstrated that whether mothers thought their neighbors thought they should have their children immunized for polio was more significantly related to having their children immunized than was social class (a known predictor of compliance).

Fass, Green and Levine [57] have reported on a study in progress on the education of another family member in which they hope to enhance compliance with an antihypertensive drug regimen through the influence of education of another family member.

Evidence is mounting that the family exerts a more significant influence on compliance behavior than had been recognized heretofore. Becker and Green [58] list three reasons for this:

1. Non-ill family members must assume responsibility for compliance with medical regimens on the part of dependent family members such as children, the aged, and the disabled. Up until now, reviews have summarized results

---

††*Because of the impossibility of reviewing the large number of research studies which have been conducted investigating various aspects of the use of fear communications in motivating health behavior, the reader is referred to three excellent reviews of this literature: Higbee,[78] Janis,[79] and Leventhal.[53]*

of compliance studies where the patient is responsible for his medication regimen with those where another family member, especially a mother, is responsible for the patient's taking a medication. Combining these data may have masked the role of significant others in compliance.

2. Specific roles within the family may have important consequences for compliance with medication regimens. For example, a spouse who embraces Christian Science teachings may control the finances for the spouse in need of a particular medication, although the ill member may not be a member of the same faith.

3. Even if the cost of a medication is not an important issue, the attitude of others significant to the patient may influence the patient's medication-taking.

Becker and Green [58] suggest that research is needed where the professional appeals to the motive of family responsibility to promote increased compliance. These authors caution, however, that if the costs of compliance to the patient and/or family are great in terms of the side effects of the medication, interference with activities of daily living, monetary cost, etc., feelings of guilt and shame may be aroused. These authors suggest that the presence of chronic illness may "place a burden on family relationships," and it may be unwise to add the burden of guilt as well.

There will always be some patients under extreme stress as a result of their medical regimens. For example, Goldstein and Reznikoff [59] attribute the high suicide rate among patients with end-stage kidney disease undergoing periodic renal dialysis to the extreme stress they experience in association with their self-care regimens.

Sometimes the stress of compliance is greater for family members than for the patient himself. This is a factor not noted by Becker and Green. For example, a well-educated adult man was able to overcome paralysis resulting from polio, to such an extent that he would have been able to leave the hospital and run his business from his home. However, as the time for hospital discharge grew near, his mother committed suicide and his wife refused to have him return. The implication of this example is that appeals to family responsibility as motivation for compliance should be undertaken cautiously by any health professional. To imply, however, that the professional nurse's attempt to increase the salience of a family member's responsibility to comply for the sake of the rest of the family group can cause the family member to experience guilt and shame for failure to comply imputes more power to the nurse than she, indeed, possesses. Most patients and family members can resist feeling guilt or shame for noncompliance if, in their view, they have valid reasons for failing to comply. However, the above example illustrates that this is not always true.

Contracting

Contracting with patients has not been used in a systematic way by nurses in attempts to enhance compliance with medication or other self-care regimens (*see*

Lewis and Michnich, pages 69-75). However, the technique seems a promising one for this purpose. Sheridan and Smith [60] have reported on contracts which master's and baccalaureate level students have used with families in community health nursing settings. The kinds of content around which formal contracts were developed, and signed by nurse and family, included (1) set times for visits, (2) discussion of alternative methods to meet problems, (3) confidentiality of information, and (4) sharing of the nurse's work and/or report with a community agency. This type of contract is concerned with relationship building, development of trust and openness, and ensurance of mutual respect, all of which are necessary prerequisites to motivating health behavior.

There is a danger in certain kinds of contracts in that the behavior under consideration may become an end in itself. Meaningful content around which a contract could be developed is medication-taking, adherence to special diets, etc. Emphasis is placed on the target behaviors, but with the goal of improved health set forth clearly.

The development of a formal contract dealing with the most important aspects of the patient's health behavior as agreed upon by any health professional working with a patient, and preceded by the relationship-building approach outlined by Sheridan and Smith,[60] might stand a good chance of success. Such an approach would certainly help all health professionals as well as the patient to be sensitized to the desired behavioral outcomes in terms of the patient's health.

Behavior Modification

Only recently has behavior modification come to be seriously considered and utilized in nursing care other than in psychiatric settings and physical rehabilitation settings. The time is overdue for nurses to have a thorough orientation to the theory, techniques and applications of behavior modification in a wide variety of patient care situations.**

Application of Social Exchange Theory to Nursing

Conant [61,62] has done some beginning work to operationalize Homans' concepts of cost and reward in nurse-patient interactions. According to Homans' early formulations of Social Exchange Theory [63,64] social behavior was seen as an exchange of activity between two or more people. The exchange could be tangible or intangible, and involved costs and rewards. Conant's 1967 study was conducted in child health conference settings. For example, cost to a patient was operationalized as a question asked; reward, as a smile of the nurse, a nod of the head implying approval, a statement of acceptance or agreement with the patient, etc. Conant was particularly interested in "unsolicited participation" where the mother might initiate a discussion, elaborate on a comment, or ask the

---

** *The chapters by both Barofsky and Zifferblatt and Curry expand on these issues.*

nurse a question. Conant [62] as well as Simons [65] found positive correlations between nurse "giving behavior" (synonymous with nurse rewarding behavior described above) and unsolicited participation on the part of the mother. High nurse giving behavior and high unsolicited participation on the part of the mother were associated with high satisfaction on ohe part of both nurses and mothers. Nettle [66] adapted Conant's technique for observing nurse-patient interactions in home settings where the nurse was performing a technical nursing procedure. Nettle's findings were, for the most part, in agreement with those of Conant and Simons.

Davis [67] has pointed out that failure of the physician to give the patient adequate feedback regarding his condition is associated with noncompliance on the part of patients. Within the framework which has just been outlined, failure to give feedback may be considered as a cost to the patient. Since community health nurses often must ask many questions during early visits to new patients, especially if care is being financed by Medicare or Medicaid, the cost of the questions *may,* in a sense, be noncompliance with the medication and self-care regimens, unless the patient is provided with adequate feedback. More research is needed to determine whether this is, indeed, so.

OTHER APPROACHES WHICH MAY BE FOUND TO INFLUENCE COMPLIANCE

Beginning research on the use of body language and nonverbal communication will, in all probability, be found to have implications for compliance behavior. For certain groups of patients the laying on of hands is an essential ingredient of the nursing care provided. Nurses are just beginning to recognize and document this phenomenon.[68,69] There have, however, been no studies which examined the relationship between (1) direct physical care, (2) body language not requiring the laying on of hands, or (3) nonverbal communication on the one hand, and compliance with medication or other self-care regimens.

The development of a theory of helping behavior [70] and identification of elements of helping relationships which are most effective in changing clients' behavior are the subject of much current research and guidelines for practice,[71-75] although little evidence can be found of application of helping concepts to compliance behavior.

In order to increase cost effectiveness, in both institutions and in community health agencies, professional nurses are often replaced with nursing personnel with lesser preparation, such as diploma graduates, associate degree graduates, licensed practical nurses, nurse aides, paraprofessionals, and indigenous workers. Holder [76] has demonstrated differences between indigenous workers and professional nurses in attempts to enhance compliance with self-care regimens other than compliance with medication regimens. Thorough evaluation of the effectiveness of utilizing lesser prepared workers to enhance compliance with medication regimens has yet to be undertaken.

NEED FOR FUTURE RESEARCH
TO ENHANCE COMPLIANCE

Knowledge concerning how professional nurses as well as other health professionals can enhance compliance with medication and other self-care regimens is in its infancy. There are many promising areas for future research which are especially relevant to nursing. Some of the most important of these are:

1. Identification of critical periods when patients are most likely to discontinue their medications.
2. Identification of factors determining whether the reasons a patient assumes responsibility for taking his own medications differ from those influencing a family member to ensure that a dependent member take medications.
3. Investigation of the influence of the perceived attitudes of significant others, including health professionals, on a patient's compliance behavior.
4. Wide exploration of use of contracting to enhance patient compliance, with emphasis on the goal of achieving optimal health status.
5. Careful experimentation with threat communications in order to gather data concerning whether nurses can be effective in motivating compliance behavior using this approach.
6. Systematic manipulation of elements of the Health Belief Model to determine the effectiveness of this approach in enhancing compliance behavior with patients with long-term illnesses.
7. Investigations of the usefulness of Conant's modification of Homans' concepts of cost and reward in nurse-patient interactions utilizing compliance behavior as the dependent variable.
8. Investigations of use by nurses of behavior modification techniques with specific patient behaviors.
9. Investigations of the relationship between body language and nonverbal communication, and compliance behavior.
10. Investigations of use of compliance behavior in those situations necessitating direct patient care (i.e., laying on of hands, or touch).
11. Investigations of specific helping behavior approaches in enhancing compliance behavior.

Although the suggestions for further research on compliance have been listed as separate issues, some will probably be found to interact with each other. Basic to all of the suggested areas for further research is the assumption that the investigator must take into consideration nurse-patient relationship variables and the influence of others significant to the patient. This approach is similar to the suggestions Kasl [77] has made with respect to the physician-patient relationship and compliance behavior. Nurses may be in a somewhat better position than physicians to influence compliance because of the additional preparation many are receiving to prepare them for increased responsibility in patient management, along with their continuing opportunities for direct care giving.

SUMMARY

The primary focus of this paper has been on the nursing management of compliance with medication regimens. Compliance has been treated as one of a class of health behaviors whose aim is improved health. In actual nursing practice assisting a patient to comply with his medication regimen is an integral part of the self-care regimen. As a result, the major approaches outlined for helping patients to follow medication regimens are as applicable to medication-taking as to any other part of the self-care regimen.

In the past ten years nurses have begun to assume more responsibility for the management of patient health behaviors than ever before. The major reasons for this are: (1) the increased numbers of nurses prepared at the baccalaureate, master's, and doctoral levels; (2) delineation by the *Secretary's Report* of the wider scope of practice which nurses could and should undertake; and (3) revisions of the nurse practice acts in individual states, which provide license, in the legal sense, for expanded practice.

The present paper has reviewed alternative theoretical models and skill approaches which show promise of exerting the greatest impact on patient health behavior. The approaches reviewed can and are being used by nurses on a limited basis. Until now, nurses have persevered in the use of patient education, sometimes to the exclusion of other approaches, despite research which has demonstrated little relationship between the patient's knowledge regarding diagnosis and treatment and his compliance. With the exception of patient education, nursing is in its infancy with respect to the widespread application of the approaches suggested in this paper. Systematic testing of other nursing intervention approaches which have been outlined is badly needed. Nurses as well as all other health professionals must accord the highest priority to the promotion of health behavior at all points on the health-illness continuum.

REFERENCES

1. American Nurses' Association: First position on education for nursing. Am J Nurs 65:106-111, 1965.
2. American Nurses' Association: Facts about Nursing 74-75. Kansas City, Missouri, American Nurses' Association, 1975.
3. Sadler AN, Sadler BL, Bliss AA: The Physician's Assistant — Today and Tomorrow. New Haven, Yale University Press, 1972.
4. American Nurses' Association: Definition: Nurse Practitioner, Nurse Clinician and Clinical Nurse Specialist. Mimeographed statement prepared by Congress for Nursing Practice, May 8, 1974. Kansas City Missouri, American Nurses' Association.
5. Extending the scope of nursing practice: a report of the Secretary's Committee to study extended roles for nurses. USDHEW Publ No. (HSM) 73-2037 (Nov) 1971.
6. Maas ML: Nurse autonomy and accountability in organized nursing services. Nurs Forum 12:237-259, 1973.
7. Stevens BJ: Accountability of the clinical specialist: the administrator's viewpoint. J Nurs Admin 6:30-32, 1976.
8. Bowar-Ferres S: Loeb Center and its philosophy of nursing. Am J Public Health 75:810-815, 1975.

9. Bullough B: The law and the expanding nursing role. Am J Public Health 66:249-254, 1976.
10. Leavell HR, Clark EG: Preventive Medicine for the Doctor in his Community, 3rd ed. New York, McGraw Hill, 1965.
11. Kelman HC: Processes of opinion change. Public Opin Q 25:57-78, 1961.
12. Rosenstock IM: Historical origins of the health belief model. Health Educ Monogr 2(4):328-335, 1974.
13. Kiesler CA, Kiesler SB: Conformity. Reading, Massachusetts: Addision-Wesley Publ Co, 1969.
14. Orne MT: On the social psychology of the experiment: with particular reference to demand characteristics and their implications. Am Psychologist 17:776-783, 1962.
15. Rosenthal R: Experimenter Effects in Behavioral Research. New York, Appleton-Century-Crofts, 1966.
16. Marston MV: Compliance with medical regimens: a review of the literature. Nurs Res 19:312-323, 1970.
17. Twaddle AC: The concept of health status. Soc Sci Med 8:29-38, 1974.
18. Kasl SV, Cobb S: Health behavior, illness behavior and sick role, I and II. Arch Environ Health 12:246-266, 534-541, 1966.
19. Roy SrC: A diagnostic classification system for nursing. Nurs Outlook 23:90-94, 1975.
20. American Nurses' Association: Standards for Practice. Kansas City Missouri, American Nurses' Association, 1973.
21. Mundinger MO, Jauron GD: Developing a nursing diagnosis. Nurs Outlook 23:94-98, 1975.
22. Bircher AU: On the development and classification of nursing diagnoses. Nurs Forum 14:10-29, 1975.
23. Abruzzese RS: The nursing process and the problem-oriented system. *In* The Problem-Oriented System — A Multidisciplinary Approach. New York, National League for Nursing Publ No. 20-1546, 1974, pp 11-21.
24. Beisser AR: Models of helping behavior. Am J Orthopsychiat 43:586-594, 1973.
25. Parsons T: The Social System. London, Free Press of Glencoe, 1951.
26. Kassebaum GG, Baumann BO: Dimensions of the sick role in chronic illness. J Health Hum Behav 6:16-27, 1965.
27. Parsons T: The sick role and the role of the physician reconsidered. Milbank Mem Fund Q: 257-277, 1975.
28. Rotter JB: Generalized expectancies for internal versus external control of reinforcement. Psychol Mono 80: Whole Number 609, 1966.
29. Green LW: Toward cost-benefit evaluation of health education: some concepts, methods and examples. Health Educ Mono 2 (Supp 1):34-65, 1974.
30. Davis MS: Variations in patients' compliance with doctors' orders: analysis of congruence between survey responses and results of empirical investigations. J Med Educ 41:1037-1048, 1966.
31. Hieb E, Wang RIH: Compliance: the patient's role in drug therapy. Wis Med J 73:152-154, 1974.
32. Orlando IJ: The Dynamic Nurse-Patient Relationship. New York, G.P. Putnam's Sons, 1961.
33. Green LW: Should health education abandon attitude change strategies? Perspectives from recent research. Health Educ Mono 1(30):25-47, 1970.
34. Becker MH: The health belief model and sick role behavior. Health Educ Mono 2(4):409-432, 1974.
35. Becker MH, Drachman RH, Kirscht JP: Predicting mothers' compliance with pediatric medical regimens. J Pediat 81:843-854, 1972.
36. Becker MH, Drachman RH, Kirscht JP: A new approach to explaining sick-role behavior in low-income populations. Am J Public Health 64:205-216, 1974.
37. Becker MH, Kaback MM, Rosenstock IM, Ruth MV: Some influence on public participation in a genetic screening program. J Community Health 1:3-14, 1975.
38. Rosenstock IM: Why people use health services. Milbank Mem Fund Q 44:94-127, 1966.
39. Hochbaum GM: Public participation in a medical screening program: A sociopsychological study. Bethesda, Maryland, Public Health Service, Publ No. 572, 1958.
40. Weiss SM: Proceedings of the National Heart and Lung Institute Working Conference on Health Behavior, Basye, Virginia, May 12-15, 1975. USDHEW Publ No. (NIH) 76-868.
41. Pender NJ: A conceptual model for preventive health behavior. Nurs Outlook 23:385-390, 1975.

42. Manno B, Marston AR: Weight reduction as a function of negative covert reinforcement (sensitization) versus positive covert reinforcement. Behav Res Ther 10:201-207, 1972.
43. James WH, Woodruff AB, Werner W: Effect of internal and external control upon changes in smoking behavior. J Consult Psychol 29:184-186, 1965.
44. MacDonald AP Jr: Internal-external locus of control and the practice of birth control. Psychol Rep 27:206, 1970.
45. Dabbs JM, Kirscht JP: "Internal control" and the taking of influenza shots. Psychol Rep 28:959-962, 1971.
46. Andrew JM: Delay of surgery. Psychosom Med 34:345-354, 1972.
47. Seeman M, Evans JW: Alienation and learning in a hospital setting. Am Sociol Rev 27:772-782, 1962.
48. Wallston BS, Wallston KA, Kaplan GD, Maides SA: Development and validation of the health locus of control (HLC) scale. 1975 (unpublished manuscript).
49. Phares EJ: Locus of Control in Personality. Morristown, New Jersey, General Learning Press, 1976.
50. MacDonald AP Jr: Internal-external locus of control change technics. Rehab Lit 33:44-47, 1972.
51. Masters JC: Treatment of "adolescent rebellion" by the reconstrual of stimuli. J Consult Clin Psychol 35:213-216, 1970.
52. Dua PS: Comparison of the effects of behaviorally oriented action and psychotherapy reeducation on intraversion-extraversion, emotionality and internal-external control. J Counsel Psychol 6:567-572, 1970.
53. Leventhal H: Findings and theory in the study of fear communications. In Berkowitz L (ed): Advances in Experimental Social Psychology. New York, Academic Press, 1970, vol 5, pp 119-186.
54. Janis IL, Feshbach S: Effects of fear-arousing communications. J Abnorm Soc Psychol 48:78-92, 1953.
55. Leventhal H, Singer R, Jones S: Effects of fear and specificity of recommendation upon attitudes and behavior. J Pers Soc Psychol 2:20-29, 1965.
56. Gray RM, Kesler JP, Moody PM: The effects of social class and friends' expectations on oral polio vaccination participation. Am J Public Health 56:2028-2032, 1966.
57. Fass MF, Green LW, Levine DM: Design of an Experimental Intervention to Increase Family Reinforcement in the Home for Patient Compliance. Paper presented at Am Public Health Assoc Meeting, Chicago, Illinois, Nov 19, 1975.
58. Becker MH, Green LW: A family approach to compliance with medical treatment: a selective review of the literature. Inter J Health Educ 18:173-182, 1975.
59. Goldstein AM, Resnikoff M: Suicide in chronic hemodialysis patients from an external locus of control framework. Am J Psychiat 127:124-127, 1971.
60. Sheridan A, Smith RA: Student-family contracts. Nurs Outlook 23:114-117, 1975.
61. Conant LH: Give-and-take in home visits. Am J Nurs 65:117-120, 1965.
62. Conant LH: Exploratory Study of Nurse-Patient Give and Take. Yale University, unpublished terminal progress report, 1967.
63. Homans GC: Social behavior as exchange. Am J Sociol 63:597-606, 1958.
64. Homans GC: Social Behavior: Its Elementary Forms. New York, Harcourt, Brace and World, 1961.
65. Simons BA: Nurse-Mother Interaction in the Child Conference Interview. School of Nursing, Case Western Reserve University, (unpublished master's thesis) 1970.
66. Nettle C: Nurse Assessment of Effectiveness and Nurse-Patient Interaction. School of Nursing, Case Wstern Reserve University, (unpublished master's thesis) 1971.
67. Davis MS: Variation in patients' compliance with doctors' advice: an empirical analysis of patterns of communication. Am J Public Health 58:274-288, 1968.
68. Durr CA: Hands that help...but now? Nurs Forum 10:392-400, 1971.
69. Krieger D: Therapeutic touch: The imprimator of nursing. Am J Nurs 75:784-787, 1975.
70. Bloom M: The Paradox of Helping: Introduction to the Philosophy of Scientific Practice. New York, John Wiley and Sons, 1975.
71. Brill NI: Working with People: The Helping Process. Philadelphia, J.B. Lippincott, 1973.

72. Carkhuff RR: Helping and Human Relations: Selection and Training, New York, Holt, Rinehart and Winston, vol 1, 1969.
73. Carkhuff RR: Helping and Human Relations: Practice and Research. New York, Holt, Rinehart and Winston, vol 2, 1969.
74. Combs AW, Avila DL, Purkey WW: Helping Relations: Basic Concepts for the Helping Professions. Boston, Allyn and Bacon, 1971.
75. Keith-Lucas A: Giving and Taking Help. Chapel Hill, University of North Carolina Press, 1972.
76. Holder L: Some theoretical and practical considerations in influencing health behavior. Health Educ Mono 1(30):49-69, 1970.
77. Kasl SV: Issues in patient adherence to health care regimens. J Hum Stress 1:5-17, 1975.
78. Higbee K: Fifteen years of fear arousal: research on threat appeals, 1953-1968. Psychol Bull 72:426-444, 1969.
79. Janis I: Effects of fear arousal on attitude change; recent developments in theory and experimental research. In Berkowitz L (ed): Advances in Experimental Social Psychology. New York, Academic Press, 1967, vol 3, pp 167-222.

C. Focus on Educational Interventions

The next five papers provide an overview and specific examples of how individual or group educational efforts can be used to increase patient compliance. Patient education, and educational approaches remain our chief methodological approach today to the management of compliance and thus deserve consideration of both evaluated research and individual practitioner experiences.

Principles of Learning, Patient Education and Hypertension

P.G. ENSOR

Department of Health Sciences
Towson State College
Towson, Maryland

S.G. ROSENBERG

Division of Long Term Care
National Center for Health Services Research
Rockville, Maryland

PRINCIPLES OF LEARNING

It is often assumed that learning is simply the process of the presentation and absorption of new material. Learning is rarely seen as a process which, although lived with, dealt with daily, and considered ordinary, can be studied by the same scientific procedures that have been used to study other subject matter. However, when learning processes have been scientifically studied, it has been discovered that how we learn is quite lawful in nature. From this we can conclude that a body of knowledge exists,[1] consisting of learning principles which have been acquired in carefully controlled experiments and which can be applied to practical problems. The immediate task is the transformation of these facts and principles of learning to a form which will permit the development of health behavior.

Supported in part by the National High Blood Pressure Education Program.

The traditional view of learning equates knowledge and education with the acquisition of facts obtained in schools. The experience of various health educators (*e.g.,* Rosenstock and others [2-5]) reveal, however, that knowledge alone does not indicate learning, and when applied to health does not necessarily determine health behavior. Thus health professionals, instead of viewing education as a process of hammering in bits and pieces of information, should view education as a social process with learning occurring *primarily* as a result of human interaction which is based on self-knowledge and self-understanding.

Education viewed in this way is not then restricted merely to classrooms or formal educational settings. Instead, learning may occur in any setting and throughout one's life as the result of continued interactions with others. This theory of learning does not denigrate the importance of training or development of specific motor skills; instead, it changes the focus in the education process from merely the task — to the individual learning the task, and the resulting human interaction between the learner and the teacher. Thus, the nature of the relationship receives as much attention as the task.

Readers can easily identify with this approach to the education process. Each of us can remember courses in which we strove to do our best and "loved the course"; yet, in other courses every moment was dreaded. Why? Because of the teacher or medium through which we learned. As it was succinctly put by McLuhan,[6] "the medium is the massage." This example lends credence to the theory that learning is also a social process. Simplistically put, we can say that the social interactions (medium) provide impact, not the subject matter (content).[1] This implies that as educators in the area of health behavior we need to examine both the subject matter and the social interaction in the educational process. Therefore, not only what message we send but how we send it to the patient is important.

In summary, we can state that learning is best seen as a process that involves more than content or specific tasks, but content and specific tasks which are acquired in a social interaction and which for most of us will be a lifelong process.

MEANING AND LEARNING

The meaning and importance of any information supplied to a person affects the person's behavior only to the degree to which it has personal meaning or relevance to him. One of the shortcomings of teachers, whether as schoolteachers or as health professionals professing to provide patient instruction, has been that they have not given sufficient attention to the individual's perceptions of what in fact is important. The consequence is that educators often appear prescriptive, requiring for themselves and their students reproduction of subject matter rather than integration of material into an ongoing life. As Stanford and Roark state:

> Significant learning is that learning which has meaning and importance to the life of the learner. To have meaning and importance, what is learned must affect the person's life or his potential to live life. Such learning usually occurs through

human interaction, because we derive meaning from our relationships with other humans.... It's not that one person tells another the meaning of something but instead that meaning is derived from the reaction of the persons involved.[7]

Thus, education for health, to be effective, must operate on an individual at a personal level and in a social context.

In addition, educational psychologists [7] tell us that a critical element in learning is the development of an adequate self-concept. Knowledge and understanding of self imply that an individual has some sense of his needs, ways of behaving, and values. Such self-understanding of personal motives enables the individual to become more self-directed, based on informed choice rather than from rote, habit, or in response to directions from an authority figure.

An understanding of how the patient/learner sees himself is imperative to the learning process. Remedial teachers know that most academic deficiencies are traceable to negative concepts of self, which in turn are derived from negative experience. Children and many adults carry self-perceptions of themselves as "dumb," a "slow learner," or "a person who can't do things as well as everyone else." Since a self-concept is learned, negative self-concepts can be unlearned and replaced by attitudes of positive self-regard. Individuals with positive self-concepts are good learners without forcing, coaxing, pleading, demanding, manipulation, or cajoling. Individuals with negative self-concepts are poor learners. The methods and materials may be of the latest technology, but if the learner is negative to his "self," little progress will occur. Thus, any patient teaching program must pay particular attention to the self-concept and self-understanding of the patient.

Another basic principle, the principle that one learns to do by doing, is not a new concept but needs reinforcement in view of the fact that educational technology has been the focus of attention in recent years. Students in a modern school and even patients in a health care setting may be forced to become passive learners if subjected to a variety of hardware and learning devices which are "efficient." Inasmuch as any of these educational devices may provide the opportunity for active rather than merely passive learning, we suggest they be used, but first ask: "Does the method and material included have meaning for the patient and does it provide for active learn-by-doing by the patient?"

A final point is that the patient must be actively involved in his own therapy and demonstrate his participation, not only to the health care professional, but also to himself. This means that at various points the patient will stop and ask himself, "How am I doing?" Periodic self-evaluation permits the patient to assess the relevance of his therapeutic regimen to himself, and thus the meaning and significance of his own therapy to himself.

ROLE OF HEALTH PROFESSIONAL AS TEACHER

Many health professionals feel apprehensive about their expanded role as health teachers. These feelings arise from personal experiences as a student, experiences in patient teaching, and their notions of what a patient expects of them. Uneasiness with the hardware and software of modern educational technology may intimidate the health professional and inhibit the teaching/learning process. "The behavior of a teacher, like that of everyone else, is a function of his concept of self. Teachers who believe they are able will try. Teachers who do not think they are able will avoid responsibilities."[1] It is therefore suggested that health professionals examine their self-concepts as persons having responsibility for patient teaching, remembering that it is the quality of the human relationship which influences learning most, not whether the teacher always threads the movie projector right the first time. Thus, for the patient education process to succeed, the health professional, as a teacher, needs to perceive him or herself as a "helping person" or "facilitator," a "practitioner" who practices the "art of teaching" within the framework of human interaction.

From the foregoing, one may conclude that patient education may be best viewed as a social process, and that for this process to succeed any educational objectives must be meaningful and contribute to the development of positive self-concepts, for both the patient and the practitioner.

WHAT HAS BEEN DONE IN PATIENT EDUCATION?

Studies over the past 25 years related to patient education, primarily chronic diseases (diabetes, kidney failure, cardiovascular diseases, and more recently, asthma) have demonstrated that organized and disease-specific patient education programs modify compliance. Original interest was in short-term and long-term benefits to the patient. More recently, interest has also been focused on patient education as it is related to cost-effective benefits in utilization of services.

Each of the major studies illustrated the benefits of the educational component in total patient care. Rosenberg [8] discussed the types of failures in medical care: the medical failure, the clinical failure, and the educational failure. As related to hypertension, it is the educational failure which should be given primary attention. The long-term therapy which this disease requires places much of the responsibility for care on the patient himself. Medical and/or clinical failure is minimal. The lack of compliance with a therapeutic regimen over an extended period, when there may be no evident signs or symptoms of disease, is one of the major problems in the treatment of hypertension. The potential for failure in medical care in the control of hypertension is high unless the education component is built into patient care.

If we examine the literature on compliance we find that the range of noncompliance ranges from 15 to 93 per cent, regardless of the prescribed regimen or disease involved.[9,10] This illustrates the attention needed for patient education directed specifically at compliance. Unfortunately, many of the studies indicated that the problem lies not only with patients, but with physicians who "assume" that patients will follow medical advice.

Five major studies published in the last ten years present data which support the value of patient education in compliance. Egbert and coworkers [11] instituted a program of patient instruction for patients hospitalized for intra-abdominal surgery. Information and guidance, reassurance, and instructions on how to "cope with pain" were given to 47 of 97 patients by the anesthetist. Patients were in no way restricted from requesting medication for pain. The results indicated that educated patients reported less pain than the control group. Narcotic medications were used by both groups with no difference on the day of operation, but significant reduction of use for the next five days following the operation. Of note also is that educated patients were discharged 2.7 days earlier than patients who received no pre- and postoperative instruction.

The importance of family education was demonstrated by Skipper and Leonard.[12] They reported the results of instruction to the parents of children scheduled for tonsillectomies (T & A's). These parents were instructed as a group what to expect of their children following surgery. It was hypothesized that the child would exhibit less stress and postoperative symptoms, such as elevated temperatures, pulse rate and blood pressure, postoperative emesis, and disturbed sleep, if the *mother's* fears were reduced. Results of the study indicated that there was a significant reduction in the postoperative symptoms among the children whose mothers were educated about the total T & A procedure.

Reports of patient education among patients with chronic conditions such as asthma, diabetes, and hemophilia indicate reduction of visits to an emergency room for acute episodes related to their conditions. Avery, Green and Kreider [13] studied asthmatic patients (aged 15-45 years) from the inner city. They were randomly divided into study and control groups. The patients were also identified as those with repeated and frequent asthma attacks who presented themselves to the emergency room for treatment. Patients in the study group participated in small discussion groups which met under the direction of third-year medical students who emphasized factors contributing to asthma: general health measures, life style, and use of prophylactic drugs. After a 12-week follow-up period, results indicated that the control group continued in the same pattern of emergency room visits while the study group significantly reduced their visits to the emergency room. The control group had twice the number of visits as the study group. The author of this study estimated a dollar savings of $5 for every $1 spent to conduct the discussion groups.

Diabetics are another patient group with frequent acute conditions due to the nature of the disease. Miller and Goldstein [14] initiated an educational program to eliminate emergency visits for diabetics and to reduce clinic visits for diabetes-related problems which could be prevented if patients were knowledgeable about their condition and crisis-precipitating factors. The project directors hypothesized that 50 per cent of admissions could be prevented if patients had access to medical care and medical advice. The means of providing the necessary information was a diabetes "hotline" which patients could call any time for information, medical advice, and prescriptions. Patients using emergency rooms were informed of the "hotline" through emergency room personnel, and by pamphlets and posters in Spanish as well as English. This study continued from 1968 to 1970. During that time the diabetic clinic population increased from

4,000 to 6,000. In-1968, when the program began, emergency room visits totaled 2,680. In 1970, visits were reduced to 1,250. The authors report a total savings over the two-year period of $1,797,750, or savings of $1,245 per admission for an average of 8.3 days per admission. The authors did not report the personal benefits in terms of reduced anxiety, well-being, and family harmony resulting from reduction of diabetic coma and other complications; however, they are easily inferred from the dramatic results.

Levine and Britten [15] studied moderate to severe hemophiliacs who volunteered to participate in a self-treatment project. The purpose of the project was to teach patients self-infusion and thus reduce the number of hospitalized days and outpatient visits. The patients and their family members were given instructions by physicians. Two to four successful infusions under supervision were considered sufficient before allowing patients to take materials home for self-infusion. Telephone contact was available for the at-home patient if he felt the need for supervision. The mean number of outpatient visits in the study group was 23 per cent prior to the study. After the education program, the number of visits dropped to 5.5 per patient. As a group, the 45 patients spent a total of 432 days in the hospital in the year preceding compared with a total of 42 days within the year following the instruction program. Dramatic cost savings were computed for reduction in hospitalization costs (89 per cent) and outpatient professional fees (76 per cent). All patients continued with the clinic supervision for the one-year period of the study. As a result of instruction, mean cost per patient in the study group dropped from $5,780 to $3,209.

The value of patient education among patients with congestive heart failure was demonstrated by Rosenberg.[16] One hundred patients were selected: 50 were assigned to the study group while 50 patients, in three other general hospitals, served as controls. A broad-ranged educational and counseling program was offered to the patient and family members. An interdisciplinary team provided various elements of the educational package: knowledge test, group discussion, formal instruction sessions, and individualized counseling. All patients in the study group were interviewed to determine their knowledge and attitudes about their condition, and an assessment of their health behavior and habits. An *educational prescription* was designed for each patient as the basis for planning each patient's individualized educational experience. The findings indicated that the study patients increased their knowledge about the disease process, diet, medications, etc. Urinalysis revealed that there was lowered sodium excretion in study patients in the end of the study. Other medical results were the reduction in number of readmissions (five as compared to nine in the control group) and reduction in number of readmission days (82 as compared to the 238 in the control group). Thus, this patient-education program demonstrated the value of the individualized education prescriptions by reducing hospital readmissions.

In summary, these studies demonstrate the value of patient education in a variety of settings and with different diseases. Organized patient education when provided as an integral part of medical care can increase patient understanding and thus compliance to the prescribed medical regimen. In turn, the results are evident in improved health of the patient and reduced use of medications, outpatient clinics and hospitalization.

PLANNING THE PROGRAM

While the evidence for improved health through patient education is available, the question remains: how does one begin effective program planning? The planning process should involve steps and orderly progression of identifying need, in the areas of *knowledge, attitudes* and *practice* (KAP). The Committee on Educational Tasks in Chronic Illness of the Public Health Education Section, American Public Health Association, published a report in 1973 which provided such a step-by-step procedure for instituting organized and planned patient/family education programs in a variety of health care settings.[17] The planning model proposed follows a logical and sequential series of events which allows periodic evaluation of patient/family behavior change and consequent modification of the learning when indicated.

In any program, the committee agreed, staff must begin with an assessment of patient/family needs. A realistic appraisal of what the patient needs to know and do in order to cope effectively with illness should be conducted. One question which staff should constantly ask is, "Do they need to know that or do we ask them to learn it because we had to learn it?" For example, in almost every curriculum one examines for diabetes education, time is allotted for the study of anatomy and physiology and in particular to the island of Langerhans. How important is the study of such anatomy and physiology? We constantly need to ask ourselves why do we want the patient to know that? How will the information help him modify his behavior? How will it help him to make the decision to adhere?

Identifying the patient's educational needs also begins with a recognition of the uniqueness of that individual which is determined by his biological and psychological make-up and his environment and experiences. Following a definition of what the patient/family must know, the next step is to make a determination of what the patient/family know, think they know, believe, or practice: in other words, a determination of *KAP* (knowledge, attitudes, practice). It is obviously important in the KAP survey to separate information on practice the patient thinks the professional wants from actual current practice. It becomes important then to ask the questions in such a way as to get true estimates of knowledge, attitudes, and practice. For example, instead of asking the patient's wife if she uses salt in her cooking, you might ask, "How much salt do you add to the water when you cook spaghetti?" Or you might ask the hypertensive patient who is on a sodium-restricted diet, "How do you prepare your frozen peas?" In both instances, the patient might have been instructed on salt restriction, may actually know he is on such a diet, and respond with, "I don't use salt." However, when the question is phrased as above, "How do you cook your frozen peas?" and the patient responds with, "I just use 1/4 cup of water, cover and cook for five minutes," then you may be more certain the patient needs help with the problem of adherence.

Following a determination of educational goals, which is in effect a subtraction of what the patient/family needs to know from what the staff has set for him to know, a determination or a selection of the proper educational methodology becomes apparent. Once again, it is important that the professional remember that content and the learner's educational experience determine the appropriate teaching/learning methodology to be used. The hypertensive biochemist who is on a diuretic may be satisfied if simply told to eat a banana daily to replace the potassium he will lose. Then again, he may not until he has been given an explanation including data on ion exchanges, other potential salt depletion problems, corrective therapy, etc. The functional illiterate or less-educated patient may be satisfied to know how much, how often, and what might happen if he did not eat his daily banana or suitable substitute.

The question which might be asked is, "Could both the biochemist and the less-educated, possibly illiterate person receive the same information at the same time utilizing a group method or group discussion approach?" The answer is *Yes* if the discussion leader recognizes the different levels of sophistication of the two patients and responds to the questions of the biochemist in a way which does not exclude or bore the other patient. Essentially, both need to know the same fact vis-a-vis potassium depletion. The biochemist simply wants an explanation in depth.

The use of films, filmstrips, booklets, programmed instruction, and other media techniques have all been found to be effective educational methods. However, they do not work equally well with all content and learners. Some methods are simply inappropriate to effective learning; we need to recognize that fact. The use of a film to teach a subject such as preparation for an insulin injection may not be as effective as the use of a filmstrip, for example, which allows for stopped action and narration to suit the needs of the learner. Group discussion decision-making may be a more viable technique to effect behavior change than the lecture or the "let me tell you want you need to know for your own good" method.

After the program has been carried out and teaching/learning has taken place, evaluation of both cognitive and effective behavior (knowledge and practice) should be carried out. Data related to staff assessment of knowledge and skills needed by patients should be carefully scrutinized. Did they really need to know that? What else do they need to know and do? Patient/family KAP should be re-examined. What are they doing? How are they doing it? What else needs to be learned? What better way can they be taught? What new skills does the staff need?

Another approach to instituting, organizing, and coordinating patient/family health education is the *educational prescription*. The educational prescription differs from the foregoing program by emphasizing the specification of the steps in the patient-education process. For example, specific content, predetermined by staff related to what the patient/family needs to know, is listed. Through interviews an understanding of what the patient already knows and does is obtained. Gaps in knowledge and behavior are determined and the resultant difference is "ordered" by the physician in charge. Primary responsibility for content areas usually follows a discipline orientation. However, reinforcement is everyone's responsibility. Since specifics regarding medications, diet, etc., are written on the prescription, there can be no question concerning the possibility of providing the patient with differing information. Each medication, its dosage, and its frequency should be listed. If there is a potential for side effects such as might occur with overdigitilization, for example, this should appear on the prescription as information to be given by the physician, nurse, and pharmacist. Again, prime responsibility can be assigned by the physician who orders the prescription, but reinforcement can be given by all. Once the information has been given by whatever educational methodology has been deemed appropriate, it should be noted on the prescription. In effect, then, the educational prescription is considered as any other order would be; it becomes a permanent part of the patient's chart and as such functions as a legal part of the record.

The usefulness of the educational prescription has been tested in a number of projects. Rosenberg,[16] for example, tested the concept for patients with congestive heart failure; Fiori et al [18] organized educational prescriptions for patients with emphysema and mastectomies; and Ulrich and Kelley [19] developed a prescription for diabetes. In addition, Rosenberg [2] provided such prescriptions for a group of patients, regardless of their diagnosis.

CHOOSING EDUCATIONAL METHODOLOGIES

If we look at the educational problem in light of decision-making for adherence, our task becomes somewhat easier. The question is, what educational methodologies lend themselves to appropriate decision-making? Skiff [20] responded "all of them." "The answer," she continues, "is that which governs the selection of a method or particular group of methods is subject to the same basic considerations that influence choice in other situations." To paraphrase what we wrote earlier, the appropriate methods depend upon the variables inherent in the content to be taught and the sum total of the learner's experience and ability to learn, given physical, emotional, intellectual, linguistic, cultural, and other influencing handicaps. Skiff listed a series of educational methods which she has employed in her work at the Staten Island Public Health Service hospital. They are not exhaustive, but are illustrative of methodologies which have been used by Fiori et al [18] and Rosenberg [16] in New Jersey, Avery et al [13] in Baltimore, and other health educators in countless programs for disease- and illness-oriented programs. Francis Storlie,[21] in her new text written primarily for nursing personnel, provides an additional list of effective educational methods.

- **Individual Instruction:** This is the method most commonly used by health professionals. These sessions offer maximum opportunity for assuring the patient, but unfortunately, the method also creates problems for some learners who become anxious and do not "hear." Individual instruction can also be inefficient use of valuable staff time. Also, family members may not be available for instruction when staff teaches.

- **Programmed Instruction:** Data available reveal that programmed instruction can be a valuable teaching adjunct. However, the cost of programming and the paucity of trained programmers as well as the cost of the teaching machines have proven to be deterrents to effective use of this technique.
- **Group Discussion:** In this method, a facilitator leads the group into areas of mutual interest and concern. Decisions regarding appropriate topics for discussion, direction of the discussion, and the ability to satisfy the group's need-to-know so they can effectively make appropriate decisions are dependent upon the skills and training of the facilitator.
- **Coaching Utilizing Members of Self-Help Groups:** Coaching by volunteers or others who have experienced the same problem has been an acceptable teaching method for many years. In the health field the use of volunteers is fairly new but now seems to be entrenched in practice. As examples of such programs we would cite the "Reach to Recovery" and ostomy education programs of the Cancer Society.
- **Multi-Media:** The use of films, slides, and closed-circuit television have all been considered as part of the armamentarium used to teach patients and their families. Sometimes these have been combined with other methods, and sometimes teaching instruments unto themselves.
- **The Learning Experience:** All the methods which we have discussed (*i.e.,* Individual Instruction, Programmed Instruction, Group Discussion, etc.) have taken cognizance of basic principles of adult education which make the learner part of the experience. In other words, the experience is learner- and not teacher-oriented. These principles may be cited by other authors in a slightly different sequence and phrased somewhat differently; however, they are basic to learning.
- **Participation:** The student learns by doing, by practicing, by using his own hands. This is also known as experiential learning.
- **Usefulness:** The student needs to satisfy himself that the information has value to him.
- **Progression from the Simple to the Complex:** The student learns a simple task or concept, and demonstrates mastery of that task or concept before moving on to the next skill or conceptual level.
- **Continuity and Reinforcement:** The student needs an opportunity to practice learned skills.
- **Appraisal and Evaluation:** The student needs an opportunity to evaluate his skills and knowledge against a set of standards.

APPLICATION TO HYPERTENSION

It is obvious that the foregoing methodologies have application for any hypertension education programming. The question one might ask relates to what content area or skills area might best be used with what educational methodology.

The questions do not lend themselves to simple solutions. However, approaches based on practice are applicable. For example, if the physician orders a 2,500 g sodium-restricted 1,200 calorie diet, devoid of coffee and tea, and a weight loss of 25 pounds for the patient as well as an antihypertensive drug and diuretic, the educational content is obvious. The question becomes: how best can we work with the patient/family to obtain the desired behaviors? Since we know the patient/family must feel they are involved, what approaches will ensure involvement? After the educational diagnosis has been made in the case of drug therapy, content concerning dosage, the rationale for the choice of medication, etc., can be provided through the use of film-sound cassette units, pamphlets, booklets, or some other audiovisual device. The patient should be given the opportunity to write questions which should be responded to by a member of the treatment team. The patient is made to understand that the opportunity to ask questions is part of his therapy. He or she is expected to ask questions. Data available reveal that many patients do not ask questions because they fear embarrassment or because they do not want to bother the busy doctor or nurse.[16, 21] Giving the patient the opportunity to write questions will demonstrate the team's expectations for having questions and answering them.

The use of group discussion methods seems to provide one of the better strategies for involvement. The opportunity for the patient to problem-solve on his own level with others who share the same problem ensures self-actualization and appropriate decision-making to insure adherence.

Since improved patient care is the primary task, the focus of evaluation should be related to the progress made by the patient in terms of his own adherence. It is imperative that progress be measured against goals and objectives which are realistic and identifiable. For example, if the goal to be measured is couched in terms of "to live a happier, more fruitful life," then the goal is not written as a measurable behavioral objective. If, however, the goal is written in terms of "to reduce and maintain a weight loss of 30 pounds within six months," the goal is both measurable and specific.

Following this reappraisal or evaluation of patient progress a new definition of needs can be evolved, a new prescription written, and a new learning program begun. Thus, we are viewing patient/family education as a process which is never completed but rather one which continues as long as the patient remains a patient.

RESEARCH

Although data cited in this paper do not specifically apply to methodologies for patient/family education for hypertensives, we firmly believe the principles do. Research, however, still has to tell us which methodologies yield the best results with which groups and under what conditions. Examples of these questions include: Will inner city residents respond more favorably to individualized instruction than group discussion methods? Can a programmed instruction format be used, and if so at what reading level? Can a health educator provide assistance to more than a single facility providing services for hypertensive patients? To what extent does the involvement of the family in the treatment plan modify adherence? What strategies provide a better adherence to prescribed regimens for the inner city poor, the single, and the social isolate? What staffing needs are minimal for effective programming? What techniques are necessary to cost-benefit the educational component of a hypertension treatment program?

SUMMARY

Because of the implicit teaching role of all health professionals, some general concepts of learning have been presented. In addition, applicable data related to the efficacy of organized and planned patient/family education programs as well as a rationale and methodology for planning teaching programs and the selection of appropriate teaching techniques have been presented. The need for applicable research is also discussed.

REFERENCES

1. Combs AW, Syngg D: Individual Behavior: A Perceptual Approach to Psychology. New York, Harper and Row, 1959, p 59.
2. Dowell LJ: The relationship between health knowledge and practice. J Educ Res 62:201-202, 1969.
3. Hochbaum GM: Measurement of effectiveness of health education activities. Int J Health Educ 14:54-59, 1971.
4. Keyes LL: Health education in perspective — an overview. Health Educ Monogr 31:13-17, 1972.
5. Rosenstock I: Why people use health services. Milbank Mem Fund Q 44:94-127, 1966.
6. McLuhan M, Fiore Q: The Medium is the Massage. New York, Bantam Books, 1967.
7. Stanford G, Roark AE: Human interaction in education. Boston, Allyn and Bacon, 1974.
8. Rosenberg SG: A case for patient education. Hosp Form Manag 6:1-4, 1971.
9. Davis M, Eichorn R: Compliance with medical regimens: a panel study. J Health Hum Behav 4:240-249, 1963.
10. Marston M: Compliance with medical regimens: a review of literature. Nur Res 19:312-323, 1970.
11. Egbert LD, Batlit GE, Welch CE, Bartlett MK: Reduction of postoperative pain by encouragement and instructions of patients. N Engl J Med 270:825-827, 1964.
12. Skipper JK Jr, Leonard RC: Children, stress and hospitalization: a field experiment. J Health Soc Behav 9:275-287, 1968.
13. Avery C II, Green LW, Kreider S: Reducing emergency visits of asthmatics: an experiment in patient education. Testimony before the President's Committee on Health Education, Pittsburgh, Pa (Jan 11) 1972.
14. Miller L, Goldstein J: More efficient care of diabetic patients in a county hospital setting. N Engl J Med 286:1388-1391, 1972.
15. Levine P II, Britten AF: Supervised patient management of hemophilia. Ann Intern Med 78:105-201, 1973.
16. Rosenberg SG: Patient education leads to better care for heart patients. HSMHA Health Rep 86:793-802, 1971.
17. Report of the Committee on Educational Tasks in Chronic Illness: A Model for Planning Patient Education, An Essential Component of Health Care. Public Health Education Section, Am Publ Health Assoc HEW Publication HSM 73-4028.
18. Fiori FB, de la Vega M, Vacarro MJ: Health education in a hospital setting: Report of a public health service project in Newark, NJ. Health Educ Mon 2:11-29, 1974.
19. Ulrich MR, Kelley KM: Patient care includes teaching. Hospital 40:59-75, 1972.

20. Strategies for Patient Education. Report of the Second Invitational Conference. Chicago, Amer Hosp Assoc, 1969, p 35.
21. Skiff A: Experiences with methods for patient teaching in a public health service hospital. Health Educ Mono 21:48-53, 1974.
22. Storlie F: Resources for patient education. *In* Patient Teaching in Critical Care. New York, Appleton-Century Crofts, 1975, pp 170-176.

Group Treatment and Management of the Hypertensive Patient*

ALISA ROSA KASACHKOFF

American Health Foundation
New York, New York

GROUP THERAPY AND MEDICAL PRACTICE

Despite well-defined and well-understood therapy, many hypertensive patients fail to comply with their medical treatment regimen. Patients, attempting to ward off their anxieties, fears, and/or depressive feelings regarding the possible outcomes of having hypertension, may rationalize that the perils of this disease do not apply to them. An approach therefore is needed to aid hypertensive patients in accepting the emotional realities of their disease and in instituting life-style modifications necessary to reduce the risks associated with elevated blood pressure. One approach which, to date, has not been given a great deal of attention is that of group therapy. This seems unfortunate because the nature of the group therapy process appears well suited for dealing with the hypertensive patient. In addition, group therapy is efficient in terms of treating more than one

---

The contents of this paper grew out of my experience as Director of Group Treatment and Head Behavioral Scientist of the Boston University Medical Center, Multiple Risk Factor Intervention Trial.

patient at the same time and in using both medical and nonmedical personnel, *e.g.,* nurses and technicians, social workers and psychologists.

The group approach refers to seeing a certain number of patients together over a specified period of time, the common ground being the necessity to deal with common issues. A group organized to deal with hypertensive issues, would, therefore, discuss issues ranging all the way from pill-taking to losing weight to coming for follow-up medical check ups, etc. The group setting allows for examination of any individual participant's behavior in a nonthreatening constructive manner and also provides an opportunity to have clarified presented material and issues raised for discussion. Critical in this process is the fact that the more articulate participants can clarify issues for those less articulate, and a process of peer teaching and learning occurs. Furthermore, a setting of this type may promote active compliance because the feeling of group spirit and cohesiveness which is generated by a consistent group of people sharing common experiences induces motivation to achieve the overall group goals and/or objectives.[1] An example may be seen in the hypertensive patient who has never listened to his physician's advice regarding the management of hypertension but complies in the group, feeling that he cannot betray the members by acting otherwise. He may reason that such an attitude might break down the feeling of togetherness and furthermore may lead to noncompliance on the part of other members, a responsibility few people, hypertensive or not, would wish to assume. As life styles are extremely difficult to change, the foregoing characteristics of group therapy seem to be an attractive way of getting people to comply to a hypertension-management regimen.

The obvious advantages of group therapy approach contrast sharply with its actual integration into medical practice. In fact, patient groups are in general rarely used except in specialized settings (see chapter by Budman, pages 189-194). Reasons for this include the limited availability of nonmedical (paramedical and behavioral) personnel to run such groups. However, a second, possibly critical, reason is that both physicians and patients are generally more comfortable with the present relationship than with change even though the status quo may be unproductive or even destructive.[2] Any change in this customary mode may produce a state of anxious uncertainty in both patient and physician.

Replacing the traditional one-to-one relationship by another mode of treatment (*e.g.,* group) may be seen by the physician as bearing the inherent implication that both he and his mode of treatment are inadequate. Moreover, the physician, feeling satisfied with his progress in hypertension management, may not see any necessity to change.

To admit that something done by a previous generation of physicians was incorrect or could be improved is to take pride in the constant improvement of medical practice, but to admit that the treatment of one's own patients has been inadequate is ego-damaging.[3]

Many people who enter the medical profession do so to achieve prestige and power.[4] To recognize and accept management of the hypertensive patient by nonmedical personnel (*e.g.,* psychologists or social workers) may represent a self-defacing loss of this heightened social status. Furthermore, if nonphysicians are able to contribute to the treatment of hypertensives, serious questions about the extent and limits of this nonphysician involvement might be raised. Clearly, physicians (as would be true for any professional) would feel threatened by such a prospect and would resist change. Thus the combination of psychological inertia, the threat of loss of social status, and the natural avoidance of ego damage are sufficient psychological reasons for physicians not to consider experimenting with the physician-patient relationship.

At another level, treating patients in groups is less expensive per patient treatment. Because of the constantly repeated issue concerning the "exorbitant" prices charged by physicians for individual treatment, the treatment by a less expensive modality seems to open a Pandora's box which physicians might wish to shut as quickly as possible. In addition, using economic reasons as the justification for changing some aspects of the health-care process raises the spectre of using nonmedical reasons in general to change any part of medical practice.

One might think that to change the traditional physician-patient relationship, having withstood the test of time, would require at least minimal demonstration of its deficiencies.

What appears to be required, however, is solely a demonstration of the superiority of another method. For example, one does not need to demonstrate the deficiencies of an injection (*e.g.,* Salk injection) to promote the advantages of something administered orally (Sabin vaccine). This exact same reasoning can be utilized when promoting the group method of treatment for hypertension management. It is *not* to say that the one-to-one physician-patient relationship is ineffective, but rather that the group method appears to be more effective.

In light of the potential effectiveness of the group therapy treatment, all hypertensive patients (regardless of compliance) should be referred except when contraindicated. These contraindications refer to patients who would use the group nonproductively or who would not use it for its designated function. These persons include psychotics (*e.g.,* schizophrenics), severe neurotics (group-related phobics, those with interfering paranoid features), and those with character disorders (*e.g.,* psychopaths).

Factors involved in referring hypertensive patients to group treatment should include the following:

1. The physician's assessment of any personality contraindications to group treatment;
2. An exploration of any patient feelings regarding possible characteristics of group leaders, for example, feelings regarding the sex of the group leader, his race, religion, etc.,
3. An emphatic statement(s) that because the physician is concerned with optimal care, he is referring the patient to the group treatment method, the method he believes to be the treatment of choice for hypertensives;
4. A concerned, interest statement that he expects to see the patient on follow-

up visits † and will periodically confer with the group leader so as to maintain total treatment continuity.

As confidentiality is an inherent assumption in the physician-patient relationship and since groups appear to alter this relationship, there is a necessity for the direct discussion of this issue with the patient. Thus, besides explaining the purpose of the group, the physician should also explain that the ground rules for group participation (e.g., mandatory attendance and honesty) also include confidentiality. Confidentiality in a group refers to the discussion of material only among group members, the group leader(s), and those physicians involved with the patient: any discussion with outsiders is considered to be a betrayal.

THE USE OF GROUP TREATMENT DURING
A HYPERTENSION INTERVENTION TRIAL

Concern with the growing incidence of myocardial infarction and the demonstration of adequate, prophylactic agents for the treatment of hypertension and hypercholesterolemia [5,6] prompted the federal government to fund the Multiple Risk Factor Intervention Trial (MRFIT). What follows is a brief history and description of the MRFIT Program.

Starting twenty-five years ago under the directorship of Thomas R. Dawber, M.D., and William Kannel, M.D., the Framingham Heart Study began a longitudinal epidemiological study of those factors present in people who eventually suffer from a heart attack versus those who did not. To date three factors statistically differentiate the two groups: cigarette smoking, serum cholesterol levels, and blood pressure. Those suffering from heart attacks demonstrated higher figures for one or more of these factors than those who did not. Hence rose the question: If one were to lower these factors, would the incidence of heart attack decrease? It was with this in mind that MRFIT began a study designed to lower these three specific factors in a population highly prone to develop heart disease as predicted by the Framingham Heart Study Data.

The MRFIT program includes twelve thousand men in the top percentages of the risk categories for developing heart disease, as predicted by the Framingham Heart Study.[7] These men are to be studied over a five-year period, with six thousand accepted into the Center run by MRFIT and monitored by MRFIT physicians, while the other half are to be followed by their own family physicians. Twenty MRFIT Centers were created across the United States (six hundred men followed by each center) so as to provide broad sampling of the country's male population. One such program, the program created at Boston University Medical Center, provides our setting for illustrating how group therapy processes can aid in the treatment of hypertensive patients.

The MRFIT program at Boston University Medical Center sees hypertension

---

†The frequency of visits should be dependent both on the patient's personality and his hypertension-related problems and difficulties.

raising many broad behavioral issues as well as specific issues related to cigarette smoking, nutrition (serum cholesterol), and taking medication. Thus, it was important to provide our patients with a group setting that avoided the anger, anxiety, and ultimate group withdrawal that can come from raising fundamental psychological issues without dealing with them, but yet dealing with the behaviors that could affect the probability of a heart attack, cardiovascular accident, etc. The method used for achieving the goal blood pressure revolved around the development of a normative system within the group where noncompliance to hypertension management has no place. It was predicted that this norm, once internalized in each member of the group, would result in compliance even when participants were away from the group.[8]

These are, however, important reasons why it is necessary to help in this internalization process. Besides not wanting to face the fact that one has a disease, one is taught by present-day society to comply to medical management only in the face of "felt" illness. Hypertensives often feel well; in fact, they often cannot remember feeling better or more active. Taking medication or going on a weight control program when they are asymptomatic makes no sense. Because of this, the norm that is to be internalized must center around the preservation of optimal health regardless how one is feeling.

Reasons for preserving optimal health are plentiful and particular to the individual at hand. To some, it may be a religious value that preaches care of the body to such an extent that no damage can result because of lack of attention. To others, it may be a value in which the family unity is held in high regard: consequently, the care of one's health is a responsibility of each family member to his overall unit. Still another value leading to hypertensive management may be that potential pain or discomfort should be avoided at all costs. Yet still another may be "vanity" of maintaining the body in an intact state: any thought of possible effects of illness induced or caused by high blood pressure may cause potential conflict with this value system.

For groups of hypertensive patients run at the Boston University Medical Center, the actual process [9] for achieving the norm includes:

1. Regular sessions in which all members can get to know one another and develop a feeling of confidence and trust;
2. Sessions that begin and end at a specified time (allowing this to occur regardless of how many members are present, even if it is only one, implies that the hypertension issue set aside for discussion will not be treated in a haphazard manner and that each single member represents a significant part in the carrying out of this program);
3. Common values among members, whether they are religious, cultural, social or racial (similar ideas precipitate a feeling of warmth and commonality — a necessity for sharing painful, intimate issues);
4. Common habits that serve to create a looser, more human atmosphere;
5. A group leader(s) who will not only prevent his or her own personal conflicts from getting involved in the group process, but who will also not permit domination or persecution of any member by another;

6. A supportive atmosphere where all members feel that they will develop an avenue of resolution, strength, and knowledge by sharing their weaknesses, faults, conflicts, and doubts. This support is a natural consequence of being among people who have the same general purpose and share the same feelings.

Both the time and rate at which certain material is presented are important factors in the running of groups. Only when a sense of trust and acceptance has been developed among group members will an atmosphere of mutuality arise. Only within this receptive atmosphere can discrepancies between lack of care of a diagnosed illness and the various relevant value systems be pointed out in a nonthreatening way.

In the group, there is constant reiteration by the group leader of ways in which members can alleviate their hypertension, whether it be by weight control, taking medication, etc. Definite plans are continually set up for continued care. Plans may vary from going to a movie for every five-pound loss, to buying a new necktie for each month in which medication compliance is diligently followed, to reassuring oneself by stating aloud that the guarantee against untimely death is slowly being increased as he continues to follow the medical regimen prescribed, to finding someone who will continually compliment the patient on his success at mastering hypertension compliance. Effective planning appears to take place as the group leader becomes aware of that which is meaningful to each member. Planning also includes the use of self-monitoring devices, ranging from requiring each member to take his weight, to charting it regularly, to having him write an account for each scheduled time for taking medication that was missed.

There appear to be several reasons for nonresponsiveness. The experiences of not feeling well, of being poorly treated by his family, or of fearing a dependency on medication for the rest of his life may cause a member to have an underlying wish to die. Becoming fearful of having his mind changed as a result of the group sessions may cause a patient to stop attending.

To guard against this possibility, our participants are told that there will be a specified number of sessions, attendance at which is mandatory if they are accepted into the program. The groups are large enough in size to provide for a diversity of discussion, yet at the same time small enough to permit every member to get to know one another's problems and how those problems relate specifically to him. A manageable size appears to range from six to eight members and the length of each session between 1 1/4 to 1 3/4 hours.

Supplies necessary to run this type of group session are minimal. Basic literature or other instructional materials, such as films on hypertension and how the disease can be controlled, are utilized. Monitoring and control devices such as blood pressure cuffs, a weighing scale, and an ecolyzer (to measure the amount of carbon monoxide in the blood of smokers) are also present. These tools are used in diagnosis as well as in modifying and evaluating participant progress. They are constantly used as an adjunct to intensify the goal of high blood pressure reduction.

As heart attack prevention is the underlying aim, any reason(s) for avoiding a heart attack is adopted as motivation for hypertension management. These may range from wanting to outlive a brother who has a lower blood pressure to accepting a dare from some acquaintance questioning the ability to lower one's blood pressure to feeling guilty over the possibility of leaving a young widow and/or children.

In addition to the foregoing, the following recommendations might be considered for improving management of the hypertensive patient:

1. A buddy system to check on participant progress and encountered difficulties;
2. The use of relaxation as a technique of self-control to reduce tension [10];
3. The use of behavior rehearsal (role playing) to train participants to deal more effectively with situations that in the past induced a rise in blood pressure [11];
4. The use of bio-feedback techniques so that participants can monitor their own blood pressures.

SUMMARY

The objectives and goals of group therapy appear compatible with an extension to medical practice and in particular in the treatment of the hypertensive patient. While the group setting should provide a supportive atmosphere whereby patients can feel free to express themselves, it should also create a feeling of discomfort should they neglect to care for their hypertension. The purpose of the group is to develop a new normative system which, as it is internalized, should open patients to new ways in which they can care for their high blood pressures. Normative internalization, once it is accomplished during group treatment, should continue in a sustained manner independent of and long after the group has discontinued.

REFERENCES

1. Festinger L, Schechter S, Bach K: Social Pressure. New York, Harper and Row, 1950, p 91.
2. Berlson B, Steiner GA: Human Behavior: An Inventory of Scientific Findings. New York, Harcourt, Brace and World, 1964, p 614.
3. Krech D, Crutchfield RS, Ballachey EL: Individual in Society. New York, McGraw-Hill Book Co, 1962, p 83.
4. McDermott JR, Char WF, Hensen MJ: Motivation for medicine in the seventies. Am J Psychol 130:253, 1973.
5. VA Cooperative Study: Effects of treatment on morbidity in hypertension: I. Results in patients with diastolic blood pressure averaging 115 through 129 mm Hg. JAMA 202:1028-1034, 1967.
6. VA Cooperative Study: Effects of treatment on morbidity in hypertension: II. Results in patients with diastolic blood pressure averaging 90 through 114 mm Hg. JAMA 213:1143-1152, 1970.
7. Kannel WB, Gordon T, Schwartz MJ: Systolic versus diastolic blood pressure and risk of coronary heart disease. Am J Cardiol 27:335-346, 1971.
8. Sherif M, Sherif C: An Outline of Social Psychology. New York, Harper and Brothers, 1948, pp 246-247.

9. Berelson B, Steiner GA: Human Behavior: An Inventory of Scientific Findings. New York, Harcourt, Brace and World, 1964, pp 325-339.
10. Cautela JR: Behavior therapy and self control: techniques and implications. *In* Frank CM (ed): Behavior Therapy: Appraisal and Status. New York, McGraw Hill, 1969, pp 323-340.
11. Wolpe J: The Practice of Behavior Therapy. New York, Pergamon Press, 1969, pp 68-70.

Psychoeducational Groups with Medical Patients

SIMON H. BUDMAN

Harvard Community Health Plan
Harvard Medical School
Boston, Massachusetts

The medical patient with a chronic condition, such as diabetes, hypertension, or blindness, and people experiencing life changes such as childbirth, mid-life or menopause, often feel alone and different from others not undergoing such illness or change.[1] They also feel anxious and uninformed about their situation and its significance. The physician or nurse who sees such people usually can provide only limited support, information and encouragement in the course of his/her own busy work schedules. An invaluable and little used resource in medical practice is found in groups of patients with similar health problems or life situations. Such groups may be used to provide an efficient social support and information system otherwise unavailable to these patients.

A group setting provides the opportunity for the health care provider to efficiently inform a number of patients simultaneously about various important aspects of their life situations or medical conditions. "Will my hypertension ever be cured?" "How will my heart attack affect my sex life?" "Is breast feeding or bottle feeding better?" These are the types of questions often raised in the groups to be described.

In answering these questions in a group, patients discover that they have the same health problems as others and that there are answers to these problems.[2,3] The feelings of loneliness, oddness, and isolation that frequently exist in the individual patient-doctor relationship give way to feelings of communality and unity with the group.[4],[5] Thus, a group provides a patient with the opportunity for both educational and interpersonal growth and development.

The usefulness of groups to the individual patient and in managing adherence seems obvious. For example, the patient who expects to be "cured" of his hypertension, or who views hypertension as an "inner weakness or oddness," or who continues a strenuous life style to prove he or she is normal illustrates the kind of common human responses to the discovery of an illness and the task required to adhere to the therapy. The advantage of the group is that it greatly increases the chances that the unspoken will be stated, and the patient's assumptions concerning his illness evaluated. This alone justifies considering what it would take to develop a group approach to managing medical patients.

A PROGRAM OF INTERVENTION

The intervention program to be described is called a *psychoeducational group approach.* This type of group intervention is neither a self-help group like Alcoholics Anonymous which is run by and for alcoholics, with no professional input,[6] nor is it a "class" on health and illness or a professionally led psychotherapy situation.[7] Rather, psychoeducational groups combine elements of self-help, educational, and psychotherapy groups.

The unique characteristic of psychoeducational groups is that the problems dealt with generate from the immediate experience of patients (in this case health-related issues), and the solutions generated are meant to be directly applied. Thus, health-oriented psychoeducational groups function to promote "health growth" but, more specifically, health behavior.

Based on eight years of experience with psychoeducational groups in a variety of inpatient and outpatient medical settings, it is possible to describe the growth phases of these groups, and the issues involved in their implementation and utilization. There seem to be four major phases in the life of these groups.

Coming Together

In this first phase, since the group members are aware of their common issue, there is a general coming together around this issue with comparisons and examination of similarities and differences. For example, there may be comparisons of childbirth experiences, time spent in Vietnam, or comparing the severity of, and medication for, one's hypertension. In a group of returning disabled Vietnam veterans, much time in the early sessions was spent determining who had been in what unit, how many "fire fights" one had been in, where rest and recreation time was spent, etc., for example:

Mr. J: Were you at Phu Bin?
Mr. S: Yeah, we got hit bad there.
Mr. J: Was that where you saw your first action? It wasn't for me; our unit got hit just as soon as we got in. It was a helluva mess.
Mr. T: Same happened to me, my unit. I wasn't in Nam for two weeks before we saw action. We just got processed at Da Nang, and went right out.

Similarly, in a group of new parents, the initial phase involved frequent comparisons and sharing around their common experience. For example:

Mr. K: How much does Sammy weigh now?
Mrs. F: He's pretty small compared with Amy: she's really big. What are you feeding her? Is she on solid foods already? Our doctor recommends we wait a little longer.
Mrs. K: The pediatrician told us to start cereal the second week. The baby just seemed too hungry without it.

Who is the Leader of the Group?

In the next major phase, the group usually turns toward the leader(s) for specific information regarding the stress around which the group was organized. The leader should steer a course somewhere between the "all-knowing" expert on child development, divorce, or any other topic and the "blank-screen" therapist.

Physicians or nurses inexperienced in leading groups may have a tendency to simply hold a "class." This should be avoided. Although valuable informational input can and should be made by the leader(s), members should be encouraged to use one another for input, information and support. If the leader does not really respect the usefulness of group members to one another, and communicates that truth resides only in her or him, it is unlikely that the group will ever really pull together and move on to Phase 3.

Mrs. A: I'm reading [names a book] which says you shouldn't overstimulate infants. Josh doesn't even have a mobile. Doesn't it seem that there can be too much stimulation for a kid? There are so many kids these days who are so wild. There's no calming them down.
Mr. A: I'm not, well I don't really know how you can really overstimulate kids, but maybe Jan [his wife] has a point; it's really confusing. All I know is that I'd rather have him calmed down than all hyper like some kids. What do you two think?
Dr. B: I really don't think that you can overstimulate kids, at least not with a mobile. Maybe if it was a matter of waking up a child to have him look at it...
Mrs. N: Not letting him get his rest...
Dr. B: Actually what we know about infant growth and development indicates that visual and auditory stimulation is useful to the baby. I think the kinds of kids you were talking about [Mrs. A] really have other kinds of difficulties. Maybe we can talk some about what you mean when you say "wild kids." What are they like?

Learning about Yourself and Others

At this point, if group interaction has been supported and encouraged, members begin to examine their own and other's psychological characteristics in dealing with a particular life stress. A hypertensive patient, for example, may see that he or she is assuming a "sick role" and withdrawing due to illness. A new father may be able to see that as he becomes anxious when his infant cries, he deals with this anxiety by becoming exceedingly critical of his wife's handling of the child, and so on. There are strong similarities between the issues examined during this phase and issues usually examined in group psychotherapy. For example, in a group of hypertensive patients, a young woman stated that whenever excessive demands and pressures were placed on her by friends, neighbors, or relatives, she would submit. She did this to avoid an argument and thereby "push up my pressure." She came to realize that the subsequent self-directed anger and depression were far worse for her than any confrontation could have been.

United We Stand

In the closing phase of these groups, a strong cohesiveness and mutual support develop. Often members become friends outside of the group; thereby they develop a mutual support network that can operate without the leaders. The group leaders become less and less prominent. Several of these groups have continued as "clubs" long after the formal group meetings have ended. A parents' group continues to meet informally more than two years after "termination."

Implementation

The increasing proportion of patients with chronic (*e.g.,* hypertension) as opposed to acute illnesses implies that the quality of health care delivery will inevitably become more dependent on patient health behavior. This alone justifies integrating psychoeducational groups into the health delivery system. Whether it be clinic, health maintenance organization (HMO) or private practice the human demands of patients require management and support, and psychoeducational groups offer one means of meeting these demands.[8]

How Do We Get Started?

Psychoeducational groups can operate with not less than five and not more than twelve patient members, plus one or two leaders. One should be prepared for a drop-out rate of about 20-25 per cent (this can vary with group composition and leader experience).

One needs adequate space to run the group. This space may be the waiting room of general medical practice, a church meeting room, or even a private home. It is most important that the location be comfortable, accessible, and not overly stiff or formal.

Fees should be determined if the group will be paid for on a fee-for-service basis. In general, fees for such groups are kept at a minimum, as what is being provided is in fact an "optional" service, not an acute or crisis service.[9] Many patients may be reluctant to spend a great deal of money on themselves when they are not clearly in need of medical care, and the drop-out rate could be quite high.

Patients should be actively recruited for the group. It is singularly important not to portray psychoeducational groups to patients as "therapy groups." If they are portrayed as such, people feel stigmatized and often insulted.[10] Rather, the group should be described as a setting where one can discuss and share concerns around a particular illness or life change with others experiencing the same situation.

Leaders for such groups need not be specially trained mental health professionals, but physicians, nurses, clergy or others can assume the leadership role. Pharmacists, for example, would seem to be in a particularly good position to lead such groups. They are readily available at a direct community level, see many patients with similar medical issues, and could be a major locus of information and support.

It is always important for the leader(s) to maintain a listening, responsive, and available position, without imposing a set of beliefs, or a "way it must be done."

Health professionals without extensive experience in group situations may feel, because of their inexperience, reluctance to begin psychoeducational groups. However, the potential benefits for helping alleviate loneliness and pain and enhancing health behavior would seem to outweigh the risks.

How psychoeducational groups can be integrated into a practice will vary as a function of the practice, type of patients, and illness involved. For example, hypertensive patients usually return to the physician every two weeks or so during the initial states of adjustment to their therapy. This schedule provides a convenient basis for scheduling psychoeducational groups. Other illnesses offer other opportunities during which health care and health care behavior can be integrated.

Summary

Through what is called psychoeducational groups, medical patients can be brought together for mutual support and information. The four phases of development of such groups are described, as well as specific issues around implementation. The opportunity exists through such groups to make a significant contribution to humanizing health care.

REFERENCES

1. Budman SH: A strategy for preventive mental health intervention. Professional Psychol 6:394-398, 1975.
2. Farkas A, Shivachman H: Psychological adaptation to chronic illness; a group discussion with cystic fibrosis patients. Am J Orthopsychiat 43:259-260, 1973.
3. Hollon T: Modified group therapy in the treatment of patients on chronic hemodialysis. Am J Psychiatry 26:501-510, 1972.
4. Bilodeau C, Hackett T: Issues raised in a group setting by patients recovering from myocardial infarctions. Am J Psychiat 128:105-110, 1971.
5. Bouchard V: Hemiplegic exercise and discussion group. Am J Occup Ther 26:330-331, 1972.
6. Hurvitz N: Peer self-help psychotherapy groups: Psychotherapy with psychotherapists. In Rowan PM, Trice HM (eds): The Sociology of Psychotherapy. New York, Aronson, 1974, p 84-132.
7. Yalom I: The Theory and Practice of Group Psychotherapy. New York, Basic Books.
8. Moore P: Not by medicine alone. Am Psychol Assoc Monitor, 6:1 (Nov) 1975.

9. Broskowski A, Baker F: Professional organizational and social barriers to primary prevention. Am J Orthopsychiat 44:707-719, 1974.
10. Sugar M: Premature withdrawal from group therapy: parents of intellectually retarded girls. Group Process 4:60-72, 1971.

Patient Education: A Nurse's Perspective

A. MAHONEY

Massachusetts General Hospital
Boston, Massachusetts

THE PATIENT AND HIS MEDICATION

Patients are discharged every day from hospitals with the expectation that they will assume the responsibility for carrying on the treatment program prescribed for them by their physicians and administered by health care-takers during their hospital stay. Their prescribed regimens may involve special diets, activity restrictions, treatments, and often a complicated array of medications.

Various studies have shown that between 40 and 90 per cent of all patients take their medications in error.[1-4] The types of errors described in the literature include:

1. Patients who do not take medications as prescribed by the physician:
   a. Prescriptions given to the patient at discharge and not filled because of financial reasons.
   b. Refills not obtained when the initial prescription expires or not obtained in time to prevent missed doses.
   c. Medications discontinued due to self-evaluated physical improvement (this seems to happen most often with antibiotics).
   d. Medications discontinued due to apparent lack of improvement.
   e. Medications discontinued due to side effects of the drug as observed by the patient.

2. Patients who take the wrong dose of medications:
   a. Underdosage due to forgetfulness (or to make the pills "last longer," etc.)
   b. Wrong dose due to misunderstanding instructions.
   c. Overdosage due to duplication of prescriptions (medications from previous illness as in the case of the patient who has several medications with the same action).
3. Patients who take medications not prescribed by the physician.
   a. Medications prescribed during a previous illness.
   b. Over-the-counter drugs.
   c. Drugs belonging to relatives or friends (This can result in problems with drug interactions — a decreased effect of the prescribed drug or increased effects of either prescribed or nonprescribed medications).
4. Patients who take medications at the wrong time, due to lack of sufficient information about spacing doses.

It can be assumed that many of these errors could be avoided through adequate preparation of the patient and/or family for carrying out the prescribed medication regimen at home.

Patients have a *need* and a *right* to an explanation of their care. Often, they are not given adequate instructions about their medications; they do not fully understand their diagnoses and the reasons for taking drugs and prescriptions; and directions are often given without an understanding of the patient's individual needs related to life style.

As an anonymous British physician wrote a couple of years ago: "to discharge a patient from the hospital without detailed and adequate instructions.....has always seemed to me like rescuing a man from the seas, resuscitating him and putting him back on his raft without even a paddle to get to safety."[5] Patient teaching is part of the practice of all health care professionals. We are often not held sufficiently accountable for this aspect of our practice. Yet, it is the intervention which often means the difference between success and lack of success in restoring the patient to maximum well-being. We can assume that a patient who knows why he is taking a drug, how and when to take it, what effects are to be expected, and how to recognize adverse effects will be better able to participate in a prescribed program than the patient who is merely given a prescription.[6]

HOSPITAL PATIENT EDUCATION

There are many reasons why patient education efforts in a hospital do not succeed, including lack of teaching skills on the part of the doctor and/or nurse, lack of a clear division of labor among personnel who teach the patient, poor communication among members of the health team about what is to be taught the patient, and, most frequently, lack of time. Of these variables, probably the time available between the patient and the health care provider, more than any other, determines the outcome of a patient education effort.

As is true in most hospital settings, the doctor reviews the medication regimen with the patient; still it may be done superficially or at a time when the patient is distracted by his plans for going home. Also, the doctor may use terminology which the patient does not understand, and/or the patient may have questions which he is unable or afraid to ask. All of this increases the chances that the patient will not comply with the regimen.

Nurses may or may not participate in instructing patients about their medications. Many feel constrained from giving factual information to patients about their diagnoses or treatment. This is often a result of the attitudes of physicians who feel that they alone should give information to their patients. The hospital pharmacist is normally not on the scene to help with patient instruction although in some cases he is able to take an active teaching role in the outpatient setting.

The important issue is not *who* should do the teaching, but rather that the right of the patient/client to know his diagnosis and the proposed modalities of therapy is now recognized as a legal right.

THE NURSE'S ROLE IN HOSPITAL PATIENT EDUCATION

In our hospital we believe that the nurse has an important contribution to make in the area of medication teaching; not only because of the continuity of her contact with the patient throughout his hospitalization but also because of the "caring" nature of the nurse-patient relationship. Our philosophy of nursing practice states that the professional responsibility of the nurse includes:

- **Assessment** of those life patterns which are pertinent to the patient's in- and post-hospital care, including his perception of his illness.
- **Planning** of his nursing care based on the nursing and medical histories, nursing and medical findings and the planned medical regimen.
- **Collaboration** with the patient, family, nurse colleagues, physicians, social workers and other members of the health-care team.
- **Maintenance and support of normal patterns** (or deviations secondary to illness).
- **Teaching** essential to maintenance of health and adjustment to illness or disability.

In preparation for carrying out her teaching role the nurse must know and understand the physician's goals for treatment; she must be familiar with the drug, its actions and side effects. In addition, the nurse must understand the patient's goals and how the patient's life style, attitudes, and capabilities will affect acceptance of the therapy. Finally, the nurse must involve the patient's family as "partners in his care." With this, the nurse should be able to make judgments about what the individual needs to know, what he is capable of learning, how he can best be taught, and how what he has learned can be assessed.

A nursing history should be obtained early in the patient's hospitalization. These data help to identify nursing care needs as a basis for planning and giving care. Indeed, much of it is pertinent to planning for the patient's management of his medication regimen after discharge.

The nurse obtains information concerning:

1. The patient's perception of his illness — what he already knows about his diagnosis.
2. Cultural background, home setting, family or other significant persons, as well as financial resources.
3. Occupation, level of education, and previous health behavior.
4. The patient's normal life style, patterns of rest/sleep, daily activities, and meals.
5. Finally, the physical capabilities of the patient (e.g., vision, reading, memory, manual dexterity).

IMPLEMENTING A PATIENT EDUCATION PROGRAM

A teaching program begins early in hospitalization, depending upon the patient's condition and the nurse's assessment of his readiness to learn. Some patients are not ready to absorb information until after discharge because of the emotional stresses of the disease, and level of denial.

In these cases, post-discharge arrangements must be made to ensure that they are able to comply with the prescribed regimen.

We usually begin by helping the patient to understand his diagnosis as a basis for understanding the purposes of his medications and other aspects of his treatment. It is helpful if the nurse can be present when the doctor gives information or instructions to the patient; this will allow her to clarify and/or reinforce the physician's comments as well as evaluate the patient's level of understanding. Health information literature can be used, but is usually used only as a supplement to verbal teaching. Use of a patient teaching guide, with a corresponding check list and notes inserted in the patient's record, provides a means of communicating patient education efforts with other members of the health care team and thereby ensuring continuity and consistency of approach.

Patient teaching does not have to be a formalized process.[7,8] We normally discuss the patient's medications with him during our medication administration rounds. For example, we might say, "This is your digoxin — it is a heart pill," or, "It slows and strengthens your heartbeat." Using the pill as a visual aid can be effective. In discussing the medication as we administer it we can relate it to the diagnosis or a symptom and can also point out side effects when they occur.

In some cases it has been useful to write out instructions concerning the name, action, dosage and frequency of administration of a medication on a card and give it to the patient to keep at his bedside. Then, while we are on our medication-administration rounds, we ask the patient to tell us about the medication he is to take.

In the same vein, a self-medication program during hospitalization would probably do much to enhance the patient's learning. The existence of unit dose systems would lend to the development of such programs.

Discharge teaching is done as early as possible but often it is not until the day of discharge that the patient's post-discharge medications are available to us. We try to have a family member present during this instruction.

The patient receives a copy of a booklet *Taking Medicines at Home*. In addition to reviewing the contents of the booklet with the patient (Figure 1), written instructions pertaining to the patient's specific drug program are included in the back of the book (Figure 2). The written directions available in the book are for reference at home and for discussion at revisit to help fill in any gaps in information that may have occurred during the excitement of the discharge process.

Our patient teaching programs in the area of medication administration are developed within the framework of the following objectives:

1. *To know the name and purpose of the drug*— the generic and trade name of each drug are included in the written instructions. Our pharmacy labels the bottle with the generic name but we have found that the physician often uses the more common trade name when he talks to the patient about his medication in follow-up visits or over the telephone. The action of the drug is described, with the terminology varying depending upon the level of understanding of individual patient.

2. *To know the dosage and frequency of administration* — the dosage and number of pills are indicated. The times of administration are planned with the patient when possible, to fit in with his daily patterns.

3. *To know the side effects* — expected side effects are mentioned: "You may feel sleepy," or "Your bowel movements may appear black in color."

4. *To know when to notify the physician* — *adverse* side effects are described, depending upon the drug and the patient: "Call the doctor if...you are nauseated, etc."

Most importantly, the nurse assists the patient in intelligently manipulating the medical program within his life style. Patients respond most positively when they are involved in planning how to carry out their medical regimens at home. Even when the medical program cannot be altered to the patient's patterns, the nurse works with the patient in modifying his behavior as needed.

We have been able to use resources within the hospital to have instructions and labels translated into Italian, Portuguese, Spanish and other languages, a small but essential step in the process of helping the patient comply with his or her therapeutic regimen.

The nurse must evaluate the patient's understanding of the instructions. An effective way is to ask him to describe his plans for carrying them out: that is, at what time of day he will take the medications, where he will keep them, what reminders he might use, etc.

The nurse should assess the patient's ability to read the label on the bottle and to measure the dosage accurately. In some cases, it is necessary to evaluate the

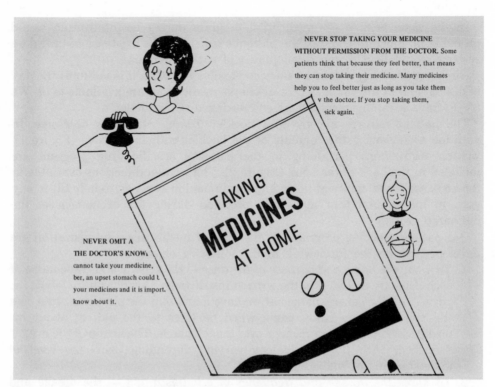

NEVER STOP TAKING YOUR MEDICINE
WITHOUT PERMISSION FROM THE DOCTOR. Some
patients think that because they feel better, that means
they can stop taking their medicine. Many medicines
help you to feel better just as long as you take them
v the doctor. If you stop taking them,
sick again.

NEVER OMIT A
THE DOCTOR'S KNOW,
cannot take your medicine,
ber, an upset stomach could t
your medicines and it is import.
know about it.

Figure 1: The cover and selected pages of the pamphlet "Taking Medications at Home," a pamphlet distributed to all patients when they leave the hospital.

CHLOROTHIAZIDE
(DIURIL)

500 mg.
Take *1* tablet
Every morning
(at breakfast time)

This is a "fluid pill" or diuretic. Helps your body get rid of excess fluid—lessening the workload on your heart and lowering your blood pressure.

— It will make you urinate more often.
— Weigh yourself every day in the morning and keep a record.

Call your doctor if you notice a rash, weakness, muscle pains or cramps—if you gain or lose more than 3 pounds in one day, or if your feet get swollen.

Figure 2: A description of a common diuretic. Included is an example of the pill plus instructions on how to take the pill.

patient's ability to *open* the bottles: *i.e.,* the patient with physical handicaps and/or the new child-safe caps appearing on many medication bottles.

Based on assessment of the patient's abilities and level of understanding, further steps may be taken. A patient with a memory problem may need to use a calendar or may have his medications placed in separate envelopes for each time of day that they are to be taken. A family member or the visiting nurse can assist in carrying this out on a daily basis. Sometimes relatives or friends are asked to assume responsibility for administering the medications.

The patient and/or family is provided with the name and telephone number of a physician and a nurse and are encouraged to call when there are questions or problems. Patients often seem to feel more comfortable in calling the nurse than the physician to describe a possible side effect or to ask questions about their medications.

The results of our teaching efforts are recorded in the patient's record for the benefit of the doctor and nurse who will see him on follow-up visits. It is often necessary to initiate a referral to the Visiting Nurse to evaluate the patient's ability to follow his medical regimen and to reinforce teaching as needed. We have had reports from the Visiting Nurse that patients have their booklets in a prominent place at home. Most are careful to bring the booklets with them when they come to visit the doctor after discharge. It seems that most of our patients *want* to comply with the doctor's recommendations. Giving them adequate information about their medications and about their diagnoses seems to have a positive influence on their ability to comply.

SUMMARY

Although this type of intervention has not been formally evaluated it appears to have many of the elements of programs that have succeeded.[2,6] We believe that this type of nursing intervention can be the answer to many of the problems that patients have in following prescribed medical regimens given them in hospitals. The physician continues to discuss his goals and plans for treatment with the patient and family, but the nursing staff has the primary responsibility for the educational process necessary to help ensure that these plans are carried out.

REFERENCES

1. Curtis E: Medication errors made by patients. Nurs Outlook 9:290, 1961.
2. Marston MV: Compliance with medical regimens: a review of the literature. Nurs Res 19:321-323, 1970.
3. Schwartz D: Medication errors made by aged patients. Am J Nurs 62:57, 1962.
4. Schwartz D: The elderly patient and his medications. Geriatrics 29:517-520, 1965.
5. Editorial: 15, Jan. Lancet 1:147, 1972.
6. Rosenberg SG: A case for patient education. Hosp Form Manag 6:1-4, 1971.
7. Palm MI: Recognizing opportunities for informal patient teaching. Nurs Clincs North Am 6:1971.
8. Redman BK: The Process of Patient Teaching in Nursing. St. Louis, CV Mosby, 1968.

One Physician's Approach to the Teaching of Patients

P. YURCHAK

Massachusetts General Hospital
Harvard Medical School
Boston, Massachusetts

My father was a lawyer. Behind the desk in his office hung a framed quotation from Abraham Lincoln: "A lawyer's time and advice are his stock in trade." The same can be said of physicians, but the importance of this fact is often ignored in practice. Two ingredients are involved — *time* and *advice.* One needs time to listen to what the patient says, time to reflect upon what he does *not* say, time to observe the "nonverbal" signs manifest as he talks, and finally, time to reflect and to synthesize. Furthermore, time spent in this way implies that the physician cares enough about the patient to accord him an all too precious commodity. Everyone in business or the professions is "busy," and many consider themselves all *too* busy. This is universally true of physicians, and patients often complain: "He is too busy to take time to explain what is going on."

It is axiomatic that people cooperate best when they understand the reasons for a course of action. They *may* acquiesce in a paternalistic attitude on the part of the physician: "Do as I tell you and don't ask questions." They may do this if they are frightened enough, respectful enough of the physician's reputation, or if it fits a life-long pattern of their own attitudes. But they will always resent this stance, however careful they may be to conceal this resentment.

It is important that the patient understands the nature of his problem and cooperates fully with the program prescribed. With this in mind, I spend perhaps

INSTRUCTIONS TO PATIENTS
TAKING MEDICATIONS FOR HIGH BLOOD PRESSURE

GENERAL REMARKS:

It is important to realize that treatment of high blood pressure is a long-term affair. It is not like treating pneumonia with penicillin, where the treatment is stopped after a week or two. You must continue taking the medication and coming for a check on your blood pressure over a period of months and years. Treating this condition is like taking out an insurance policy—the goal is to avoid *complications* of untreated high blood pressure, such as strokes, heart attacks and kidney failure. It is important to realize that high blood pressure *can* be effectively treated in the great majority of patients who cooperate with the doctor in following their treatment program.

There are a number of medications available today for treatment of high blood pressure. These act in different ways to lower the blood pressure, and are often used in combination. In this way the smoothest control of blood pressure can be achieved with the fewest side effects. All medications have some side effects, although most patients do not experience them. They are listed on the special information sheet which you will receive. One feature common to most of the agents is a tendency for the blood pressure to drop when you are in the standing position. This may be associated with slight and temporary lightheadedness, and if this occurs repeatedly you should let the doctor know. One cannot anticipate all possible effects of the medication, and if you should notice *anything* unusual while taking your treatment, report it to your doctor. It is a sound principle of treatment to use only as much of a medication as is required to control the blood pressure. For this reason the dose used at the start of treatment may be increased over the course of time, depending upon the response of the blood pressure. A second agent or even a third may be added as needed. Sometimes smaller doses of two medications achieve good control of the blood pressure while avoiding side effects seen with full doses of one medication alone. Some medications have effects on your system that can only be detected by blood tests, which will be ordered periodically.

Many blood pressure medications are taken two to four times daily. A convenient way to take all of the doses is to place the medication bottle next to your place at the table. Thus three of the four doses can be taken at meal time. Individuals who are away from home during the day should carry a supply of the medication with them. If the doctor prescribes a tablet *four* times daily it is important to take it *that* number of times, not two or three times, or all at once. Adequate control of your blood pressure depends upon taking the medications as directed. Some consider taking pills a nuisance, but the long-term benefit in avoiding complications of high blood pressure is well worth the trouble.

MEMORANDUM TO PATIENTS WHO
HAVE RECENTLY SUSTAINED A HEART ATTACK

This memorandum concerns members of your family, particularly your children. As you may or may not know there is sometimes a tendency for coronary heart disease to run in families. This inherited tendency may be reinforced by the presence of what has been termed "risk factors." These include: (1) abnormal elevation of blood cholesterol or triglycerides (another blood fat substance related to cholesterol); (2) overt diabetes, or even a *tendency* toward it manifest by abnormal elevation of blood sugar levels; (3) high blood pressure; (4) obesity (more than 20 per cent above ideal body weight, as recorded in the table below); (5) heavy cigarette smoking(more than 1 pack per day).

Weight reduction should be planned as indicated. The hazards of cigarette smoking are well publicized and should impel discontinuance of the habit. As for the first three items listed above, your children should consult their personal physicians to have their blood pressures checked and obtain the appropriate laboratory tests. If they do not have a personal physician at this time I am prepared to arrange for the necessary blood tests. I will also measure their blood pressure at the time of their visit to the laboratory here. If some abnormality is turned up in this way they should place themselves under the care of a physician who can pursue the matter further. This offer on my part is *not* a solicitation of new patients, since I have more than enough to take care of already. It is being offered as a service to you and your family. Please let me know if anyone cares to accept this offer.

IDEAL WEIGHTS FOR WOMEN
AGES 25 AND OVER

Height (with shoes)		Weight in Pounds (as ordinarily dressed)	
		Medium Frame	Large Frame
Feet	*Inches*		
4	11	114±4	122±5
5	0	116±4	124±5
5	1	118±4	126±5
5	2	121±4	129±6
5	3	124±4	132±6
5	4	128±4	136±6
5	5	131±4	139±6
5	6	135±5	144±6
5	7	139±5	148±6
5	8	142±5	151±7
5	9	146±5	155±7
5	10	151±5	159±7
5	11	153±5	162±7
6	0	157±6	167±7

IDEAL WEIGHTS FOR MEN
AGES 25 AND OVER

Height (with shoes)		Weight in Pounds (as ordinarily dressed)	
		Medium Frame	Large Frame
Feet	*Inches*		
5	2	125±4	136±6
5	3	132±4	138±6
5	4	135±5	143±6
5	5	139±5	147±6
5	6	142±5	151±6
5	7	146±5	155±7
5	8	151±5	159±7
5	9	155±5	163±7
5	10	159±5	168±7
5	11	162±5	172±8
6	0	167±6	174±8
6	1	172±6	182±8
6	2	177±7	187±9
6	3	183±7	193±9

fifteen minutes at the close of an office consultation explaining the problem to the patient and discussing the treatment options. This is usually reinforced by some written memorandum for the patient's perusal. More about this shortly. This explanation is carried out with the help of a teaching handbook, which contains a collection of color illustrations by the noted medical artist, Dr. Frank Netter. These illustrations depict both the normal anatomy of the external surface of the heart and cut-away views of its interior. The heart valves, both normal and diseased, are clearly shown. Congenital heart lesions are considered, as well as the surgical techniques involved in correcting both congenital and acquired vascular disease. Finally, there are illustrations of the evolutionary process of atherosclerosis and its complications. Selective illustrations dealing with coronary arteriography and coronary bypass surgery have been drawn from several sources.

Each patient is shown the normal anatomy of the heart and its component structures, and then the pathological process concerned in his particular case is considered. Visual and verbal understanding go hand in hand. To be sure, the patient may retain only a fraction of what he sees and is told. But he presumably understands the process better than he can on the strength of a verbal explanation alone. In addition, the patient has had the novel and (it is to be hoped) exhilarating experience of receiving a first-hand explanation of his problem and the treatment options open to him. He is grateful for the time and effort involved and optimally motivated to cooperate in further evaluation of his problem and in its management.

Over the years I have evolved a series of mimeographed "hand-outs" for patients. These reinforce what the patient has been told verbally, and compensate in part for the inability of the human mind to retain much new material for very long. The patient is encouraged to refer to these memoranda from time to time. The idea is not original with me. I learned it from my older colleagues, who for years have written out instructions for patients at the time of their discharge from the hospital. I found that instructions to patients with certain cardiac problems tended to be almost identical from patient to patient. Furthermore, it was time-consuming to complete a full set of instructions covering such items as diet, activity, medications, etc., for individual patients. For this reason a standard mimeograph instruction memorandum evolved. The margins of the instruction sheet are purposely left wide enough for comments that are unique to a given patient. Selections having no application can simply be stricken out. Examples (Figures 1 and 2) of these hand-outs are appended. The subjects which can be covered embrace a wide range of topics and are available from the author upon request.

Moreover, the American Heart Association has for some years made available various patient-information pamphlets, and I have a complete stock of these. Certain drug companies whose products are used in the treatment of hypertension have generated similar pamphlets dealing with hypertension and its management. These can be used to good advantage as well.

I have conducted no assessment of the efficacy of the foregoing measures, but believe they are worth the time and effort entailed. Patients frequently comment that the explanation was a novel event for them and express their appreciation for it.

D. Focus on the Health Delivery Systems:

No overview of the management of noncompliance would be complete without considering system-wide changes and how such changes can contribute to patient adherence to a therapeutic regimen. Frank Finnerty pioneered both identifying the nature of the delivery system problem and what could be done about it.

The D.C. General Hospital Experience

FRANK A. FINNERTY, JR.

*Georgetown University School of Medicine
and the
Georgetown University Medical Division
Washington, D.C.*

Our original interest in patient compliance stems from several drug studies where we found a 42-43 per cent evidence in drop-out rate. This obviously shocked us as well as the pharmaceutical companies, particularly since our permanent staff and not hospital personnel operated the clinic.

A sociologist and myself attempted to evaluate this drop-out problem. We interviewed 200 patients who had failed to keep appointments and were surprised by our findings. These patients failed to keep appointments for very real reasons.

1. Far and away the most common complaint was the long waiting time. Indeed, the average waiting time to see the doctor was four and one-half hours. If you have ever been in a city hospital clinic you know that this is no exaggeration.
2. The second objection was that even though we brought our own doctors and fellows down to the clinic, the same doctor did not see the patient regularly.

As you know, in a city or university hospital clinic, physicians are usually rotated, *e.g.,* one doctor one month, another doctor the next. This prevents the establishment of any doctor/patient relationship. In contrast to the four and one-half hour waiting time to see the doctor, the average time the patient spent with the doctor was seven and one-half minutes.

During these few minutes, the doctor obviously only had time to give the patient a "brush-off" and there was certainly no time for any doctor-patient relationship. He then wrote a prescription and the waiting time started again since the patient waited an average of one and one-half hours at the pharmacy. At one time during the 1968-1969 period, there was a rule that the pharmacy could only give a week's supply; he then had to go downtown for the rest. Finally, he had to take public transportation home — surely a wasted day at the clinic. If the patient had to put up with this nonsense two or three times, he soon did not come back to the clinic; and not to sound rhetorical, the next time he was seen in any medical facility was frequently in an emergency room with some kind of catastrophe.

Considering these complaints, the long waiting time, lack of doctor-patient relationship, waiting time at the pharmacy, etc., and using them as guidelines, we reorganized our clinic. First, we began using a meaningful appointment system; instead of having a high blood pressure clinic on Monday mornings, we gave the patient an appointment at 8:10 and/or 8:20 A.M. Second, we assigned each patient to a particular paramedic; more often than not, the paramedic was someone from the inner city and her background was such that she could really relate to them. Our operation was and is paramedically-run and nurse-supervised. The doctor is used in consultation only.

When the patient first comes to the clinic, he is greeted by a friendly receptionist who knows immediately whom to call "Mr. Jones" or whom to call "Joe." She then assigns him to his own paramedic who can spend as much time as he or she needs. There is relatively no waiting time and, just as important, there is ample opportunity to develop a good relationship. If there is any question about changes in medication, the patient is seen by the nurse; of course if she has any question or feels unsure, the doctor is called. Supplying the medication at the clinic obviously bypasses the waiting time at the pharmacy and reduces the time spent in the clinic to about 15 or 20 minutes. The patient, therefore, goes home very happy and satisfied.

Let me make some generalities regarding follow-up. Poor follow-up is not peculiar to a city hospital situation. Schoenberger et al [1] reported that 51 per cent of newly discovered hypertensive patients in the offices of cardiologists and internists were not even given a second appointment. What I am saying is that the average "intelligent" doctor out in practice does not express much concern about the mild hypertensive; indeed, he may not even give these patients a second appointment. So, the average doctor in practice really does not realize how many of his patients do not return.

The simplicity of therapy has been touched upon by many others. Regardless of the type of compliance study, whether it has to do with infectious diseases, rheumatic fever, or hypertension, there is no question that the more the pills the less the compliance; and the fewer the pills, the more the compliance. We who have been in the clinic for years are surely familiar with the middle-aged woman who comes in with a paper bag full of pills. She really needs a small boy to carry the pills around. She takes seven of these and four of these and two of these, and you know that she is not taking most of them. Obviously the ideal, as far as the therapy of any chronic disease is concerned, particularly an asymptomatic one such as hypertension, is a pill a day. Two studies need emphasis in this regard. As you know, in the V.A. Cooperative Study [2,3] there were three study drugs, e.g., reserpine, a thiazide, and hydralazine. This was a study conducted on men with moderately severe and severe disease. When the third study drug, hydralazine, was added, there was further reduction in diastolic pressure; but further reduction was only an average of 4 mm Hg. If the V.A. physicians could control the arterial pressure in these men with moderately severe and severe disease with such simple therapy (and two of those ingredients, the reserpine and thiazide, can be combined in the same pill), then surely 75 per cent of the 23 million hypertensive patients out there who have mild disease can be controlled with simple therapy. Said in another way, most of the patients who are taking six pills of this and four pills of that really do not need them.

Let us put side effects into their proper place! You hear people say, "Oh, those blood pressure lowering drugs; they ruin the bowels, ruin sex, ruin everything." As the potency of antihypertensive agents increases, so does the toxicity. The milder the drug the less obnoxious are the side effects. What follows is the obvious generality that patients with mild disease should receive a mild antihypertensive agent and certainly should not be given potent agents and possibly subjected to adverse side effects. To repeat again, 75 per cent of those 23 million hypertension subjects have mild or moderate disease and those people do not need potent, obnoxious drugs. They certainly do not need guanethidine. In the patients with mild disease, it is a matter of enjoying or not enjoying. In the small percentage of people (15 per cent) who have severe disease, or a large heart, or congestive heart failure, who have had a stroke or some serious disease, the choice is different. It is not a matter of enjoying or not enjoying; it is a matter of living or having a stroke and dying. Potent agents are necessary in these patients, and unfortunately side effects are frequent. Individualizing dosage, increasing the dosage slowly, willingness to change medications, and tailoring the therapeutic regimen to the individual patient are necessary. Thus, all the advances in therapy are not going to be realized — and strokes, congestive heart failure, heart attacks, and renal failure are not going to be prevented — unless the patient continues to remain under medical care and takes his medication.

It has been my experience, both in private practice and in the hypertension clinic, that patients (particularly those who are asymptomatic) will not remain under medical care and on medication unless they are properly motivated. Such motivation can only result from a good doctor-patient relationship.

Recent experience with an inner city population [4] has attested to the fact that a well-trained, understanding paramedical person may be substituted for the physician in this relationship. Once this relationship has been established, time can be spent in educating the patient rather than merely reassuring him.

REFERENCES

1. Schoenberger JA, Shekelle RB, Shekelle S, Stamler J: Current status of hypertension control in an industrial population. JAMA 222:559-562, 1972.
2. V.A. Cooperative Study: Effects of treatment on morbidity in hypertension: I. Results in patients with diastolic blood pressures averaging 115 through 129 mm Hg. JAMA 202:1028-1034, 1967.
3. V.A. Cooperative Study: Effects of treatment on morbidity in hypertension: II. Results in patients with diastolic blood pressure averaging 90 through 114 mm Hg. JAMA 213:1143-1152, 1970.
4. Finnerty FA, Mattie EC, Finnerty III FA: Hypertension in the inner city. Circulation 47:73-75, 1973.

Summary

I. BAROFSKY

Department of Behavioral Sciences
Massachusetts College of Pharmacy
Boston, Massachusetts

The purpose of this book is to summarize for you the state of the art in the management of patient behavior, in general, and the behavior of the hypertensive, in particular. We have reviewed a broad range of factors that may contribute to noncompliance and what we currently think may work in increasing compliance with therapeutic regimens. The stimulus for concern with patient behavior comes in part from the realization that many of the deaths due to cardiovascular accidents are attributable to the way the hypertensive patient cares for himself. Another equally important reason for concern with such behavior is the realization that complete access to health care, in and of itself, does not ensure an improvement in the state of health of a particular population. This observation can be derived from a recent evaluation of the impact of national universal Medicare in Canada, where it was found that universal prepaid health insurance had virtually no impact on mortality rates.[1] Instead, it appeared to the evaluation group that life-style and environmental influences contributed so greatly as to constitute the key to effective control. The papers presented in this book provide the options available to any health planner on how to approach management of this aspect of the health delivery process.

One problem facing each author, whether directly or indirectly stated, was the definition of the phrase *compliance with a medication regimen*. Most authors assumed that we were discussing the behavior of patients taking their medication, and that somehow we were concerned with factors that influence a

215

patient's decision to take the medication. The word *compliance* can imply the coercion of one individual by another, and some, responding to the aversive connotations of the word, have suggested the use of the word *adherence* instead. By using the term *adherence* we shift our emphasis from how one person effects change in the behavior of another, to how an individual adjusts his behavior relative to some standard. Another definition, suggested by Zola, was to think of the physician-patient relationship as a *therapeutic alliance,* where both physician and patient participate in the health care process. All three of these definitions make it clear that we are dealing with an example of the social control of behavior, but compliance was retained in the title of the book because it was felt it accurately reflected the current status of this aspect of the health care process.

The question of whether noncompliance is a problem determining the effectiveness of a medication regimen was virtually taken for granted. Our task instead was in identifying the factors that contribute to noncompliance with a medication regimen and suggesting approaches to the management of such factors. Table I summarizes the various proposed determinants of medication compliance. The division of these determinants into structural and functional components reflects the degree of manipulability and optimum time of manipulation of these variables, and provides an initial basis for the development of policy and selection of intervention strategies. As became clear from the papers, structural determinants were considered the key to ultimate elimination of the problem of noncompliance.

Finnerty, in his paper (*see also* Finnerty et al [2]), demonstrated to us that patient drop-out and noncompliance can be significantly reduced by prompt, reliable access to a hypertension clinic where patients can be assured of a stable relationship with a nurse-practitioner or physician. McKenney and his coworkers [3] have demonstrated the same effect, using pharmacists as the health care provider. Sufficient data appear available, therefore, to justify the

TABLE I

DETERMINANTS OF MEDICATION COMPLIANCE

I. Structural Determinants

    a. Patient Access and Management Factors
    b. Economic Factors
    c. Pharmaceutical Factors
    d. Biological Variables

II. Functional Determinants

    a. Patient Factors
    b. Health Care Professional Variables
    c. Interpersonal Relationship Variables

---

conclusion that properly designed and managed procedures whereby patients can gain access to health care will reduce noncompliance. Whether the physician in private practice can simulate what has been demonstrated so clearly in the clinic remains to be determined. Some of the obstacles to replicating such efforts includes training and use of nurse-practitioners to manage what may be a limited portion of a physician's patient population (e.g., of hypertensive patients), coordinating the efforts of physically separated health professionals (e.g., the Visiting Nurse, the community pharmacist, and the physician), and in general reluctance on the part of the physician to share in the care of the patient.

The key question is how *continuity of care* can be established and maintained. Ultimate solution of this problem may also require the development of primary care units at the community level. An interesting example of how this can be done is occurring in the Canadian city of London, Ontario. In this community, a committee entitled the "London Health Council Committee on Primary Care" was formed and generated a series of 47 recommendations. One such recommendation was the formation of experimental neighborhood primary care committees consisting of all the health workers in the area: physicians, dentists, pharmacists, social workers, etc.[4,5] The purpose of such committees, at one level, could be to enhance communication and professional relationship between health professionals in the same neighborhood and, at another level, to provide solutions to the problem of how continuity of care can be provided.

Besides patient complaints about the inconvenience created by being on a medication regimen (e.g., having to remember to take one's medication, the side effects, etc.), the cost of purchasing the medication is often of such a magnitude as to threaten what Whiston called "purchase compliance." Whiston was referring to the fact that a written prescription is not necessarily a filled prescription, and that this is especially true for the elderly, poor, and minority group member. Thus, economic pressure to noncompliance can exist, although the data presented only permitted indirect estimates of the magnitude of this pressure.

Whiston also points out that, contrary to most other aspects of the health care process, there are few alternatives to managing the economic pressure created by a medication regimen. Thus, one does not find health insurance plans in the United States providing for the cost of medication and only in the case of the welfare patient, Medicare, Medicaid, or some private health care plans will the cost of medication be provided. The importance of managing the economic pressure to noncompliance may in fact be underestimated since in the past the costs of drugs have remained relatively stable. This cost stability has in part been due to advances in preparative techniques, but also to the development and maintenance of the community pharmacy. The community pharmacy remains an optimal access point, although not necessarily the only access point, whereby patients can efficiently acquire their medications. Full utilization of the community pharmacist by developing his capacity to select between products and provide various services designed to maximize patient monitoring and self-care could also help reduce the economic pressure to noncompliance.

It may be relevant at this point to recall that at one time the pharmacist and the physician were physically located together, permitting direct distribution of drugs. Some physicians are known to continue this tradition, dispensing a limited variety of medications at their office independent of the legality. They, as Finnerty learned, have found that providing medications at the site of prescription remains a viable approach to minimizing purchase and usage noncompliance.

We all assume that when a physician prescribes and a pharmacist dispenses a bottle of 100 pills, that the contents of the bottle will be pretty much the same — one pill to the other, one batch to the other. Yet, preparative variability and its effect on bioavailability remain a potential source of patient noncompliance. If drugs vary in terms of their dissolution characteristics, absorptivity, potency, and receptor binding ability, it is equivalent to varying the dose of a drug, and patients knowingly or not will adjust their self-administration of a medication to compensate for such differences.

Clearly, certain types of drugs are more vulnerable to preparative variability than others. For example, it would be expected that drugs with narrow therapeutic margins, drugs which are designed for controlled time release, or release in specific environments (*e.g.,* in specific portions of the gastrointestinal tract), or drugs that are susceptible to microbial inactivation would be more affected by preparative variability than drugs that require less precision in preparation. This is so, even though quality control procedures exist for both within and between manufacturers. The magnitude of product variability is, of course, the key issue in the currently raging debate about the relative value of generic versus proprietary drug preparations. Hopefully, one of the end results of this debate will be the generation of the kind of data required to objectively estimate preparative variability and in this way determine if such a variable could contribute to noncompliance with a therapeutic regimen.

People differ in size and shape and weight and not too surprisingly such biological differences between people affect how well a drug acts. Tempero in his paper reviewed some of the biological variables which can determine the effectiveness of a particular medication including genetic variables (*i.e.,* pharmacogenetics), developmental variables (*i.e.,* you cannot assume that children require the same dose of a drug as adults), environmental variables (*i.e.,* smoking, drinking, and drugs don't mix), and variables reflecting the disease state of the patient. Knowing that such factors can play a role in determining a drug's action, Tempero asks how we can tailor a medication regimen to maximize its therapeutic effect? He discusses a number of examples of systems that permit individualizing of the drug therapy including systems that make drugs available as a function of the time of day (*i.e.,* chronopharmacology), or at the site of action (*e.g.,* intravaginal devices that prevent implantation of the fertilized ovum).

Many physicians who deal with the hypertensive patient adopt the operating philosophy of giving the patient the least of the weakest antihypertensive agent available that has a reasonable chance of lowering the patient's blood pressure.

Thus, antihypertensive therapy appears empirical although it is probably more correct to say that the practicing physician is tailoring the medication regimen for the patient as a product of a series of successive approximations. Clearly, before a medication regimen can be tailored to a patient, it has to be "tried on for size," but even suits of clothing have multiple sizes which narrow the margin of the adjustment required. In this context, Kock-Weser [6] has suggested that the practicing physician determine whether the patient's hypertension is due to abnormalities of peripheral vascular resistance, cardiac output, intravascular volume, the renin-angiotension-aldosterone system or the sympathetic nervous system, and on the basis of this determination select the medication that will best manage the disorder. Whether this is a practical suggestion or something that will be limited to the hospitals, where the appropriate diagnostic investigations can be performed, remains to be determined.

Procedures which can be initiated independent of the patient have been referred to as *structural determinants* of medication compliance, since they provide the *context* wherein patients and various health professionals interact. Factors which are dependent on the individual patient or health professional and which determine the *quality* of their interaction we have referred to as the *functional component* of medication compliance.

Each patient enters a doctor's office or a pharmacy with a particular past history relative to physicians, nurses, pharmacists, medications, illnesses, etc. It is the inability to measure the extent or nature of this past history at the time a therapeutic regimen is being established that confounds the prediction of noncompliance. Add to this variables dealing with a patient's age, sex, social status, cultural background, life-style, etc., and the extent of the potential factors interacting to produce the decision to take a drug becomes clear. One process, *interoceptive conditioning,* has probably received the least attention although the empirical basis for it is extensive.[7] Interoceptive conditioning refers to the fact that we are learning something about the medications, as we take them, that determine (whether we are aware of it or not) whether we will take the drug again. Consider the phenomenon known as *rebound congestion* (or "nose drops nose"). It is not uncommon for patients with nose congestion due to a cold to take some form of drops containing phenylephrine for symptomatic relief. What has been observed is that patients continue to take the medication beyond the time when other measures indicate that the cold is no longer present. The pharmacological rationale for this phenomenon is that the continued congestion occurs because of a local edema developed in response to the continued application of a vasoconstrictive substance *(i.e.,* phenylephrine). Behaviorally, what has happened is that the previously neutral (we will assume) stimulus (the nose drops) has become conditioned to the process leading to relief so that self-administration of the drops is the most probable response, although clearly not the only response. The specific behavior *(i.e.,* applying the nose drops) persists because it is reinforced *(i.e.,* relief of symptoms). Thus, conditioning principles can account for this phenomenon as readily as pharmacological principles, illustrating how the patient's behavior can determine usage of a medication.

Other patient-related factors include the development of specific behaviors that may contribute to lowering of blood pressure. These behaviors range from the relaxation response discussed by Blackwell, to self-control procedures described by Zifferblatt and Curry. Again, as with interoceptive conditioning, we are dealing with what a patient has learned or can learn. In all these examples, however, how to apply these techniques at the site of health delivery (*i.e.,* the patient health provider interaction) remains to be discussed. One suggestion to solve this implementation problem was the use of a patient health provider contract (*see* Lewis and Michnich) or the patient package insert (*see* Morris and Gagliardi). The advantage of the contract is that it provides the patient with the opportunity to participate in defining the therapeutic regimen while the insert provides information concerning the disease and the medication and what the patient should expect. The usefulness of these strategies has yet to be determined.

Physicians and other health care practitioners also enter a relationship with a patient with extensive past histories. You will find that physicians, in particular, have learned to approach behavioral problems, like medication compliance, with a different set of rules from those they use when they deal with physical dysfunctions. For example, physicians do not hesitate to inquire of patients concerning symptoms that may have some physical basis, but tend to avoid taking the time to ask the kind of questioning, suggested by Hingson, that would provide the necessary information to estimate compliance. In addition, physicians are taught that they have a unique responsibility in caring for a patient which predisposes them against sharing with the patient in decisions, as suggested by Zola, relative to the therapeutic regimen. In both cases, a physician's attitude can be traced to the nature of his education. The physician is taught diagnostic and therapeutic skills that, in their ideal, are applications of various basic sciences, while training in psychiatry and behavioral sciences are qualitatively and quantitatively more limited. This duality in education is probably why a double standard in treatment appears to exist. The situation is worse in pharmaceutical education where only in the last few years has there been any recognition of the importance of preparing students to deal with patients. A reverse bias exists in nursing education, where students are prepared to care for the patient at the expense of preparation in the scientific basis of disease and its treatment. Thus, no one health professional appears to be adequately educated to manage all aspects of a patient's needs.

The last determinant of compliance, clearly the most difficult to manage and most widely implicated in medication noncompliance, deals with factors that determine and govern the interpersonal relationships between the patient and various health providers. Zola, Jenkins, and Hingson described these factors in detail, while Barofsky emphasized some of the psychological mechanisms that might mediate these processes. In addition, the variables discussed above are also assumed to be present when the physician and patient come together. Even so there are some unique features to the interaction itself that deserve our attention: consider the emotional climate surrounding the diagnostic process, the magic and ritual of the therapeutic regimen, and the clear distinction in status and role (possibly more so than any other social relationship) between physician and patient. Together these characteristics sum to create a social situation, distinct in its character and potential for malfunction.

A final set of papers, dealing with patient education and group approaches to patient management, provide continued definition of the options available to improve compliance with a therapeutic regimen. Naturally, what can be done will vary as a function of the practitioner involved, where he works, what his resources are, etc. Still, it is safe to say that as long as primary health care delivery remains as fragmented as it currently is, noncompliance with a therapeutic regimen will remain a problem. Bringing a physician and pharmacist, or pharmacist and nurse, together to work together is immediately burdened with differences in education, role, status, and the stereotyped notions that each practitioner has of the other. Yet this book, and the Workshop it was in part based on, was organized with the explicit assumption that the task of helping a hypertensive patient better care for himself was of sufficient magnitude that the problem of prerogative and responsibility was incidental to the more important issues of alleviating what is a public health problem: the noncompliance of the hypertensive patient to his medication regimen. If various health professionals can be brought together to consider the options available in managing noncompliance, then maybe the time is not too far in the future when they may meet together to plan a common assault on such a problem.

REFERENCES

1. Pomerleau O, Bass F, Crown V: Role of behavior modification in preventive medicine. N Eng J Med 292:1277-1282, 1975.
2. Finnerty FA, Mattie EC, Finnerty III FA: Hypertension in the inner city. Circulation 47:73-75, 1973.
3. McKenney JM, Slining J, Henderson R, Barr M, Devens D: The effect of clinical pharmacy services on ambulatory hypertensive patients. Circulation 48:1104-1110, 1973.
4. Bass M: The pharmacist as a provider of primary care. Can Med Assoc J 112:60-64, 1975.
5. Bass M: Personal communication. June 10, 1975.
6. Kock-Weser J: Individualization of antihypertensive drug therapy. In Reidenberg MM (ed): Symposium on Individualization of Drug Therapy. Med Clinics N Am 58:1027-1036, 1974.
7. Garcia J, Hankins WG, Rusiniak KW: Behavioral regulation of the milieu interne in man and rat. Science 185:824-831, 1974.